Introduction to Algorithms

Joe Oswald

STATES
ACADEMIC PRESS
www.statesacademicpress.com

Published by States Academic Press,
109 South 5th Street,
Brooklyn, NY 11249, USA

ISBN: 978-1-63989-300-3

Cataloging-in-Publication Data

Introduction to algorithms / Joe Oswald.
p. cm.
Includes bibliographical references and index.
ISBN 978-1-63989-300-3
1. Algorithms. 2. Algebra. 3. Arithmetic--Foundations.
I. Oswald, Joe.
QA9.58 .A44 2022
518.1--dc23

For information on all States Academic Press publications visit our website at www.statesacademicpress.com

Contents

Permissions

Index

Preface

Finite sequences of well-defined instructions are known as algorithms. These are used to perform various computations, calculations, data processing and solve classes of problems. Algorithms are unambiguous and computer implementable in nature. These can be represented in many different forms such as flow charts, natural languages, drakon-charts, pseudo code and control tables. These representations can be classified into high level description, implementation description and formal description. Algorithms can be broadly categorized on the basis of implementation, design and complexity. The means of implementation of algorithms are further divided into recursive algorithms, logical algorithms, serial algorithms, parallel algorithms, deterministic algorithms, exact and quantum algorithm. According to the level of complexity, they can be divided into constant time, logarithmic time, linear time, polynomial time and exponential time algorithms. This book presents the complex subject of algorithms in the most comprehensible and easy to understand language. Different approaches, evaluations and methodologies and advanced studies on algorithms have been included herein. This book is a complete source of knowledge on the present status of this important field.

To facilitate a deeper understanding of the contents of this book a short introduction of every chapter is written below:

Chapter 1- Computer algorithms are a sequence of well-defined computer-implementable instructions used to perform computations or solve problems. Some significant aspects of computer algorithms are stages of problem solving, algorithm writing and analysis of algorithms. This is an introductory chapter which will introduce briefly all these aspects of computer algorithms.

Chapter 2- In computer science and mathematics, algorithms are designed in a step-by-step manner to solve problems. This chapter discusses in detail how to design different types of algorithms such as brute force algorithms, greedy algorithms, branch and bound algorithms, transform and conquer algorithms, and backtracking algorithms.

Chapter 3- The method of solving problems in which a complex problem is split into simpler steps to find a solution to the complex problem is termed as dynamic programming. Some of the areas of study within dynamic programming are shortest path algorithm, and knapsack problem and flow scheduling. This chapter has been carefully written to provide an easy understanding about dynamic programming.

Chapter 4- Sequencing the elements of a list in a certain order is known as sorting algorithms. Some of the major types of sorting algorithms are comparison sort, comb sort, insertion sort, shell sort, selection sort, hybrid sorting algorithm, etc. This chapter closely examines these sorting algorithms to provide an extensive understanding of the subject.

Chapter 5- Search algorithms are algorithms used to solve a search problem in order to retrieve the information stored in a data structure having discrete or continuous values. The appropriate search algorithm often depends on the data structure being searched. The concepts discussed in this chapter will help in gaining a better perspective about search algorithms and hash function.

Finally, I would like to thank the entire team involved in the inception of this book for their valuable time and contribution. This book would not have been possible without their efforts. I would also like to thank my friends and family for their constant support.

Joe Oswald

Introduction to Computer Algorithms

Computer algorithms are a sequence of well-defined computer-implementable instructions used to perform computations or solve problems. Some significant aspects of computer algorithms are stages of problem solving, algorithm writing and analysis of algorithms. This is an introductory chapter which will introduce briefly all these aspects of computer algorithms.

The word Algorithm means "a process or set of rules to be followed in calculations or other problem-solving operations". Therefore Algorithm refers to a set of rules/instructions that step-by-step define how a work is to be executed upon in order to get the expected results.

It can be understood by taking an example of cooking a new recipe. To cook a new recipe, one reads the instructions and steps and executes them one by one, in the given sequence. The result thus obtained is the new dish cooked perfectly. Similarly, algorithms help to do a task in programming to get the expected output. The Algorithm designed is language-independent, i.e. they are just plain instructions that can be implemented in any language, and yet the output will be the same, as expected.

Characteristics of an Algorithm

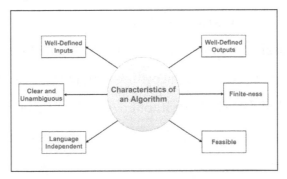

As one would not follow any written instructions to cook the recipe, but only the standard one. Similarly, not all written instructions for programming are an algorithm. In order for some instructions to be an algorithm, it must have the following characteristics:

- Clear and Unambiguous: Algorithm should be clear and unambiguous. Each of its steps should be clear in all aspects and must lead to only one meaning.

- Well-Defined Inputs: If an algorithm says to take inputs, it should be well-defined inputs.

- Well-Defined Outputs: The algorithm must clearly define what output will be yielded and it should be well-defined as well.

- Finiteness: The algorithm must be finite, i.e. it should not end up in an infinite loops or similar.

- Feasible: The algorithm must be simple, generic and practical, such that it can be executed upon will the available resources. It must not contain some future technology, or anything.

- Language Independent: The Algorithm designed must be language-independent, i.e. it must be just plain instructions that can be implemented in any language, and yet the output will be same, as expected.

Advantages of Algorithms

- It is easy to understand.

- Algorithm is a step-wise representation of a solution to a given problem.

- In Algorithm the problem is broken down into smaller pieces or steps hence, it is easier for the programmer to convert it into an actual program.

Disadvantages of Algorithms

- Writing an algorithm takes a long time so it is time-consuming.

- Branching and Looping statements are difficult to show in Algorithms.

Need of Algorithm

- To understand the basic idea of the problem.

- To find an approach to solve the problem.

- To improve the efficiency of existing techniques.

- To understand the basic principles of designing the algorithms.

- To compare the performance of the algorithm with respect to other techniques.

- It is the best method of description without describing the implementation detail.

- The Algorithm gives a clear description of requirements and goal of the problem to the designer.

- A good design can produce a good solution.

- To understand the flow of the problem.

- To measure the behavior (or performance) of the methods in all cases (best cases, worst cases, average cases).

- With the help of an algorithm, we can also identify the resources (memory, input-output) cycles required by the algorithm.

- With the help of algorithm, we convert art into a science.

- To understand the principle of designing.

- We can measure and analyze the complexity (time and space) of the problems concerning input size without implementing and running it; it will reduce the cost of design.

How to Decide which Algorithm is Best Suited?

- It depends on how efficient the algorithm when higher order of inputs is given.

- The possible restrictions/constraints on the values.

- The architecture of the computer and the kind of storage devices to be used.

- Another important aspect is the correctness of the algorithm implying that algorithm is correct if, for every instance, it produces correct output. An incorrect algorithm might not halt at all on some input instances, or give incorrect output.

Practical Applications of Algorithms

The Internet without which it is difficult to imagine a day is the result of clever and efficient algorithms. With the aid of these algorithms, various sites on the Internet are able to manage and manipulate this large volume of data. Finding good routes on which the data will travel and using search engine to find pages on which particular information is present.

Another great milestone is the Human Genome Project which has great progress towards the goal of identification of the 100000 genes in human DNA, determining the sequences of the 3 billion chemical base pairs that make up the human DNA, storing this huge amount of information in databases, and developing tools for data analysis. Each of these steps required sophisticated and efficient algorithms.

The day-to-day electronic commerce activities are hugely dependent on our personal information such as credit/debit card numbers, passwords, bank statements, OTPs and so on. The core technologies used include public-key cryptocurrency and digital signatures which are based on numerical algorithms and number theory.

The approach of linear programming is also one such technique which is widely used like:

- In manufacturing and other commercial enterprises where resources need to be allocated scarcely in the most beneficial way.

- Or an institution may want to determine where to spend money buying advertising in order to maximize the chances of their institution to grow.

Shortest path algorithm also has an extensive use as:

- In a transportation firm such as a trucking or railroad company, may have financial interest in finding shortest path through a road or rail network because taking shortest path result in lower labour or fuel costs.

- Or a routing node on the Internet may need to find the shortest path through the network in order to route a message quickly.

Even an application that does not require algorithm content at the application level relies heavily on algorithms as the application depends on hardware, GUI, networking or object orientation and these entire make an extensive use of algorithms.

Stages of Problem Solving

Problem solving is both an art and science. As there are no guidelines available to solve the problem, the problem solving is called an art as high creativity is needed for solving problems effectively. Thus by art, we mean one has to be creative, novel and adventurous and by science, we mean the problem solving should be based on sound mathematical and logical guidelines. The problem solving stages are; Problem Understanding, Algorithm Planning, Design of algorithms, Algorithm Verification and Validation, Algorithm analysis, Algorithm Implementation and Perform post-mortem analysis.

Problem Understanding

Is it possible to solve the given problem? This falls under the domain called computability theory. Computability theory deals with the solvability of the given problem. To deal with the solvability, one requires analytical thinking. Analytical thinking deals with the ways of solving the given problems. It is not possible to solve the problem if the problem is ill-defined. Often puzzles depict the limitations of computing power. Sometimes, there may be some solution but one doesn't have the knowledge or means to analyze the algorithms. Thus problems can be as follows:

- Computationally hard problems: It is not possible to solve this problem.

- Analytically hard problems: These problems, like Traveling salesperson problem, runs effectively for small instances. But for larger problems, it may be computationally feasible. Also for some problems analysis is difficult.

In computability theory, these sorts of problems are often considered. The problem solving starts with understanding of the problem and aims at providing a detailed problem statement. There should not be any confusion in the problem statement. As the mistakes in understanding the problem may affect the development of algorithms.

Planning of an Algorithm

Once problem statement is produced, the planning of algorithm starts. This phase requires selection of computing model and data structures. Computational model is the selection of a computing device. A computational model is a mathematical model. Why? It is meaningless to talk about fastness of the algorithm with respect to a particular machine or environment. An algorithm may run faster in machine A compared to machine B. Hence, analysis of algorithms based on a particular brand of machines is meaningless. Hence, the algorithm analysis should be should be independent of machines. Normally, two theoretical machines are used – One is called Random Access Machine (RAM) and another is called Turing machine.

Data Structures

Second major decision in algorithm planning is selection of a data structure. Data structure is a domain that deals with data storage along with its relationships. Data structures can have impact on the efficiency of the algorithms. Therefore, algorithms and data structures together often constitute important aspect of problem solving.

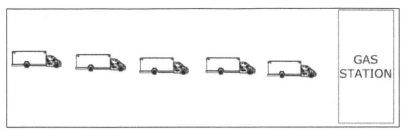

Example of a Queue.

Data organization is something we are familiar with in our daily life. The Figure above shows a data organization called „Queue". A Gas station with one servicing point should have a queue like above to avoid chaos. A queue (or FCFS – First Come First Serve) is an organization where the processing (filling of gas) is done in one end and addition of a vehicle is done in another end. A popular statement in computer science is "Algorithm + Data structure = Program" as a wrong selection of a data structure often proves fatal in problem solving.

The planning of a data structure can be based on the solution also as some of the problems can be solved exactly. Sometimes, getting the exact solution is impossible for computationally hard problems. Therefore, for such problems approximate solutions are planned.

Design of Algorithms

Algorithm design is the next stage of problem solving. Algorithm design is a way of developing the algorithmic solutions using the appropriate design strategy. Different types of problem demands different strategies for finding the solution. Just imagine, searching a name in a telephone directory. If one has to search for a name "Qadir", then the search can be done from starting page to the end page. This is a crude way of solving the problem. Instead, one can prefer to search using indexed entries. It can be done using interpolation search also. Thus design strategy selection plays an important role in solving problems effectively.

After the algorithm is designed, it should be communicated to a programmer so that the algorithms can be coded as a program. This stage is called algorithm specification. The choices of communication can be natural language, programming language and pseudocode. Natural language is preferable, but has some disadvantages such as lack of precision and ambiguity. Programming language may create a dependency on that particular language. Hence, often algorithm is written and communicated through pseudocode. Pseudocode is a mix of natural language and mathematics.

Algorithm Verification and Validation

Algorithm verification and validation is the process of checking algorithm correctness. An algorithm is expected to give correct output for all valid inputs. This process is called algorithm validation. Once validation is over, program proving or program verification starts. Verification is done by giving mathematical proofs. Mathematical proofs are rigorous and better than scientific methods. Program correctness itself a major study by itself. Proofs are given as follows:

- Proof by assertion: Assertion asserts some facts. It can be given throughout the program and assertions expressed are in predicate calculus. If it can be proved that, if for every legal input, if it leads to a logical output, then it can be said that the given algorithm is correct.

- Mathematical Induction: Mathematical induction is a technique can be used to prove recursive algorithms.

Algorithm Analysis

Once the algorithm is proved correct, then the analysis starts. Analysis is important for two reasons. They are as follows:

- To decide efficiency of algorithms.

- To compare algorithms for deciding the effective solutions for a given problem.

Algorithm analysis as a domain is called Algorithmic Complexity theory. What is a complexity? Well, complexity is assumed to be with respect to size of the input. Sorting of an array with 10 numbers is easy: but the same problem with 1 million is difficult. So there is a connection with the complexity and the size of the input. The complexity of two or more algorithms can be done based on measures that can be categorized into two types:

- Subjective measures include factors like ease of implementation or style of the algorithm or understandability of algorithms. But the problems with the subjective measures are that they vary from person to person. Hence Objective measures are preferable.

- Objective measures include factors like time complexity, space complexity and measures like disk usage and network usage. By and large, algorithmic analysis is the estimation of computing resources.

Out of all objective measures, two measures are popular:

- Time complexity: Time complexity refers to the time taken by the algorithm to run for scaled input. By time, it is often meant run time. Actually, there are two time factors. One is execution time and another is run time. Execution (or compile time) does not depend on problem instances and compilers often ignore instances. Hence, time always refers to run or execution time only.

- Space Complexity: Space complexity is meant the memory required to store the program.

Implementation of Algorithm as a Program and Performance Analysis

After the algorithms are designed, it is implemented as a program. This stage requires the selection of a programming language. After the program is written, then the program must be tested. Sometimes, the program may not give expected results due to errors. The process of removing the errors is called debugging. Once program is available, they can be verified with a bench mark dataset. It is called experimental algorithmic. This is called performance analysis. Thus, Profiling is a process of running a program on a datasets and measuring the time/space requirement of the program.

Postmortem Analysis

Problem solving process ends with postmortem analysis. Any analysis should end with the valuable insight. Insights like is the problem solvable? Are there any limits of this algorithm? And is the algorithm efficient? Are asked and collected.

A theoretical best solution for the given problem is called lower bound of the algorithm. The worst case estimate of behaviour of the algorithm is called upper bound. The difference between upper and lower bound is called algorithmic gap. Technically, no algorithmic gaps should exist. But practically, there may be vast gap present between two bounds. Refining the algorithms is to bring these gaps short by reefing planning, design, implementation and analysis. Thus problem solving is not linear but rather this is a cycle.

Algorithm Writing

Algorithms can be written using natural language or pseudocode. There is no standard way of writing algorithms in pseudocode. So there is a need for basic guidelines for writing algorithms. The problem solving starts with stepwise refinement. The idea of stepwise refinement is to take a problem and try to divide it into many subproblems. The subproblems can further be divided more subproblems. The subdivision will be carried out till the problem can't further be divided. Hence, the idea of stepwise refinement is to evolve structures that can be directly implemented in a programming language. The kinds of structures thus evolved are sequence, decision and Iteration. These are called control structures and are described below:

Sequence

Sequence is a structure whereby the computer system executes tasks one by one. This is given as follows:

- Task P

- Task Q

- Task R

Here, the task P is executed first, followed by tasks Q and R.

Decision or Conditional Branching

This is a control structure where the condition is evaluated first and based on its condition the course of action is decided. The control structure for decision is given as follows:

```
IF (Condition C) Then

        Perform Task A

Else

Perform Task B
```

It can be observed that the condition C is evaluated first. Then based on the results of the condition, task P is performed if the condition is true or task Q is performed if the condition is false.

Repetition

Computers are known for their effectiveness in solving repetitive tasks. Repetition control structure is given as follows:

```
While (condition C) do
     R
```

For example, informally we say often in English language "Perform the task 100 times". This is a kind of repetition.

There are two types of iteration. Iteration like saying "Perform task A exactly 500 times" is called a bounded iteration. Programming languages do provide a 'For – Statement" that implements a bounded iteration. On the other hand, statements like performing a task for a specific condition are called unbound iteration. Good examples of unbounded iteration are statements like "While... End while" and "repeat .... until".

Once the control structures are evolved, then it has to be written as an algorithm. There are only three ways of writing algorithms:

- Using a natural language like English.

- Using a programming languages, say C++ or Java.

- Pseudocode.

English, or any natural language, is obvious choice for writing algorithms. But the problem is most of the natural languages are ambiguous as a wrong interpretation of a word may lead to imprecise implementation. Hence, natural languages are not considered suitable for algorithm writing. Similarly, the usage of a programming language makes algorithm dependent on a particular language. Hence, pseudocode is preferable for writing algorithms. Pseudocode is a mix of natural language like English and mathematical constructs. Let us evolve pseudocode conventions so that the algorithm can be written. The pseudocode conventions of the algorithms are specified below:

1. Assignment Statement: Assignment statement is a statement for assigning a value or expression to a variable. For example, the following assignment statements are valid.

$$x = 20$$
$$z = r + k$$

2. Input/output Statements: Input statement is used by the user to give values to the variables of the algorithm. For example, the following statement is right.

Input x, y

Similarly, the print or write statement is used to print the values of the variables. For example, the following statement is used to print the value of the variable x and y.

Print x, y or Write x, y

3. Conditional Statements: Algorithm can have conditional statement. The syntax of the conditional statement can be shown as:

```
If (condition) then

    Statement (s)

End if
```

Here, the condition (True or false type) is evaluated first. If the condition is true, then statement(s) are executed. "If- Endif" serves as brackets for the conditional statement. Conditional statement can have else part also as shown below:

```
If (condition) then

    Statement A ;

else

    Statement B

End if
```

Here, If the condition is true, then statement A (This can be a set of statements also) are executed. Otherwise, if the condition is false, then statement B (This also can be a single or multiple statements) is executed.

4. Repetition Statement: Algorithms can have repetitive statements. Three repetitive statements are supported by most of the programming languages. Unconditional repetitive statement is 'For' statement. This is an example of bounded iteration. The syntax of this statement is given as follows:

```
For variable = value1 to value2 do

    Statement(s)

End for
```

Computer system executes this statement like this: First the variable is to value1. Value1 and value2 can be a value or an expression. Then the statement(s) is executed till the variable values reaches value 2.

Conditional Loop

One useful repetitive statement is "While" statement that provides a conditional loop. The syntax of the statement is given below:

```
While (Condition) do begin

    Statement(s);

End while.
```

Until also provides repetition control structure. The difference between this statement and While statement is that "repeat – until" statement first executes the task and then checks condition of the statement. The syntax of repeat statement is given below:

```
repeat
        Statement(s)
until (condition)
```

Using these statements, some elementary algorithms can be designed.

Let us practice some elementary algorithms and let us consider the problem of converting Fahrenheit to Celsius. The problem can be directly solved using a simple formula. The formula for conversion is given as,

$$\text{celsius} = \frac{5}{9} \times \left(\text{Farenheit} - 32\right)$$

The algorithm can be written informally as follows:

- Input Fahrenheit temperature.
- Apply the formula for temperature conversion.
- Display the results.

The algorithm can be given formally as follows:

Algorithm FtoC(F)

```
Input: Fahrenheit F

Output: Celsius

Begin
        Celsius = (5/9)* (F-32)

        Return Celsius;
End.
```

Let us practice one more algorithm for finding the count and sum of even/odd numbers of an array. The algorithm can be given informally as follows:

- Initialize oddcount, evencount, oddsum and evensum.
- Read the sumber.
- If it is odd or even, then increment the appropriate counters.
- Display the results.

The algorithm is formally given as follows:

```
Algorithm sumoddeven (A[1..n])
```

```
Input: An array A[1..n]

Output: sum on odd and even number count

oddcount = 0

evencount = 0

oddsum = 0

evensum = 0

for i = 1 to n

        reminder = A[i] mod 2

     if (reminder = 0) then

              evensum = evensum + A[i]

            evencount = evencount + 1

        else

              oddsum = oddsum + A[i]

              oddcount = oddcount + 1

         End if

        End for

        Return evensum, evencount, oddsum, oddcount

        End
```

Another popular algorithm is linear search. Here, a target is given and the objective of the linear search is to display whether the target is present in the given array, if so where? And failure message is the target is not present in the array. The informal algorithm is given as follows:

```
1. Read the value of the target and array A

2. Index = 1, found = false

3. Repeat until found = true of index > n

        if the value at index = target then

                return the index and set found = true

         else index = index + 1

4. If (not found) then output message that target is not found

5. Exit
```

It can be seen that initially index and flag found is initialized to 1 and 'false' respectively. Every value guided by index pointer is checked and if the target is found, then the flag is set true and the corresponding index is sent. Otherwise, the failure message to find target is printed.

Formally this can be written as follows:

```
Algorithm Search(list, n, target)
Begin
index = 1
found = false
repeat until found = true of index > n
     if (list_index = target) then
          print "target found at", index
            found = true
       else index = index + 1
     if (not found) then print 'Target is not found'
     End
```

Thus one can conclude that after stepwise refinement, the control structures are evolved and can be written suitable as a pseudocode. Now let us discuss about recursive algorithms.

Basics of Recursion

Recursion is a way of defining an object using the concept of self-reference. The statements like "A length of the linked list of size N is 1 plus the length of the remaining linked list of size N-1" are examples of recursive definition. Let us start with recursive definitions. The basic components of a recursive algorithm definition are given as follows:

- Base case: This is also known as initial values. This is the non-recursive part.

- Recursive step: It is the recursive part of the algorithm. Often this is a rule used for calculating a function in terms of the previous values of the function.

- Step for progress towards base case: This is a condition that ensures the algorithm eventually converges by bringing the recursive step towards the base case. Let us discuss some recursive algorithms now.

Let us consider the problem of finding summation problem given as $\sum_{i=1}^{n} n$. The recursive definition of summation can be given compactly as follows:

$$\text{Sigma}(n) = \begin{cases} 0 & \text{if } n = 0 \\ n + \text{Sigma}(n-1) & \text{if } n > 1 \end{cases}$$

A simple recursive algorithm for implementing the above recursive formula is given as follows:

Algorithm Sigma (N)

```
Program: Compute sum recursively

Input: N
```

```
Output: Sum of N numbers
Begin
      if (N == 0)
      return 0;
      else
      return N + Sigma(N - 1);
   End if
End
```

The above algorithm can also be written as an iterative algorithm. The iterative algorithm is given as follows:

Algorithm Iterative-sigma(N)

```
Program: Compute sum recursively
Input: N
Output: Sum of N numbers
Begin
      sum = 0;
      for i = 1 to N do
            sum = sum + I
      end for
End
```

It can be observed that both versions give identical answers. It can be observed that recursive algorithms are compact and it is easier to formulate the algorithms. But, the disadvantage is that recursive algorithms take extra space and require more memory.

Let us discuss about one more recursive algorithm for finding factorial of a number. The recursive function for finding the factorial of a number is given as follows:

$$\text{Factorial}(n) = \begin{cases} 1 & \text{if } n = 0 \\ n \times \text{factorial}(n-1) & \text{if } n \geq 1 \end{cases}$$

The pseudocode for finding factorial of a number is given as follows:

Algorithm MFactorial(m)

```
Begin
If m < 0 then
print "factorial for negative numbers is not possible"
```

```
End if
If ((m=0) OR (m = 1) then
     Return 1;
Else
     Return m * MFactorial(m-1);
End If
End.
```

Another important problem is towers of Hanoi. There are three pegs – source, intermediate and destination. The objective of this problem is to move the disks from source peg to the destination peg using the intermediate peg with the following rules:

- At any point of time, only one disk should be moved.

- A larger disk cannot be placed on the smaller disk at any point of time.

The logic for solving this problem is that, for N disks, N-1 disks are moved to the intermediate tower and then the larger disk is moved to the destination. Then the disks are moved from the intermediate tower to the destination.

The formal algorithm is given as follows:

Algorithm Towers of Hanoi (A, B, C, n)

```
Input: Source Peg A, intermediate Peg B and Destination Peg C, n disks
Output: All the disks in the tower C
Begin
if n = 1 the move disk from A to C
lse
towersofhanoi (A,C,B,n-1);
move disk from A to C
towersofhanoi (B,A,C,n-1);
End if
End.
```

Classification Algorithms

We use the training dataset to get better boundary conditions which could be used to determine each target class. Once the boundary conditions are determined, the next task is to predict the target class. The whole process is known as classification.

Basic Terminology in Classification Algorithms

- Classifier: An algorithm that maps the input data to a specific category.

- Classification model: A classification model tries to draw some conclusions from the input values given for training. It will predict the class labels/categories for the new data.

- Feature: A feature is an individual measurable property of a phenomenon being observed.

- Binary Classification: Classification task with two possible outcomes. Example: Gender classification (Male/Female).

- Multi-class classification: Classification with more than two classes. In multi-class classification, each sample is assigned to one and only one target label. Example: An animal can be a cat or dog but not both at the same time.

- Multi-label classification: Classification task where each sample is mapped to a set of target labels (more than one class). Example: A news article can be about sports, a person, and location at the same time.

Applications of Classification Algorithms

- Email spam classification.

- Bank customer's loan pay willingness prediction.

- Cancer tumor cell identification.

- Sentiment analysis.

- Drugs classification.

- Facial key points detection.

- Pedestrian detection in automotive car driving.

Types of Classification Algorithms

Logistic Regression

Logistic regression is a machine learning algorithm for classification. In this algorithm, the probabilities describing the possible outcomes of a single trial are modeled using a logistic function.

- Advantages: Logistic regression is designed for this purpose (classification), and is most useful for understanding the influence of several independent variables on a single outcome variable.

- Disadvantages: Works only when the predicted variable is binary, assumes all predictors are independent of each other and assumes data is free of missing values.

```
from sklearn.svm import SVC
svm = SVC(kernel="linear", C=0.025,random_state=101)
svm.fit(x_train, y_train)
y_pred=svm.predict(x_test)
```

Naive Bayes

Naive Bayes algorithm based on Bayes' theorem with the assumption of independence between every pair of features. Naive Bayes classifiers work well in many real-world situations such as document classification and spam filtering.

- Advantages: This algorithm requires a small amount of training data to estimate the necessary parameters. Naive Bayes classifiers are extremely fast compared to more sophisticated methods.

- Disadvantages: Naive Bayes is known to be a bad estimator.

```python
from sklearn.naive_bayes import GaussianNB
nb =  GaussianNB()
nb.fit(x_train, y_train)
y_pred=nb.predict(x_test)
```

Stochastic Gradient Descent

Stochastic gradient descent is a simple and very efficient approach to fit linear models. It is particularly useful when the number of samples is very large. It supports different loss functions and penalties for classification.

- Advantages: Efficiency and ease of implementation.

- Disadvantages: Requires a number of hyper-parameters and it is sensitive to feature scaling.

```python
from sklearn.linear_model import SGDClassifier
sgd =  SGDClassifier(loss='modified_huber', shuffle=True,random_state=101)
sgd.fit(x_train, y_train)
y_pred=sgd.predict(x_test)
```

K-Nearest Neighbours

Neighbours based classification is a type of lazy learning as it does not attempt to construct a general internal model, but simply stores instances of the training data. Classification is computed from a simple majority vote of the k nearest neighbours of each point.

- Advantages: This algorithm is simple to implement, robust to noisy training data, and effective if training data is large.

- Disadvantages: Need to determine the value of K and the computation cost is high as it needs to compute the distance of each instance to all the training samples.

```python
from sklearn.neighbors import KNeighborsClassifier
knn = KNeighborsClassifier(n_neighbors=15)
knn.fit(x_train,y_train)
y_pred=knn.predict(x_test)
```

Decision Tree

Given a data of attributes together with its classes, a decision tree produces a sequence of rules that can be used to classify the data.

- Advantages: Decision Tree is simple to understand and visualise, requires little data preparation, and can handle both numerical and categorical data.

- Disadvantages: Decision tree can create complex trees that do not generalise well, and decision trees can be unstable because small variations in the data might result in a completely different tree being generated.

```
from sklearn.tree import DecisionTreeClassifier
dtree = DecisionTreeClassifier(max_depth=10, random_state=101,
                               max_features = None, min_samples_leaf = 15)
dtree.fit(x_train, y_train)
y_pred=dtree.predict(x_test)
```

Random Forest

Random forest classifier is a meta-estimator that fits a number of decision trees on various sub-samples of datasets and uses average to improve the predictive accuracy of the model and controls over-fitting. The sub-sample size is always the same as the original input sample size but the samples are drawn with replacement.

- Advantages: Reduction in over-fitting and random forest classifier is more accurate than decision trees in most cases.

- Disadvantages: Slow real time prediction, difficult to implement, and complex algorithm.

```
from sklearn.ensemble import RandomForestClassifier
rfm = RandomForestClassifier(n_estimators=70, oob_score=True, n_jobs=-1,
                             random_state=101, max_features = None, min_samples_leaf = 30)
rfm.fit(x_train, y_train)
y_pred=rfm.predict(x_test)
```

Support Vector Machine

Support vector machine is a representation of the training data as points in space separated into categories by a clear gap that is as wide as possible. New examples are then mapped into that same space and predicted to belong to a category based on which side of the gap they fall.

- Advantages: Effective in high dimensional spaces and uses a subset of training points in the decision function so it is also memory efficient.

- Disadvantages: The algorithm does not directly provide probability estimates, these are calculated using an expensive five-fold cross-validation.

```
from sklearn.svm import SVC
svm = SVC(kernel="linear", C=0.025,random_state=101)
svm.fit(x_train, y_train)
y_pred=svm.predict(x_test)
```

Clustering Algorithms

Clustering is the task of dividing the population or data points into a number of groups such that data points in the same groups are more similar to other data points in the same group than those in other groups. In simple words, the aim is to segregate groups with similar traits and assign them into clusters.

Let's understand this with an example. Suppose, you are the head of a rental store and wish to understand preferences of your costumers to scale up your business. Is it possible for you to look at details of each costumer and devise a unique business strategy for each one of them? Definitely not. But, what you can do is to cluster all of your costumers into say 10 groups based on their purchasing habits and use a separate strategy for costumers in each of these 10 groups. And this is what we call clustering.

Types of Clustering

Broadly speaking, clustering can be divided into two subgroups:

- Hard Clustering: In hard clustering, each data point either belongs to a cluster completely or not. For example, in the above example each customer is put into one group out of the 10 groups.

- Soft Clustering: In soft clustering, instead of putting each data point into a separate cluster, a probability or likelihood of that data point to be in those clusters is assigned. For example, from the above scenario each costumer is assigned a probability to be in either of 10 clusters of the retail store.

Types of Clustering Algorithms

Since the task of clustering is subjective, the means that can be used for achieving this goal are plenty. Every methodology follows a different set of rules for defining the 'similarity' among data points. In fact, there are more than 100 clustering algorithms known. But few of the algorithms are used popularly:

- Connectivity models: As the name suggests, these models are based on the notion that the data points closer in data space exhibit more similarity to each other than the data points lying farther away. These models can follow two approaches. In the first approach, they start with classifying all data points into separate clusters and then aggregating them as the distance decreases. In the second approach, all data points are classified as a single cluster and then partitioned as the distance increases. Also, the choice of distance function is subjective. These models are very easy to interpret but lack scalability for handling big datasets. Examples of these models are hierarchical clustering algorithm and its variants.

- Centroid models: These are iterative clustering algorithms in which the notion of similarity is derived by the closeness of a data point to the centroid of the clusters. K-Means clustering algorithm is a popular algorithm that falls into this category. In these models, the no. of clusters required at the end has to be mentioned beforehand, which makes it important to have prior knowledge of the dataset. These models run iteratively to find the local optima.

- Distribution models: These clustering models are based on the notion of how probable is it that all data points in the cluster belong to the same distribution (For example: Normal, Gaussian). These models often suffer from over fitting. A popular example of these models is Expectation-maximization algorithm which uses multivariate normal distributions.

- Density Models: These models search the data space for areas of varied density of data points in the data space. It isolates various different density regions and assigns the data points within these regions in the same cluster. Popular examples of density models are DBSCAN and OPTICS.

K Means Clustering

K means is an iterative clustering algorithm that aims to find local maxima in each iteration. This algorithm works in these five steps:

1. Specify the desired number of clusters K: Let us choose k=2 for these 5 data points in 2-D space.

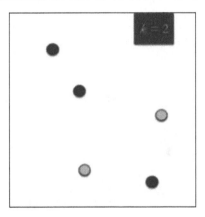

2. Randomly assign each data point to a cluster: Let's assign three points in cluster 1 shown using red color and two points in cluster 2 shown using grey color.

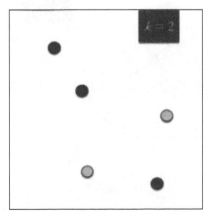

3. Compute cluster centroids: The centroid of data points in the red cluster is shown using red cross and those in grey cluster using grey cross.

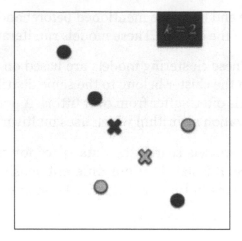

4. Re-assign each point to the closest cluster centroid: Note that only the data point at the bottom is assigned to the red cluster even though it's closer to the centroid of grey cluster. Thus, we assign that data point into grey cluster.

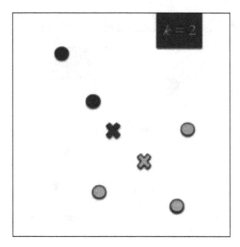

5. Re-compute cluster centroids: Now, re-computing the centroids for both the clusters.

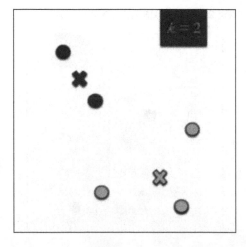

6. Repeat steps 4 and 5 until no improvements are possible: Similarly, we'll repeat the 4th and 5th steps until we'll reach global optima. When there will be no further switching of data points

between two clusters for two successive repeats. It will mark the termination of the algorithm if not explicitly mentioned.

Hierarchical Clustering

Hierarchical clustering, as the name suggests is an algorithm that builds hierarchy of clusters. This algorithm starts with all the data points assigned to a cluster of their own. Then two nearest clusters are merged into the same cluster. In the end, this algorithm terminates when there is only a single cluster left. The results of hierarchical clustering can be shown using dendrogram. The dendrogram can be interpreted as:

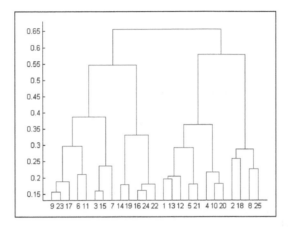

At the bottom, we start with 25 data points, each assigned to separate clusters. Two closest clusters are then merged till we have just one cluster at the top. The height in the dendrogram at which two clusters are merged represents the distance between two clusters in the data space.

The decision of the no. of clusters that can best depict different groups can be chosen by observing the dendrogram. The best choice of the no. of clusters is the no. of vertical lines in the dendrogram cut by a horizontal line that can transverse the maximum distance vertically without intersecting a cluster. In the above example, the best choice of no. of clusters will be 4 as the red horizontal line in the dendrogram below covers maximum vertical distance AB.

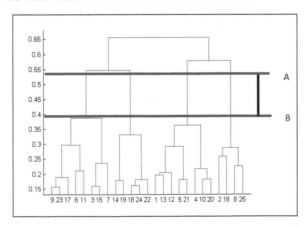

Two important things that you should know about hierarchical clustering are:

- This algorithm has been implemented above using bottom up approach. It is also possible to follow top-down approach starting with all data points assigned in the same cluster and recursively performing splits till each data point is assigned a separate cluster.

- The decision of merging two clusters is taken on the basis of closeness of these clusters. There are multiple metrics for deciding the closeness of two clusters:

  ○ Euclidean distance: $\|a - b\|_2 = \sqrt{(\Sigma(a_i - b_i))}$.

  ○ Squared Euclidean distance: $\|a - b\|_2^2 = \Sigma((a_i - b_i)^2)$.

  ○ Manhattan distance: $\|a - b\|_1 = \Sigma |a_i - b_i|$.

  ○ Maximum distance: $\|a - b\|_{INFINITY} = \max_i |a_i - b_i|$.

  ○ Mahalanobis distance: $\sqrt{\left((a - b)^T S^{-1} (-b)\right)}$ {where, s : covariance matrix}.

Difference between K Means and Hierarchical Clustering

- Hierarchical clustering can't handle big data well but K Means clustering can. This is because the time complexity of K Means is linear i.e. $O(n)$ while that of hierarchical clustering is quadratic i.e. $O(n^2)$.

- In K Means clustering, since we start with random choice of clusters, the results produced by running the algorithm multiple times might differ. While results are reproducible in Hierarchical clustering.

- K Means is found to work well when the shape of the clusters is hyper spherical (like circle in 2D, sphere in 3D).

- K Means clustering requires prior knowledge of K i.e. no. of clusters you want to divide your data into. But, you can stop at whatever number of clusters you find appropriate in hierarchical clustering by interpreting the dendrogram.

Applications of Clustering

Clustering has a large no. of applications spread across various domains. Some of the most popular applications of clustering are:

- Recommendation engines,

- Market segmentation,

- Social network analysis,

- Search result grouping,

- Medical imaging,

- Image segmentation,

- Anomaly detection.

Algorithm Analysis

Algorithm analysis is a process of determining the resources required when executing an algorithm. The resources considered include memory, communication bandwidth and computational time, The last resource is usually considered the most important. The running time of an algorithm is almost always independent of the programming language. Now let us understand the purpose of analyzing an algorithm. Basically the algorithm is analysed to estimate how long a program will run by analyzing an algorithm's running time without coding it. Analyzing an algorithm will also help to estimate the largest input that can reasonably be given to the program. It also helps to compare the efficiency of different algorithms and to focus on the parts of code that are executed the largest number of times. Finally the analysis of an algorithm helps to choose an appropriate algorithm for an application.

Algorithmic Performance

When we discuss about algorithmic performance there are two aspects to be considered namely time and space requirements. Instructions of an algorithm take time to be executed. We generally discuss how fast the algorithm performs and what are the components that affect its runtime. The other aspect is the space requirement. In general, data structures take space to be represented and so the kind of data structures that can be used and how the choice of data structure affects the runtime are important considerations.

We will focus on the time aspect of algorithmic performance. In this case the main questions to be answered include how to estimate the time required to run an algorithm, how to reduce the time required for implementing an algorithm by considering the factors affecting the running time including computer used, compiler and algorithm used and finally what is the input to the algorithm for implementing an algorithm by considering the factors affecting the running time including computer used, compiler and algorithm used and finally what is the input to the algorithm. We assume that in the machine model considered the instructions are executed one after another, with no concurrent operation that is we do not consider parallel computation. Example below shows the comparison of two algorithms.

Example of Time Taken by an Algorithm: A city has n stops. A bus driver wishes to follow the shortest path from one stop to another. Between every two stops, if a road exists, it may take a different time from other roads. Also, roads are one-way, i.e., the road from point 1 to 2, is different from that from point 2 to 1. How to find the shortest path between any two pairs?

A Naïve approach to the problem is to list all the paths (e) between a given pair of points and then compute the travel time for each. After this process we choose the shortest one.

The number of paths will be $n! \cong \left(\dfrac{n}{e} \right) n$

It will be impossible to run your algorithm even for a value of n = 30.

Examples of Two Algorithms for the Selection Problem Time Complexity: Given a list of N numbers, we need to determine the kth largest, where k ≤ N. There are two algorithms which can accomplish the given task.

Algorithm 1:

- Read N numbers into an array.

- Sort the array in decreasing order by some simple algorithm.

- Return the element in position k.

Algorithm 2:

- Read the first k elements into an array and sort them in decreasing order.

- Each remaining element is read one by one.

  ◦ If smaller than the kth element, then it is ignored.

  ◦ Otherwise, it is placed in its correct spot in the array, bumping one element out of the array.

- The element in the kth position is returned as the answer.

Now the question is which algorithm is better when N = 100 and k = 100? What happens when N = 1,000,000 and k = 500,000? Now the above two algorithms are not the only ones there exists better algorithms.

Time Complexity

Time complexity is a function that specifies how the running time of an algorithm depends on the size of the input. Now we have to understand the concept of time in the context of analyzing algorithms. Time can be defined as number of seconds. However this definition of time makes the analysis machine and implementation dependent.

Another way to define time is in terms of the lines of code executed so that algorithms performance can be compared independent of the machine used and the actual implementation methodology. It can also be defined as the number of times a specific operation is performed, example being the number of times addition is performed.

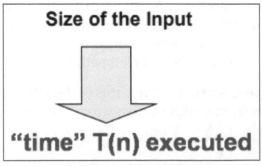

Function Mapping.

Running-time of Algorithms

The time bounds that we define are for the algorithms and not for programs. Programs are just implementations of an algorithm, and almost always the details of the program do not affect the bounds since they are defined in a relative manner. Similarly bounds are for algorithms not for the problems the algorithms solve. A problem can be solved with several algorithms some are more efficient than others and have different bounds.

Efficiency of an Algorithm

Normally when we want to analyze an algorithm we do not consider the actual run time using the computer. This running time is basically machined dependent. The solution to the problem is to carry out machine independent analysis. We also make the simplifying assumption that every basic operation takes constant time. Examples of such basic operations include addition, subtraction, multiplication, memory access operations. Non-basic operations such as sorting, searching, etc. are normally defined using basic operations. The efficiency of an algorithm is the number of basic operations it performs. In fact we do not distinguish between the basic operations for the purpose.

Theoretical Analysis of Time Efficiency

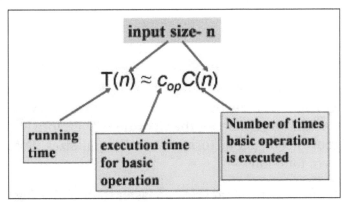

Running time.

Time efficiency is analyzed by determining the number of repetitions of the basic operation as a function of input size. Basic operation is defined as the operation that has the most influence in determining the running time of the algorithm. However different basic operations may cost differently. Figure above shows that running time of an algorithm is defined in terms of the input size and is the product of the execution time of a basic operation and the number of times the basic operation is executed.

Table: The input size and basic operation for different problems.

Problem	Input size measure	Basic operation
Search for key in list of n items	Number of items in list n	Key comparison
Multiply two matrices of floating point numbers	Dimensions of matrices	Floating point multiplication
Compute a^n where a is a floating point number	n	Floating point multiplication
Graph problem	#vertices and/or edges	Visiting a vertex or traversing an edge

For example, when analysing the worst case running time of a function that sorts a list of numbers, we are interested in determining the time taken in terms of the length of the input list and expressed as a function of this length. For example, the standard insertion sort takes time $T(n)$ where $T(n)= c*n^2+k$ for some constants c and k.

In fact, we do not worry about the exact values, but will look at 'broad classes' of values, or the growth rates. In case we consider the size of the input to be n. If an algorithm needs n basic operations and another algorithm needs 2n basic operations, we will consider them to be in the same efficiency category. However, we distinguish between exp(n), n, log(n).

Asymptotic Algorithm Analysis

The asymptotic analysis of an algorithm determines the running time in big-Oh notation. To perform the asymptotic analysis we first determine the worst-case or maximum number of primitive operations executed in terms of the function of the input size. We express this function with big-Oh notation. Since constant factors and lower-order terms will eventually be dropped, we can ignore them when counting the number of primitive operations. When we express the running time of an algorithm as $T(n)$, we mean that $T(n)$ is an upper bound on the running time that holds for all inputs of size n. This is called worst-case analysis. The algorithm may take less time on some inputs of size n, but we consider the worst case.

Asymptotic Growth Rate

The asymptotic behaviour of a function $f(n)$ (such as $f(n)=c*n$ or $f(n)=c*n^2$, etc.) refers to the growth of $f(n)$ as n gets large. In general we are not interested in small values of n, since what is crucial is the estimation of how slow the performance of the program will be on large inputs. The slower the asymptotic growth rate, the better the algorithm. Therefore we need a method of comparing functions that ignores constant factors and small input sizes. Before we go further let us some define some classes of functions:

- $O(g(n))$: Class of functions $f(n)$ that grow no faster than $g(n)$ – Big Oh.

- $\Theta(g(n))$: Class of functions $f(n)$ that grow at same rate as $g(n)$ – Big Theta.

- $\Omega(g(n))$: Class of functions $f(n)$ that grow at least as fast as $g(n)$ – Big Omega.

In general we use Big-Oh notation in the context of time analysis of algorithms.

Asymptotic Notation: Big-Oh

In estimating the running time of an algorithm we do not know the values constants associated with the function. A convenient notation for hiding the constant factor is the Big-Oh notation such as $O(n)$ (read: ''order n'') instead of ''cn for some constant c.'' Thus an algorithm is said to be $O(n)$ or linear time if there is a fixed constant c such that for all sufficiently large n, the algorithm takes time at most cn on inputs of size n. An algorithm is said to be $O(n^2)$ or quadratic time if there is a fixed constant c such that for all sufficiently large n, the algorithm takes time at most cn^2 on inputs of size n. $O(1)$ means constant time. The Big-Oh notation is a notation that concisely captures the important differences in the asymptotic growth rates of functions. One important advantage of big-O notation is that it makes algorithms much easier to analyse, since we can conveniently ignore low order terms. For example, an algorithm that runs in time say $16n^3 + 20n^2 + 4n \log n + 100$ is still a considered as a cubic algorithm of the order $O(n^3)$. This means that any two linear algorithms will be considered equally good by this measure. This is one of the main issues associated with asymptotic analysis and big-O notation. In summary in the case of Big-Oh notation to simplify the running time estimation, for a function f(n), we ignore the constants and lower order terms.

Growth Rate Functions

Some typical growth rate functions in the context of analysis of algorithms:

- $O(1)$: That of the order of 1 – here time requirement is constant, which means the time taken by the algorithm is independent of the size of the problem.

- $O(\log_2 n)$: That is of the order of logn – here the time requirement has logarithmic growth in terms of n (size of the problem) and increases slowly as the problem size increases.

- $O(n)$: That is of the order n – here the time requirement has linear growth in terms of the size of the problem n and increases directly with the size of the problem.

- $O(n*\log_2 n)$: That is of the order of nlogn that is the time requirement has a growth of nlogn and increases more rapidly than a linear algorithm.

- $O(n^2)$: That is of the order of n^2 - here the time requirement has quadratic growth in terms of the size of the problem n and increases rapidly with the size of the problem.

- $O(n^3)$: That is of the order of n^3 - here the time requirement has cubic growth in terms of the size of the problem n and increases very rapidly with the size of the problem.

- $O(2n)$: That is of the order of 2^n - here as the size of the problem increases, the time requirement experiences an exponential growth and increases too rapidly to be practical.

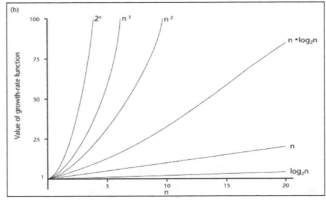

Comparison of Growth Functions.

Primitive Operations

The basic computations performed by an algorithm are identifiable in pseudocode. However an algorithm is specified such that these operations are largely independent from the programming language. The exact definition of the operations is not important. It is assumed to take a constant amount of time in the RAM model. The RAM model is used for the purpose of analysis and is assumed to have one processor, execute one instruction at a time where each instruction takes "unit time", has fixed-size operands, and has fixed size storage (RAM and disk). Examples of these basic operations include:

- Evaluating an expression.

- Assigning a value to a variable.

- Indexing into an array.

- Calling a method.

- Returning from a method.

Now let us consider an example shown in figure below. As can be seen from the example for loops the maximum time required is at most the running time of the statements inside the for-loop (including tests) times the number of iterations.

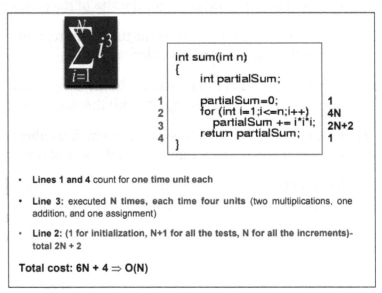

- **Lines 1 and 4** count for one time unit each

- **Line 3:** executed N times, each time four units (two multiplications, one addition, and one assignment)

- **Line 2:** (1 for initialization, N+1 for all the tests, N for all the increments)- total 2N + 2

Total cost: 6N + 4 ⇒ O(N)

An example showing the Calculation of Time Complexity.

In the case nested for loops the running time of the statement multiplied by the product of the sizes of all the for-loops and hence will result in time complexity of the order of $O(N^2)$.

```
for (i=0;i<n;i++)
    for (j=0;j<n;j++)
        k++;
```

A piece of code with nested for loop.

Consecutive statements just add to the overall time complexity. If there are n such statements then they add to the time complexity of nested for loops.

$$O(N)+O(N^2)=O(N^2)$$

In the case of If/Else statements the time complexity is never more than the running time of the test plus the larger of the running times of S1 and S2 where S1 is the set of statements in the then part of If/Else and S2 is the set of statements in the else part of If/Else.

Best-case, Average-case and Worst-case

Now let us discuss the various cases of time complexity analysis. These three cases arise because not all inputs of a given size take the same time to run.

- Worst case: W(n): Maximum over inputs of size n – this is the maximum time complexity for the given input size. Worst-case running time of an algorithm is the longest running time for any input of size n. In other words it is an upper bound on the running time for any input and in fact guarantees that the algorithm will never take longer than this time. Example: Sort a set of numbers in increasing order; and the data is in decreasing order. Nevertheless the worst case can occur fairly often.

- Best case: B(n): Minimum over inputs of size n.

- Average case: A(n): "Average" over inputs of size n. We can calculate the average case complexity under some assumption about the probability distribution of all possible inputs of size n, and calculate the weighted sum of expected C(n) (numbers of basic operation repetitions) over all possible inputs of size n.

Let us consider an example of sequential search and another example for searching a database to illustrate these aspects.

Sequential Search for K in an Array of n Integers

Begin at first element in array and look at each element in turn until K is found.

- Best case: Find at first position. Cost is 1 for the comparison operation.

- Worst case: Find at last position. Cost is n compares.

- Average case: (n+1)/2 compares IF we assume the element with value K is equally likely to be in any position in the array.

Sorting the Elements in an Array

- Best-case running time: Sort a set of numbers in increasing order; and the data is already in increasing order.

- Average-case running time: May be difficult to define what "average" means.

Recursive Algorithms: Analysis

In order to analyze recursive algorithms, we require more sophisticated techniques. Specifically, we study how to define and solve recurrence relations. We use the example of Factorial to explain these concepts.

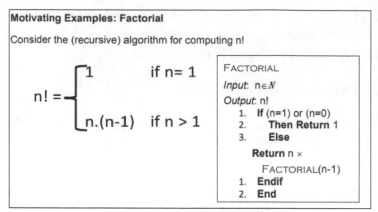

Motivating Examples: Factorial

Consider the (recursive) algorithm for computing n!

$$n! = \begin{cases} 1 & \text{if } n = 1 \\ \\ n.(n-1) & \text{if } n > 1 \end{cases}$$

FACTORIAL

Input: $n \in N$

Output: n!
1. **If** (n=1) or (n=0)
2.   **Then Return** 1
3.   **Else**

    Return n ×

      FACTORIAL(n-1)
1. **Endif**
2. **End**

Recursive Algorithm for Factorial.

In order to analyze the recursive algorithm we need to find out the number of multiplications performed by the factorial F(n)? When n=1 we do not perform any multiplication. In other cases we perform one plus how many ever multiplications we perform in the recursive call (Factorial(n-1)). The number of multiplications can be expressed as a formula:

$$F(0) = 0$$
$$F(n) = 1 + F(n-1)$$

This relation is known as a recurrence relation.

Recurrences and Running Time

Now let us discuss how to find out the running time in terms of recurrence equations. A recurrence equation gives a function of a value n in terms of functions on smaller inputs (lesser than n). This is given below:

$$T(n) = T(n-1) + n$$

Recurrences arise when an algorithm contains recursive calls to itself. Now we need to find out the actual running time of the algorithm. In order to do this we need to solve the recurrence equation by finding an explicit formula of the expression by binding the recurrence by an expression that involves n. Let us understand this using the example of Binary Search and the corresponding algorithm.

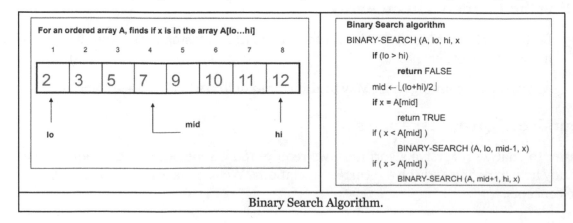

Binary Search Algorithm.

Now let us discuss the recurrence equation for the above binary search algorithm. The algorithm can be analysed as given. $O(1)$ is the time taken to do the comparisons. After this process the search range is divided into two halves. Therefore,

$$T(N) = T(N/2) + 1$$

On applying the recurrence repeatedly we get,

$$T(N) = T(N/4) + 2$$
$$= T(N/8) + 3 \dots$$
$$= T(N/2k) + k$$

Let this be rounded to nearest power of 2. That is let $N \leq 2m$

$$T(N) \leq T(2m/2k) + k$$

Let $k = m$.

Then $T(N) \leq T(2m/2m) + m = T(1) + m = 1 + m = O(m)$

If $N = 2m$, then $m = \log N$. So $T(N) = O(\log N)$

Thus, the running time is $O(\log N)$.

References

- Introduction-to-algorithms: geeksforgeeks.org, Retrieved 14, April 2020

- Daa-need-of-algorithm: javatpoint.com, Retrieved 17, January 2020

- The-role-of-algorithms-in-computing: geeksforgeeks.org, Retrieved 04, August 2020

- Introduction-to-classification-algorithms: dzone.com, Retrieved 27, March 2020

- 7-types-classification-algorithms: analyticsindiamag.com, Retrieved 07, May 2020

- An-introduction-to-clustering-and-different-methods-of-clustering: analyticsvidhya.com, Retrieved 18, July 2020

Algorithm Design

In computer science and mathematics, algorithms are designed in a step-by-step manner to solve problems. This chapter discusses in detail how to design different types of algorithms such as brute force algorithms, greedy algorithms, branch and bound algorithms, transform and conquer algorithms, and backtracking algorithms.

Algorithm design technique is a specific approach to create a design process for solving problems. These techniques can be applied to different computing problems. These general techniques provide guidelines for designing algorithms for new problems and to represent a useful collection of tools. Before we proceed further let us list out some generally used techniques.

Commonly used Techniques

- Brute force,

- Decrease and Conquer,

- Divide and Conquer,

- Transform and Conquer,

- Greedy Techniques,

- Dynamic programming,

- Backtracking,

- Genetic Techniques.

Recursive Algorithms

A recursive algorithm is based on replying the algorithm to sub-problems. A recursive algorithm is defined as an algorithm which contains at least one recursive call with "smaller (or simpler)" input values. A recursive call is a call of the same algorithm either directly (algorithm A calls itself) or indirectly (algorithm A calls algorithm B which in turn calls algorithm A). The cascade of recursive calls is similar to iterative processing. In other words a recursive algorithm solves a problem by reducing it to an instance of the same problem with smaller input (recursive part) and having smaller instances where the solution is computed directly (base part) without the algorithm making any calls to itself. Each recursive algorithm must contain a particular case for which it returns the result without calling itself again. Recursive algorithms are easy to implement but their implementation is not always efficient (due to the supplementary space on the program stack needed to deal with the recursive calls). Figure shows the role of recursive algorithms in algorithm design.

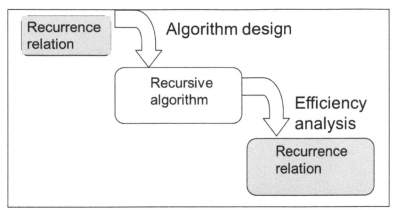

Recursion and Algorithm Design.

Brute Force Algorithms

Brute force is a straightforward approach to solving a problem, usually directly based on the problem's statement and definitions of the concepts involved. Generally it involved iterating through all possible solutions until a valid one is found.

Although it may sound unintelligent, in many cases brute force is the best way to go, as we can rely on the computer's speed to solve the problem for us. Brute force algorithms also present a nice baseline for us to compare our more complex algorithms to. As a simple example, consider searching through a sorted list of items for some target. Brute force would simply start at the first item, see if it is the target, and if not sequentially move to the next until we either find the target or hit the end of the list. For small lists this is no problem (and would actually be the preferred solution), but for extremely large lists we could use more efficient techniques.

Brute Force String Matching

The string matching problem is to find if a pattern P[1..m] occurs within text T[1..n]. Later on we will examine how to compute approximate string matching using dynamic programming. In this case we will examine how to perform exact string matching, and later we will see more efficient methods than the brute force approach. Note that string matching is useful in more cases than just searching for words in text. String matching also applies to other problems, for example, matching DNA patterns in the human genome.

Find all valid shifts of P in T using a loop:

```
Brute-Force-Match(T,P)   // T = length 1-n        P = length 1-m

    n←length[T]

    m←length[P]

    for s←0 to n-m

        do if P[1..m]=T[s+1,s+m] then P matches T at index s+1
```

Example:

```
T = ILOVEALGORITHMS

P = ALGOR
```

O(n+m) in this case, not much duplication of P in T.

```
T = AAAAAAAAAAAAAA

P = AAAAAB

    AAAAAB etc.
```

O(mn) in this case, for each of the n characters we have to go through all m chars of P.

The brute force or naïve string matcher is slow in some cases, although in many cases it actually works pretty good and should not be ignored, especially since it is easy to implement. For small n or cases when the text and pattern differ, this is one of the best methods to use.

Closest-Pair and Convex-Hull Problems

In computational geometry, two well-known problems are to find the closest pair of points and the convex hull of a set of points. The closest-pair problem, in 2D space, is to find the closest pair of points given a set of n points. Given a list P of n points, $P_1=(x_1, y_1)$, ... $P_n=(x_n, y_n)$ we simply do the following:

```
BruteForceClosest(P)

    min ← ∞

    for i = 1 to n-1

        for j = i+1 to n do

            d ← distance(P_i, P_j)        // Use sqrt(distances squared)

            if d < min then

                min ← d

                minPoints = (P_i, P_j)
```

The basic operation is computing the Euclidean distance between all pairs of points and requires $O(n^2)$ runtime. We could arrive at this value more formally by noting:

$$T(n) = \sum_{i=1}^{n-1}\left(\sum_{j=i+1}^{n} C\right) = C\sum_{i=1}^{n-1}\left(\sum_{j=i+1}^{n} 1\right) = C\sum_{i=1}^{n-1}(n-i) = C(n-1)(n-i) = \theta(n^2)$$

This requires computing the square root of the sum of squares of the difference between the coordinates in the point. For a large number of points, computing the square root is a very expensive operation and can take a long time to run.

In fact, we don't even need to compute the square root – we can simply ignore the square root and compare the values $(x_i - x_j)^2 + (y_i - y_j)^2$ themselves, since this value is strictly increasing compared to the square root of the value. This results in the same runtime, but would significantly increase the execution speed.

The Convex Hull Problem

In this problem, we want to compute the convex hull of a set of points? What does this mean?

- Formally: It is the smallest convex set containing the points. A convex set is one in which if we connect any two points in the set, the line segment connecting these points must also be in the set.

- Informally: It is a rubber band wrapped around the "outside" points.

It is an applet so you can play with it to see what a convex hull is if you like.

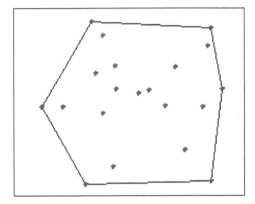

Theorem: The convex hull of any set S of n>2 points (not all collinear) is a convex polygon with the vertices at some of the points of S.

How could you Write a Brute-force Algorithm to Find the Convex Hull?

In addition to the theorem, also note that a line segment connecting two points P_1 and P_2 is a part of the convex hull's boundary if and only if all the other points in the set lie on the same side of the line drawn through these points. With a little geometry:

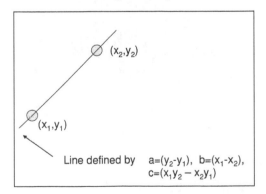

Line defined by $a=(y_2-y_1)$, $b=(x_1-x_2)$, $c=(x_1y_2 - x_2y_1)$

For all points above the line, $ax + by > c$, while for all points below the line, $ax + by < c$. Using these formulas, we can determine if two points are on the boundary to the convex hull.

High level pseudocode for the algorithm then becomes:

```
for each point P_i
        for each point P_j where P_j ≠ P_i
                Compute the line segment for P_i and P_j
                for every other point P_k where P_k ≠ P_i and P_k ≠ P_j
                        If each P_k is on one side of the line segment, label P_i
                        and P_j
                        in the convex hull
```

Exhaustive Search

Exhaustive search refers to brute force search for combinatorial problems. We essentially generate each element of the problem domain and see if it satisfies the solution. We do the following:

- Construct a way of listing all potential solutions to the problem in a systematic manner:

    ○ All solutions are eventually listed.

    ○ No solution is repeated.

- Evaluate solutions one by one, perhaps disqualifying infeasible ones and keeping track of the best one found so far.

- When search ends, announce the winner.

Traveling Salesman Problem

Find shortest Hamiltonian circuit in a weighted connected graph.

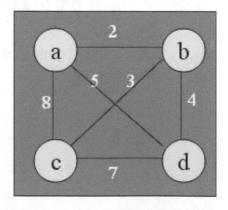

Tour	Cost
a→b→c→d→a	2+3+7+5 = 17
a→b→d→c→a	2+4+7+8 = 21
a→c→b→d→a	8+3+4+5 = 20
a→c→d→b→a	8+7+4+2 = 21

a→d→b→c→a	5+4+3+8 = 20
a→d→c→b→a	5+7+3+2 = 17
Efficiency?	

Knapsack Problem

Given n items:

weights: $w_1 w_2 \ldots w_n$

values: $v_1 v_2 \ldots v_n$

A knapsack of capacity W.

Find the most valuable subset of the items that fit into the knapsack (sum of weights ≤ W).

Example:

Item	Weight	Value
1	2	$20
2	5	$30
3	10	$50
4	5	$10
Knapsack capacity W=16		

Subset	Total weight	Total value
{1}	2	$20
{2}	5	$30
{3}	10	$50
{4}	5	$10
{1,2}	7	$50
{1,3}	12	$70
{1,4}	7	$30
{2,3}	15	$80
{2,4}	10	$40
{3,4}	15	$60
{1,2,3}	17	not feasible
{1,2,4}	12	$60
{1,3,4}	17	not feasible
{2,3,4}	20	not feasible
{1,2,3,4}	22	not feasible

Exhaustive search algorithms run in a realistic amount of time only on very small instances. In many cases there are much better alternatives. In general though we end up with an approximation to the optimal solution instead of the guaranteed optimal solution.

- Euler circuits,

- Shortest paths,

- Minimum spanning tree,

- Various AI techniques.

In some cases exhaustive search (or variation) is the only known solution.

Brute Force strengths and weaknesses

- Strengths:
    - Wide applicability.
    - Simplicity.
    - Yields reasonable algorithms for some important problems:
        - Searching.
        - String matching.
        - Matrix multiplication.
- Yields standard algorithms for simple computational tasks:
    - Sum/product of n numbers.
    - Finding max/min in a list.
- Weaknesses:
    - Rarely yields efficient algorithms.
    - Some brute force algorithms unacceptably slow.
    - Not as constructive/creative as some other design techniques.

Greedy Algorithms

A greedy algorithm, as the name suggests, always makes the choice that seems to be the best at that moment. This means that it makes a locally-optimal choice in the hope that this choice will lead to a globally-optimal solution.

How do you Decide which Choice is Optimal?

Assume that you have an objective function that needs to be optimized (either maximized or minimized) at a given point. A Greedy algorithm makes greedy choices at each step to ensure that the objective function is optimized. The Greedy algorithm has only one shot to compute the optimal solution so that it never goes back and reverses the decision. Greedy algorithms have some advantages and disadvantages:

- It is quite easy to come up with a greedy algorithm (or even multiple greedy algorithms) for a problem.

- Analyzing the run time for greedy algorithms will generally be much easier than for other techniques (like Divide and conquer). For the Divide and conquer technique, it is not clear whether the technique is fast or slow. This is because at each level of recursion the size of gets smaller and the number of sub-problems increases.

- The difficult part is that for greedy algorithms you have to work much harder to understand correctness issues. Even with the correct algorithm, it is hard to prove why it is correct. Proving that a greedy algorithm is correct is more of an art than a science. It involves a lot of creativity.

Most greedy algorithms are not correct.

How to Create a Greedy Algorithm?

Being a very busy person, you have exactly T time to do some interesting things and you want to do maximum such things. You are given an array A of integers, where each element indicates the time a thing takes for completion. You want to calculate the maximum number of things that you can do in the limited time that you have.

This is a simple Greedy-algorithm problem. In each iteration, you have to greedily select the things which will take the minimum amount of time to complete while maintaining two variables currentTime and numberOfThings. To complete the calculation, you must:

- Sort the array A in a non-decreasing order.

- Select each to-do item one-by-one.

- Add the time that it will take to complete that to-do item into currentTime.

- Add one to numberOfThings.

Repeat this as long as the currentTime is less than or equal to T.

Let A = {5, 3, 4, 2, 1} and T = 6

After sorting, A = {1, 2, 3, 4, 5}

After the 1st iteration:

- currentTime = 1

- numberOfThings = 1

After the 2nd iteration:

- currentTime is 1 + 2 = 3

- numberOfThings = 2

After the 3rd iteration:

- currentTime is 3 + 3 = 6

- numberOfThings = 3

After the 4th iteration, currentTime is 6 + 4 = 10, which is greater than T. Therefore, the answer is 3.

Implementation

```cpp
#include <iostream>
#include <algorithm>
using namespace std;
const int MAX = 105;
int A[MAX];
int main()
{
    int T, N, numberOfThings = 0, currentTime = 0;
    cin >> N >> T;
    for(int i = 0;i < N;++i)
        cin >> A[i];
    sort(A, A + N);
    for(int i = 0;i < N;++i)
    {
        currentTime += A[i];
        if(currentTime > T)
            break;
        numberOfThings++;
    }
    cout << numberOfThings << endl;
    return 0;
}
```

This example is very trivial and as soon as you read the problem, it is apparent that you can apply the Greedy algorithm to it.

Consider a more difficult problem-the Scheduling problem. You have the following:

- List of all the tasks that you need to complete today.

- Time that is required to complete each task.

- Priority (or weight) to each work.

You need to determine in what order you should complete the tasks to get the most optimum result. To solve this problem you need to analyze your inputs. In this problem, your inputs are as follows:

- Integer N for the number of jobs you want to complete.

- Lists P: Priority (or weight).

- List T: Time that is required to complete a task.

To understand what criteria to optimize, you must determine the total time that is required to complete each task.

$$C(j) = T[1] + T[2] + \ldots + T[j] \text{ where } 1 <= j <= N$$

This is because jth work has to wait till the first (j-1) tasks are completed after which it requires T[j] time for completion. For example, if T = {1, 2, 3}, the completion time will be:

- $C(1) = T[1] = 1$

- $C(2) = T[1] + T[2] = 1 + 2 = 3$

- $C(3) = T[1] + T[2] + T[3] = 1 + 2 + 3 = 6$

You obviously want completion times to be as short as possible. But it's not that simple. In a given sequence, the jobs that are queued up at the beginning have a shorter completion time and jobs that are queued up towards the end have longer completion times.

What is the Optimal way to Complete the Tasks?

This depends on your objective function. While there are many objective functions in the "Scheduling" problem, your objective function F is the weighted sum of the completion times.

$$F = P[1] * C(1) + P[2] * C(2) + \ldots + P[N] * C(N)$$

This objective function must be minimized.

Special Cases

Consider the special cases that are reasonably intuitive about what the optimal thing to do is. Looking at these special cases will bring forth a couple of natural greedy algorithms after which you will have to figure out how to narrow these down to just one candidate, which you will prove to be correct. The two special cases are as follows:

- If the time required to complete different tasks is the same i.e. T[i] = T[j] where 1 <= i, j

<= N, but they have different priorities then in what order will it make sense to schedule the jobs?

- If the priorities of different tasks are the same i.e. P[i] = P[j] where 1 <= i, j <= N but they have different lengths then in what order do you think we must schedule the jobs?

If the time required to complete different tasks is the same, then you should give preference to the task with the higher priority.

Case 1

Consider the objective function that you need to minimize. Assume that the time required to complete the different tasks is t.

$$T[i] = t \text{ where } 1 <= i <= N$$

Irrespective of what sequence is used, the completion time for each task will be as follows:

$$C(1) = T[1] = t$$
$$C(2) = T[1] + T[2] = 2*t$$
$$C(3) = T[1] + T[2] + T[3] = 3*t$$
...
$$C(N) = N*t$$

To make the objective function as small as possible the highest priority must be associated with the shortest completion time.

Case 2

In the second case, if the priorities of different tasks are the same, then you must favor the task that requires the least amount of time to complete. Assume that the priorities of the different tasks is p.

$$F = P[1]*C(1) + P[2]*C(2) + \ldots + P[N]*C(N)$$
$$F = p*C(1) + p*C(2) + \ldots + p*C(N)$$
$$F = p*(C(1) + C(2) + \ldots + C(N))$$

To minimize the value of F, you must minimize (C(1) + C(2) + ... + C(N)), which can be done if you start working on the tasks that require the shortest time to complete. There are two rules. Give preference to tasks that:

- Have a higher priority.

- Take less time to complete.

The next step is to move beyond the special cases, to the general case. In this case, the priorities and the time required for each task are different.

If you have 2 tasks and both these rules give you the same advice, then the task that has a higher priority and takes less time to complete is clearly the task that must be completed first. But what if both these rules give you conflicting advice? What if you have a pair of tasks where one of them has a higher priority and the other one requires a longer time to complete? (i.e. P[i] > P[j] but T[i] > T[j]). Which one should you complete first?

Can you aggregate these 2 parameters (time and priority) into a single score such that if you sort the jobs from higher score to lower score you will always get an optimal solution? Remember the two rules:

- Give preference to higher priorities so that the higher priorities lead to a higher score.

- Give preference to tasks that require less time to complete so that the more time that is required should decrease the score.

You can use a simple mathematical function, which takes 2 numbers (priority and time required) as the input and returns a single number (score) as output while meeting these two properties. (There is infinite number of such functions).

Let's take two of the simplest functions that have these properties:

- Algorithm #1: order the jobs by decreasing value of (P[i] - T[i]).

- Algorithm #2: order the jobs by decreasing value of (P[i] / T[i]).

For simplicity we are assuming that there are no ties.

Now you have two algorithms and at least one of them is wrong. Rule out the algorithm that does not do the right thing.

$$T = \{5, 2\} \text{ and } P = \{3, 1\}$$

According to the algorithm #1 (P[1] - T[1]) < (P[2] - T[2]), therefore, the second task should be completed first and your objective function will be:

$$F = P[1] * C(1) + P[2] * C(2) = 1 * 2 + 3 * 7 = 23$$

According to algorithm #2 (P[1] / T[1]) > (P[2] / T[2]), therefore, the first task should be completed first and your objective function will be:

$$F = P[1] * C(1) + P[2] * C(2) = 3 * 5 + 1 * 7 = 22$$

Algorithm #1 will not give you the optimal answer and, therefore, algorithm #1 is not (always) correct. Remember that Greedy algorithms are often WRONG. Just because algorithm #1 is not correct, it does not imply that algorithm #2 is guaranteed to be correct. It does, however, turn out that in this case algorithm #2 is always correct. Therefore, the final algorithm that returns the optimal value of the objective function is:

```
Algorithm (P, T, N)

    {
```

```
let S be an array of pairs ( C++ STL pair ) to store the scores and their
indices
, C be the completion times and F be the objective function
for i from 1 to N:
    S[i] = ( P[i] / T[i], i )                // Algorithm #2
sort(S)
C = 0
F = 0
for i from 1 to N:                           // Greedily choose the best choice
    C = C + T[S[i].second]
    F = F + P[S[i].second]*C
return F
}
```

Time complexity: You have 2 loops taking O(N) time each and one sorting function taking O(N * logN). Therefore, the overall time complexity is O(2 * N + N * logN) = O(N * logN).

Proof of Correctness

To prove that algorithm 2 is correct, use proof by contradiction. Assume that what you are trying to prove is false and from that derive something that is obviously false. Therefore, assume that this greedy algorithm does not output an optimal solution and there is another solution (not output by greedy algorithm) that is better than greedy algorithm.

A = Greedy schedule (which is not an optimal schedule).

B = Optimal Schedule (best schedule that you can make).

Assumption 1: All the (P[i] / T[i]) are different.

Assumption 2: (Just for simplicity, will not affect the generality) (P[1] / T[1]) > (P[2] / T[2]) > .... > (P[N] / T[N]).

Because of assumption 2, the greedy schedule will be A = (1, 2, 3, ..., N). Since A is not optimal (as we considered above) and A is not equal to B (because B is optimal), you can claim that B must contain two consecutive jobs (i, j) such that the earlier of those 2 consecutive jobs has a larger index (i > j). This is true because the only schedule that has the property, in which the indices only go up, is A = (1, 2, 3, ..., N). Therefore, B = (1, 2, ..., i, j, ... , N) where i > j.

You also have to think about what is the profit or loss impact if you swap these 2 jobs. Think about the effect of this swap on the completion times of the following:

- Work on k other than i and j.

- Work on i.

- Work on j.

For k, there will be 2 cases:

When k is on the left of i and j in B If you swap i and j, then there will be no effect on the completion time of k.

When k is on the right of i and j in B After swapping, the completion time of k is C(k) = T[1] + T[2] ⊢ .. + T[j] + T[i] + .. T[k], k will remain same.

For i the completion time: Before swapping was C(i) = T[1] + T[2] + ... + T[i] After swapping is C(i) = T[1] + T[2] + ... + T[j] + T[i].

Clearly, the completion time for i goes up by T[j] and the completion time for j goes down by T[i].

Loss due to the swap is (P[i] * T[j]).

Profit due to the swap is (P[j] * T[i]).

Using assumption 2, i > j implies that (P[i] / T[i]) < (P[j] / T[j]). Therefore (P[i] * T[j]) < (P[j] * T[i]) which means Loss < Profit. This means that swap improves B but it is a contradiction as we assumed that B is the optimal schedule. This completes our proof.

Where to use Greedy Algorithms?

A problem must comprise these two components for a greedy algorithm to work:

- It has optimal substructures. The optimal solution for the problem contains optimal solutions to the sub-problems.

- It has a greedy property (hard to prove its correctness). If you make a choice that seems the best at the moment and solve the remaining sub-problems later, you still reach an optimal solution. You will never have to reconsider your earlier choices.

Divide and Conquer Algorithms

Divide and conquer is an effective algorithm design technique. This design technique is used to solve variety of problems. In this design paradigm, the problem is divided into subproblems. The subproblems are divided further if necessary. Then the subproblems are solved recursively or iteratively and the results of the subproblems are combined to get the final solution of the given problem. These are the important components of Divide and Conquer strategy:

- Divide: In this stage the given problem is divided into small problems. The smaller problems are similar to the original problem. But these smaller problems have reduced size, i.e., with less number of instances compared to original problem. If the subproblems are big, then the subproblems are divided further. This division process is continued till the obtained subproblems are smaller that can be solved in a straight forward manner.

- Conquer: The subproblems can be solved either recursively or non-recursively in a straight forward manner.

- Combine: The solutions of the sub-problems can be combined to get the global result of the problems.

Advantages of Divide and Conquer Paradigm

- The advantages of divide and conquer approach is that it is perhaps most commonly applied design technique and its application always leads to effective algorithms.

- It can be used to solve general problems.

- Divide and conquer paradigm is suitable for problems that are inherently parallel in nature.

Disadvantages of Divide and Conquer

The disadvantage of divide and conquer paradigm is that if division process is not carried in a proper manner, the unequal division of problem instances can result in inefficient implementation. Let us discuss about one of the most popular algorithms that are based on divide and conquer, i.e., merge sort.

Merge Sort

Divide and conquer is the strategy used in merge sort. Merge sort was designed by the popular Hungarian mathematician John van Neumann. The procedure for merge sort is given informally as follows:

- Divide: Divide the n-element sequence to be sorted into two subsequences of n/2 elements each.

- Conquer: Sort the two subsequences recursively using merge sort in a recursive or non-recursive manner.

- Combine: Merge the two sorted subsequences to produce the sorted answer.

Informal Algorithm

Informally merge sort procedure is as follows:

- Divide the array A into subarrays L and R of size n/2.

- Recursively sort the subarray L gives L sorted subarray.

- Recursively sort the subarray R gives R sorted subarray.

- Combine L and R sorted subarrays give final sorted array A.

The formal algorithm is given as follows:

MergeSort (A, p, r) // sort A[p..r] by divide & conquer.

```
if p < r
        then q ← ⌊(p+r)/2⌋
        MergeSort (A, p, q)
        MergeSort (A, q+1, r)
        Merge (A, p, q, r) // merges A[p..q] with A[q+1..r]
```

It can be observed that given array A has p and r as lowest and highest indices. The midpoint p is computed so that the given array is divided into two subarrays. Then the merge sort procedure is called so that the array is recursively divided. Then the procedure uses merge to combine the sorted subarrays. The formal algorithm for merging the subarray is given as follows:

Merge(A, p, q, r)

```
n₁ ← q - p + 1
n₂ ← r - q
        for i ← 1 to n₁
                do L[i] ← A[p + i - 1]
        for j ← 1 to n₂
                do R[j] ← A[q + j]
L[n₁+1] ← ∞
R[n₂+1] ← ∞
i ← 1
j ← 1
 for k ←p to r
        do if L[i] ≤ R[j]
                then A[k] ← L[i]
                        i ← i + 1
        else A[k] ← R[j]
                j ← j + 1
```

It can be observed that the element of A is divided into the subarray L and R. Then the elements of L and R are compared and the smaller element is copied to the array A. If the subarray is exhausted, then the remaining elements of the other subarray is copied to array A. ∞ is given as sentinel so that comparison is not done for each and every time for the end of subarray.

The following Example illustrates the function of merge sort:

Example: Use merge sort and sort the array of numbers {18, 26, 32, 6, 43, 15, 9, 1, 22, 26, 19, 55, 37, 43, 99, 2}.

Solution: The first phase of merge sort is to divide the array into two parts using the middle element. The sub-arrays are divided further till one gets an array that cannot be divided further. This division process is shown figure below:

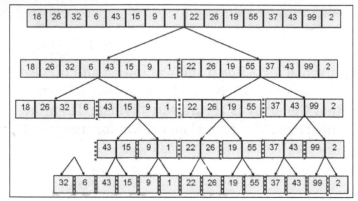

Division process.

Then, the elements are merged is illustrated for L shown in figure below:

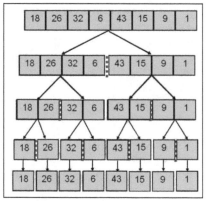

Division Process of left Subarray.

The merge process of left subarray is shown figure below:

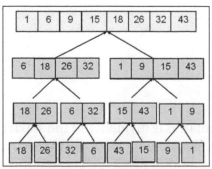

Division Process of left Subarray.

Similarly this is repeated for right subarray as well.

Complexity analysis

If T(n) is the running time T(n) of Merge Sort, then division process for computing the middle takes $\Theta(1)$, the conquering step, i.e, solving 2 subproblems takes $2T(n/2)$ and combining step, i.e., merging n elements takes $\Theta(n)$. In short, the recurrence equation for merge sort is given as follows:

$$T(n) = \begin{cases} 2T\left(\dfrac{n}{2}\right) + n - 1 & \text{for } n \leq 2 \\ 1 & \text{for } n = 2 \\ 0 & \text{where } n < 2 \end{cases}$$

Or in short,

$$T(n) = \Theta(1) \text{ if } n = 1$$

$$T(n) = 2T(n/2) + \Theta(n) \text{ if } n > 1$$

Solving this yield, the complexity of merge sort can be derived as:

$$\Rightarrow T(n) = \Theta(n \lg n)$$

Quicksort

Quicksort uses divide and conquer as a strategy for sorting elements of an array. Merge sort divides the array into two equal parts. But Quick sort unlike merge sort does not divide the array into equal parts. Instead, uses a pivot element to divide the array into two equal parts. The steps of Quicksort is given below:

- Divide step: Pick any element (pivot) p in S. This is done using a partitioning algorithm. Then, the partitioning element, partition S − {p} into two disjoint groups,

$$S_1 = \{x \in S - \{p\} \mid x <= p\}$$

$$S_2 = \{x \in S - \{p\} \mid x \geq p\}$$

- Conquer step: Recursively sort S_1 and S_2.

- Combine step: The sorted S_1 (by the time returned from recursion), followed by p, followed by the sorted S_2 (i.e., nothing extra needs to be done).

The informal Quicksort algorithm is informally given as follows:

- if left < right:

```
Partition a[left...right] such that:
  all a[left...p-1] are less than a[p], and
  all a[p+1...right] are >= a[p]
Quicksort a[left...p-1]
Quicksort a[p+1...right]
```

- Combine the subarrays and Terminate.

The formal algorithm of quicksort is given as follows:

Algorithm quicksort(A, first, last)

```
%% Input: Unsorted array A [first..last]
 %% Output: Sorted array A
 Begin
     if (first < last) then
            v = partition(A,first,last) %% find the pivot element
             quicksort([A, first,v-1])
             quicksort([A,v+1, last])
        end if
 end
```

It can be observed that the important phase of a quicksort algorithm is the partitioning stage where the given array is divided into two parts using a 'partition' procedure. While in merge sort, the middle element can be found directly. In quicksort, finding the middle element is not a straight forward process. It is done using partition algorithms.

Partitioning Algorithms

Partitioning algorithms are used to divide the given array into two subarrays. It is complicated process in quicksort compared to the division process of merge sort. There are two partitioning algorithms. One is by Lomuto partitioning algorithm and another by Hoare.

Lomuto Algorithm

Lomuto is a one directional partition algorithm. It scans from left to right and checks for the elements. If the number is less than the pivotal elements, the numbers are swapped. The following example illustrates Lomuto algorithm:

Example: Use Lomuto procedure to partition the following given array:

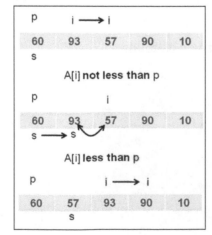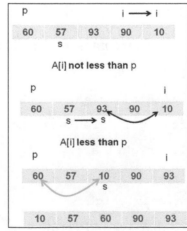

It can be observed that all the elements of the left of 60 are less than 60 and all the elements on the right hand side is greater than 60. The formal algorithm is given as follows:

ALGORITHM LomutoPartition(A[l..r])

//Partition subarray by Lomuto's algo using first element as pivot

//Input: A subarray A[l..r] of array A[0..n-1], defined by its //left and right indices l and r (l ≤ r)

//Output: Partition of A[l..r] and the new position of the pivot

```
p <- A[l]
    s <- l
    for i <- l+1 to r do
             if A[i] < p
             s <- s+1
             swap(A[s], A[i])
    swap(A[l], A[s])
    return s
```

Hoare Algorithm

Another useful partition algorithm is called Hoare partition algorithm. This algorithm has two scans. one scan is from left-to-right and another scan is from right-to-left. The left-to-right scan (using pointer i) aims to skip the smaller elements compared to the pivot and stop when an element is ≥ the pivot. Then right-to left scan (using pointer j) starts with the last element and skips over the elements that are larger than or equal to the pivot element. If i < j, in that case A[i] and A[j] are swapped and the process is continued with the increment of i and decrement of j pointers. If one encounters the situation i > j, then the pivot element is swapped with A[j].

The Hoare partition algorithm is given informally as follows:

- Choose pivot element from the array A, generally the first element.

- Search from left to right looking for elements greater than pivot.

- Search from right to left looking for elements smaller than pivot.

- When two elements are found, exchange them.

- When two elements cross, exchange pivot element such that it is in final place.

- Return the pivot element.

Formally, the Hoare partition algorithm is given as follows:

Algorithm Hoare_partition (A,first,last)

%% Input: Array A with elements 1 to n. First = 1 and last = n

%% Output: Sorted array A

```
Begin
%% First Element is the initial pivot
pivot = A [first]
%% Initialize the pointers
i = first+1
j = last
flag = false
predicate = true
While (predicate) do
      while (I ≤ j ) and (A[i] ≤ pivot) do
            i = i + 1
       End while
      while (j  ≥ pivot and j ≥ i) do
       j = j-1
      End while
       if (j < i)
            break
       else
            A[i] ↔ A[j]
            End if
      End while
A[first] ↔ A[j]
return j
End
```

It can be observed that the algorithm initializes two pointers i and j and initial pivot. The pointers are updated based on the conditions that are discussed above as an informal procedure. The following example illustrates the application of Hoare partition to a given array:

Example: Apply the Hoare portioning algorithm for the following array: 26,33,35,28,19,12,23. To apply Hoare partition algorithm, the following steps are used:

- Step 1: Start with all data in an array, and consider it unsorted.

- Step 2: Step 1, select a pivot (it is arbitrary), Let it be first element.

Step 2, start process of dividing data into LEFT and RIGHT groups. The LEFT group will have elements less than the pivot and the RIGHT group will have elements greater that the pivot.

- Step 3: If left element belongs to LEFT group, then left = left + 1. If right index element, belongs to RIGHT, then right = right − 1. Exchange the elements if they belong to the other group. The final steps are shown below:

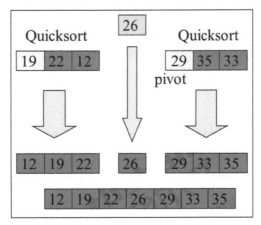

Complexity Analysis of Quicksort

Quicksort is an effective and popular algorithm and its complexity analysis is given below:

Best Case Analysis

The best case quicksort is a scenario where the partition element is exactly in the middle of the array. The best case quicksort is when the pivot partitions the list evenly. The resulting partitions of a best case are well balanced. Thus, the recurrence equation is given below:

$$T(n) = T\left(\frac{n}{2}\right) + n$$

Using the master's theorem, the complexity of the best case turns out as $T(n) \in \theta(n \log n)$. It can also be derived as follows:

$$T(N) = 2T(N/2) + cN$$

$$\frac{T(N)}{N} = \frac{T(N/2)}{N/2} + c$$

$$\frac{T(N/2)}{N/2} = \frac{T(N/4)}{N/4} + c$$

$$\frac{T(N/4)}{N/4} = \frac{T(N/8)}{N/8} + c$$

$$\vdots$$

$$\frac{T(2)}{2} = \frac{T(1)}{1} + c$$

$$\frac{T(N)}{N} = \frac{T(1)}{1} + c\log N$$

$$T(N) = c\,N\log N + N = O(N\log N)$$

Worst Case Analysis

In the worst case, it can be observed that the partitions are no longer better than a linear list. This happens because the first element is always the pivot element. Hence, there is no element in the left hand side.

$$T(N) = T(N-1) + cN$$

$$T(N-1) = T(N-2) + c(N-1)$$

$$T(N-2) = T(N-3) + c(N-2)$$

$$\vdots$$

$$T(2) = T(1) + c(2)$$

$$T(N) = T(1) + c\sum_{i=2}^{N} i = O(N^2)$$

∴ The overall size of the tree is given as,

$$1 + 2 + \cdots + (n-1) + n$$

$$= \frac{n(n+1)}{2}$$

Thus, the worst case complexity of quicksort is $\theta(n^2)$.

In short, one can conclude as part of this module 10 that:

- Divide and Conquer often leads to a better solution.

- Merge sort uses divide and conquer technique and sorts the elements in O(nlogn) time.

- Quicksort uses divide and conquer strategy and sorts the elements in o(nlogn) time.

- Master Theorem is helpful in solving recurrence equations.

Finding Maximum and Minimum Elements

Finding maximum and minimum of an array is one of the most commonly used routine in many applications. Maximum and minimum are called order statistics. The conventional algorithm for finding the maximum and minimum elements in a given array is given as follows:

```
Set largest = A[1]

Set index = 2 and N = length(A)

While (index <= N) do

      if A[index] > largest then

            largest = A[index]

Print the largest

End
```

Complexity Analysis: It can be observed that the conventional algorithm requires 2n-2 comparisons for finding maximum and minimum in an array. Therefore, the complexity of the algorithm is O(n).

Idea of Divide and Conquer Approach

One can use the divide-and-conquer strategy to improve the performance of the algorithm. The idea is to divide the array into subarrays and to find recursively the maximum and minimum elements of the subarrays. Then, the results can be combined by comparing the maximum and minimum of the subarray to find the global maximum and minimum of an array.

To illustrate this concept, let us assume that the given problem is to find the maximum and minimum of an array that has 100 elements. The idea of divide and conquer is to divide the array into two subarrays of fifty elements each. Then the maximum element in each group is obtained recursively or iteratively. Then, the maximum of each group can be computed to determine the overall maximum. This logic can be repeated for find minimum also.

Informal Algorithm

This idea can be generalized to an informal algorithm as follows:

- Divide the n elements into 2 groups A and B with floor(n/2) and ceil(n/2) elements, respectively.
- Find the min and max of each group recursively.
- Overall min is min{min(A), min(B)}.
- Overall max is max{max(A), max(B)}.

This idea is illustrated in the following Examples:

Example: Find the maximum of an array {2,5,8,1,3,10,6,7} using the idea of divide and conquer.

Solution: The idea is to split the above array into subarrays A and B such that,

$$A = \{2,5,8,1\} \text{ and}$$
$$B = \{3,10,6,7\}$$

The idea can be repeated to split subarrays A and B further. Then, it can be found that,

$$\max(A) = 8, \ \max(B) = 10.$$

Therefore, the maximum of the array is - max{max(A), max(B)} = 10.

Example: Find the minimum of the array {22,17,18,3,4,7,9,30} using divide and conquer idea?

Solution: The idea of the previous problem can be repeated. This results in the following figure:

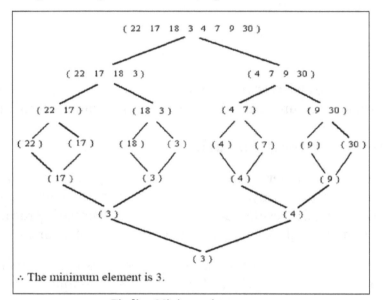

Finding Minimum in an array.

Formal Algorithm

The formal algorithm is given as follows:

Algorithm minimummaximum A(i,j)

```
Begin

        mid = floor of (i + j) / 2

        [max, min] = minimummaximum(A[i,mid])

        [max1,min1] = minumummaximum(A[mid+1,j])

        globalmax = max(max,max1)

        globalmin = min(min,min1)

End
```

It can be observed that, this algorithm formally divides the given array into two subarrays. The subarrays are subdivided further if necessary. It can be observed that only the maximum and minimum elements of the subarrays are compared to get the maximum/minimum element of the parent list.

Complexity Analysis of Finding Maximum/Minimum

The recurrence equation for the max/min algorithms can be given as follows:

$$T(n) = \begin{cases} 2T\left(\frac{n}{2}\right) + 2 & n > 2 \\ 1 & n = 2 \\ 0 & n = 1 \end{cases}$$

Assume that $n = 2^k$. By repeated substitution, one can obtain that the following relations:

$$\begin{aligned} T(n) &= 2T\left(\frac{n}{2}\right) + 2 \\ &= 2\left[\left\{2T\left(\frac{n}{4}\right)\right\} + 2\right] + 2 \\ &= 4T\left(\frac{n}{4}\right) + 4 + 2 \\ &\vdots \\ &= 2^{k-1} \cdot T(2) + \sum_{i=1}^{k-1} 2^i \\ &= 2^{k-1} + 2^k - 2 \\ &= \frac{2^k}{2} + 2^k - 2 \\ &= \frac{n}{2} + n - 2, \text{ since } n = 2^k \\ &= \frac{3n}{2} - 2 \end{aligned}$$

The solution of the recurrence equations gives $(3n/2) - 2$ comparisons.

Tiling Problem

Another important problem is Tiling problem. The problem can be stated as follows: Given a Region and a Tile T, Is it possible to tile R with T? A defective chessboard is a chessboard that has one unavailable (defective) position. A tromino is an L shaped object as shown in figure.

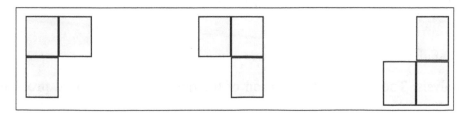

Examples of Tromino.

The idea is to tile the defective chess board with a tromino. The divide and conquer paradigm can be applied to this problem. The procedure for applying divide and conquer paradigm is given below:

If board is small, Directly tile, else:

- Divide the board into four smaller boards.

- Conquer using the tiling algorithm recursively.

- Combine it.

It can be understood as follows. If the board is small, then the tromino can be applied manually and checked. Else, divide and conquer paradigm can be applied. The board configurations can be divided further, then the subboards can be tiled, finally the results can be combined to find solution of the given larger board.

The formal Algorithm for Tiling problem is given as follows:

INPUT: n – the board size ($2^n \times 2^n$ board), L – location of the defective hole.

OUTPUT: Tiling of the board

```
Algorithm Tile(n, L)

Input : n - order of the board,

      L - Tromino

Begin

if n = 1 then

      Tile with one tromino directly

return

Else
```

Divide the board into four equal-sized boards. Place one tromino at the centre to cover the defective hole by assuming the extra 3 additional holes, L1, L2, L3, L4 denote the positions of the 4 holes:

```
 Tile(n-1, L1)

Tile(n-1, L2)

Tile(n-1, L3)

Tile(n-1, L4)

End
```

The complexity analysis of this is given below:

Complexity Analysis: The recurrence equation of the defective chess board problem is given as follows:

$$T(n) = \begin{cases} c & \text{for } n = 0 \\ 4T\left(\dfrac{n}{2}\right) + c & \text{for } n > 0 \end{cases}$$

Therefore, the complexity analysis is $O(n^2)$.

Fourier Transform

Fourier transform is used for polynomial multiplication because it helps to convert one representation of a polynomial (coefficient representation) to another representation (value representation). Thus, computation using Fourier transform can be carried out in the following two ways:

- Evaluate: Fourier transforms help in converting a coefficient representation to a value representation. This is given as follows:

  ```
  <values> = Fourier transform((coefficients), ω)
  ```

- Interpolation: After computation, conversion of a value representation to a coefficient form can be performed using inverse Fourier transform. This is given as follows:

  ```
  <coefficients> = Fourier transform((values), ω⁻¹)
  ```

One may view Fourier transform as a method of changing the representation or coding of a polynomial. Fourier transform has many applications. One of its important applications is polynomial multiplication. A polynomial is used to represent a function in terms of variables. A polynomial can be represented as follows:

$$A = a_0 + a_1 x + \cdots + a_{n-1} x^{n-1}$$

Here n is referred to as the degree bound of the polynomial and $a_0, a_1, ..., a_{n-1}$ are called its coefficients. The polynomial is said to be of degree k, if the highest coefficient of the polynomial is a_k. Fourier transform is then given as follows:

$$A_i = \sum_{k=0}^{n-1} a_k e^{-j\frac{2\pi i k}{n}}, 0 \leq i \leq n-1$$

a_k, where k ranges from 0 to n – 1, represents the set of coefficients of a polynomial $\{a_0, a_1, ..., a_{n-1}\}$; n is the length of the coefficient vector that represents the degree of the given polynomial. In other words, Fourier transform also represents a polynomial as the nth root of unity. The nth root is the solution of the polynomial $x^n - 1 = 0$, which is given as $\omega_n = e^{-j2\pi}$. The nth root at all points of input x is given as $e^{2\pi j x/n}$. Using Euler's formula, the evaluation of $e^{2\pi j x/n}$ yields $\cos\left(\frac{2\pi}{n}x\right) + j\sin\left(\frac{2\pi}{n}x\right)$, where $j = \sqrt{-1}$. The output of a Fourier transform thus can also be a complex number.

One can also design inverse Fourier transform to convert a value form to a coefficient form. Inverse Fourier transform can be given as follows:

$$a_i = \frac{1}{n}\sum_{k=0}^{n-1} A_k e^{j\frac{2\pi i k}{n}}, 0 \leq i \leq n-1$$

To multiply faster and effectively, it is better to use matrix representation for implementing Fourier transform. The matrix representation is given as follows:

$$A \quad Va$$

where V is an n × n matrix, called the Vandermonde matrix, and a is the vector of coefficients given as $\{a_0, a_1, ..., a_{n-1}\}$. Here n represents the number of coefficients of the given polynomial. The resultant vector A is a set of values given as $\{A_0, A_1, ..., A_{n-1}\}$, which represent the transformed coefficients of Fourier transform. The matrix V can be given as follows:

$$V = \begin{pmatrix} 1 & 1 & 1 & 1 & \cdots & 1 \\ 1 & \omega^1 & \omega^2 & \omega^3 & \cdots & \omega^{n-1} \\ 1 & \omega^2 & \omega^4 & \omega^6 & \cdots & \omega^{2(n-1)} \\ 1 & \omega^3 & \omega^6 & \omega^9 & \cdots & \omega^{3(n-1)} \\ \vdots & \vdots & \vdots & \vdots & \vdots & \vdots \\ 1 & \omega^{(n-1)} & \omega^{2(n-1)} & \omega^{3(n-1)} & \cdots & \omega^{(n-1)^2} \end{pmatrix},$$

Thus, the resultant matrix A of Fourier transform can be given as follows:

$$A = \begin{pmatrix} 1 & 1 & 1 & 1 & \cdots & 1 \\ 1 & \omega^1 & \omega^2 & \omega^3 & \cdots & \omega^{n-1} \\ 1 & \omega^2 & \omega^4 & \omega^6 & \cdots & \omega^{2(n-1)} \\ 1 & \omega^3 & \omega^6 & \omega^9 & \cdots & \omega^{3(n-1)} \\ \vdots & \vdots & \vdots & \vdots & \vdots & \vdots \\ 1 & \omega^{(n-1)} & \omega^{2(n-1)} & \omega^{3(n-1)} & \cdots & \omega^{(n-1)^2} \end{pmatrix} \times a$$

Inverse Fourier transform can be obtained as follows:

As A = Va, the coefficients a can be retrieved as follows:

$$a = V^{-1} \times A$$

Here, the matrix V^{-1} can be obtained by taking the complex conjugate of the matrix V by replacing ω by ϖ, as $\varpi = \dfrac{1}{\omega}$ or ω^{-1}. Complex conjugate means the sign of the imaginary component of a complex number is changed. Therefore, substituting this in the matrix, one gets the inverse matrix V (V^{-1}), which is as follows:

$$V^{-1} = 1/n \begin{pmatrix} 1 & 1 & 1 & 1 & \cdots & 1 \\ 1 & \varpi^1 & \varpi^2 & \varpi^3 & \cdots & \varpi^{n-1} \\ 1 & \varpi^2 & \varpi^4 & \varpi^6 & \cdots & \varpi^{2(n-1)} \\ 1 & \varpi^3 & \varpi^6 & \varpi^9 & \cdots & \varpi^{3(n-1)} \\ \vdots & \vdots & \vdots & \vdots & \vdots & \vdots \\ 1 & \varpi^{(n-1)} & \varpi^{2(n-1)} & \varpi^{3(n-1)} & \cdots & \varpi^{(n-1)^2} \end{pmatrix}$$

Thus, the resultant matrix a of inverse Fourier transform can be given as follows:

$$a = 1/n \begin{pmatrix} 1 & 1 & 1 & 1 & \cdots & 1 \\ 1 & \omega^1 & \omega^2 & \omega^3 & \cdots & \omega^{n-1} \\ 1 & \omega^2 & \omega^4 & \omega^6 & \cdots & \omega^{2(n-1)} \\ 1 & \omega^3 & \omega^6 & \omega^9 & \cdots & \omega^{3(n-1)} \\ \vdots & \vdots & \vdots & \vdots & \vdots & \vdots \\ 1 & \omega^{(n-1)} & \omega^{2(n-1)} & \omega^{3(n-1)} & \cdots & \omega^{(n-1)^2} \end{pmatrix} \times A$$

Let us try to design the matrix V and V^{-1} for four sample points. Therefore, n = 4 and let a = {a_0, a_1, a_2, a_3}. Then one can find ω by substituting $e^{2\pi jx/n}$ as follows:

$$\omega = e^{-j\frac{2\pi}{n}} = e^{-j\frac{2\pi}{4}} = e^{-j\frac{\pi}{2}} = \cos\frac{\pi}{2} - j\sin\frac{\pi}{2} = -j \, (as \, n = 4)$$

On substituting this value of ω in the matrix V of order 4 × 4, one gets the following matrix:

$$V = \begin{pmatrix} 1 & 1 & 1 & 1 \\ 1 & -j & (-j)^2 & (-j)^3 \\ 1 & (-j)^2 & (-j)^4 & (-j)^6 \\ 1 & (-j)^3 & (-j)^6 & (-j)^9 \end{pmatrix}$$

Here, j is a complex number and is equal to $\sqrt{-1}$. Therefore, one can observe that the resultant matrix V that involves complex numbers is as follows:

$$V = \begin{pmatrix} 1 & 1 & 1 & 1 \\ 1 & -j & -1 & j \\ 1 & -1 & 1 & -1 \\ 1 & j & -1 & -j \end{pmatrix}$$

Thus, the resultant matrix A can be given as follows:

$$\begin{bmatrix} A_0 \\ A_1 \\ A_2 \\ A_3 \end{bmatrix} = \begin{pmatrix} 1 & 1 & 1 & 1 \\ 1 & -j & -1 & j \\ 1 & -1 & 1 & -1 \\ 1 & j & -1 & -j \end{pmatrix} \times \begin{bmatrix} a_0 \\ a_1 \\ a_2 \\ a_3 \end{bmatrix}$$

The coefficients can be retrieved using inverse Fourier transform. For this case where n = 4 and $A_k = \{A_0, A_1, A_2, A_3\}$, the matrix V^{-1} of order 4 × 4 can be obtained by substituting $\varpi = \frac{1}{\omega} = e^{j\frac{2\pi}{n}} = e^{j\frac{\pi}{2}} = -j$ in the general matrix. This is the complex conjugate of the matrix V. For finding the complex conjugate, one has to change the sign of the imaginary component of the complex number. For n = 4, the inverse matrix V(V^{-1}) is given as follows:

$$V^{-1} = \frac{1}{4} \begin{pmatrix} 1 & 1 & 1 & 1 \\ 1 & +j & -1 & -j \\ 1 & -1 & 1 & -1 \\ 1 & -j & -1 & j \end{pmatrix}$$

Thus, the resultant matrix for finding coefficients from values is given as follows:

$$\begin{bmatrix} a_0 \\ a_1 \\ a_2 \\ a_3 \end{bmatrix} = \frac{1}{n} \times \begin{pmatrix} 1 & 1 & 1 & 1 \\ 1 & j & -1 & j \\ 1 & -1 & 1 & -1 \\ 1 & j & -1 & -j \end{pmatrix} \times \begin{bmatrix} A_0 \\ A_1 \\ A_2 \\ A_3 \end{bmatrix}$$

One can verify that the product of V and V^{-1} is a unit matrix as they are complex conjugates of each other. In addition, one can check that the original coefficients are obtained using inverse Fourier transform and there is no information loss. This is demonstrated in the numerical example below:

Example: Find Fourier transforms of the following four coefficients and also verify that inverse Fourier transform gives the original coefficients without any loss.

$$x = \{1,3,5,7\}$$

Solution: As there are four samples, n = 4. Fourier transform can be given as follows:

$$A = V \times a$$

$$A = \begin{pmatrix} 1 & 1 & 1 & 1 \\ 1 & -j & -1 & j \\ 1 & -1 & 1 & -1 \\ 1 & j & -1 & -j \end{pmatrix} \times \begin{pmatrix} 1 \\ 3 \\ 5 \\ 7 \end{pmatrix}$$

$$= \begin{pmatrix} 16 \\ -4-4j \\ -4 \\ -4-4j \end{pmatrix}$$

One can verify that the inverse of this gives back the original coefficients. Therefore, take the inverse kernel and multiply the Fourier coefficients:

$$a = \frac{1}{n} \times \left(V^{-1} \times A \right)$$

$$a = \frac{1}{4} \begin{pmatrix} 1 & 1 & 1 & 1 \\ 1 & +j & -1 & -j \\ 1 & -1 & 1 & -1 \\ 1 & -j & -1 & j \end{pmatrix} \begin{pmatrix} 16 \\ -4-4j \\ -4 \\ -4-4j \end{pmatrix}$$

$$= a = \frac{1}{4} \begin{pmatrix} 4 \\ 12 \\ 20 \\ 28 \end{pmatrix} = \begin{pmatrix} 1 \\ 3 \\ 5 \\ 7 \end{pmatrix}$$

It can be observed that one is able to get back the original coefficients.

Idea of FFT

One can implement a faster Fourier transform using an algorithm called an FFT algorithm. FFT is implemented using the divide-and-conquer strategy. The input array of points is divided into odd and even arrays of points. Individually, FFT is applied to the subarrays. Finally, the subarrays are merged. Informally, an FFT algorithm can be stated as follows:

- Step 1: If n = 1, then solve it directly as a_o.

- Step 2: Divide the input array into two arrays B and C such that B has all odd samples and C has all even samples. Continue division if the subproblems are large.

- Step 3: Apply FFT recursively to arrays B and C to get subarrays B' and C'.

- Step 4: Combine the results of subarrays B' and C' and return the final list.

Complexity Analysis of FFT algorithms

The recurrence equation of FFT is given as follows:

$$T(n) = 2T\left(\frac{n}{2}\right) + O(n)$$

One can use the master theorem and solve this recurrence equation. One can observe that the complexity analysis of this algorithm turns out to be O(n log n).

Polynomial Multiplication

Many polynomial operations are required in scientific applications. One of the most important applications is multiplying two polynomials. Let a(x) and b(x) be two polynomials; their product C(x) = a(x) × b(x) can be expressed as follows:

Compute C(x) = A(x)B(x), where degree(A(x)) = m, and degree(B(x)) = n. Degree(C(x)) = m+n, and C(x) is uniquely determined by its value at m+n+1 distinct points.

The informal algorithm is given as follows:

- Step 1: Let the polynomials A and B be of degree n. Then find m = 2 × n − 1.

- Step 2: Pick m points ranging from 0 to m − 1.

- Step 3: Evaluate polynomials A and B at m points.

- Step 4: Compute $C(x) = A(x) \times B(x)$ using ordinary multiplication.

- Step 5: Interpolate $C(x)$ to get the coefficients of the polynomial $C(x)$.

It can be observed that point-wise multiplication is enough to multiply polynomials. One can combine the idea of divide and conquer with this concept. The idea of division is that any function at sample points x can be divided into function samples at odd points and those at even points. Thus, a polynomial $A(x)$ can also be represented as $A_{odd}(x^2) + xA_{even}(x^2)$, where A_{odd} represents a set of odd sample points and A_{even} a set of even sample points of the given polynomials. Therefore, the advantage of using a divide-and-conquer algorithm is that only one-half of the resultant polynomial is calculated and the other half is a negative of the first half $\left(\text{i.e. } A_{odd}(x^2) - xA_{even}(x^2)\right)$.

Branch and Bound Algorithms

Branch and bound algorithms are used to find the optimal solution for combinatory, discrete, and general mathematical optimization problems. In general, given an NP-Hard problem, a branch and bound algorithm explores the entire search space of possible solutions and provides an optimal solution.

A branch and bound algorithm consist of stepwise enumeration of possible candidate solutions by exploring the entire search space. With all the possible solutions, we first build a rooted decision tree. The root node represents the entire search space:

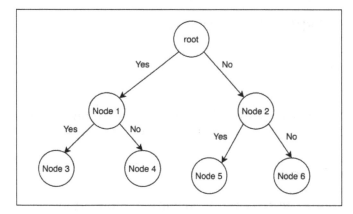

Here, each child node is a partial solution and part of the solution set. Before constructing the rooted decision tree, we set an upper and lower bound for a given problem based on the optimal solution. At each level, we need to make a decision about which node to include in the solution set. At each level, we explore the node with the best bound. In this way, we can find the best and optimal solution fast.

Now it is crucial to find a good upper and lower bound in such cases. We can find an upper bound by using any local optimization method or by picking any point in the search space. On the other hand, we can obtain a lower bound from convex relaxation or duality. In general, we want to partition the solution set into smaller subsets of solution. Then we construct a rooted decision tree, and finally, we choose the best possible subset (node) at each level to find the best possible solution set.

Branch and Bound is a Good Choice if:

- If the given problem is a discrete optimization problem, a branch and bound is a good choice. Discrete optimization is a subsection of optimization where the variables in the problem should belong to the discrete set. Examples of such problems are 0-1 Integer Programming or Network Flow problem.

- Branch and bound work efficiently on the combinatory optimization problems. Given an objective function for an optimization problem, combinatory optimization is a process to find the maxima or minima for the objective function. The domain of the objective function should be discrete and large. Boolean Satisfiability, Integer Linear Programming are examples of the combinatory optimization problems.

Example: Let's first define a job assignment problem. In a standard version of a job assignment problem, there can be N jobs and N workers. To keep it simple, we're taking 3 jobs and 3 workers in our example:

	Job 1	Job 2	Job 3
A	9	3	4
B	7	8	4
C	10	5	2

We can assign any of the available jobs to any worker with the condition that if a job is assigned to a worker, the other workers can't take that particular job. We should also notice that each job has some cost associated with it, and it differs from one worker to another. Here the main aim is to complete all the jobs by assigning one job to each worker in such a way that the sum of the cost of all the jobs should be minimized.

Branch and Bound Algorithm Pseudocode

Now let's discuss how to solve the job assignment problem using a branch and bound algorithm. Let's see the pseudocode first:

```
Algorithm : Job Assignment Problem Using Branch And Bound
Data: Input cost matrix M[][]
Result: Assignment of jobs to each worker according to optimal
        cost
Function MinCost(M[][])
while True do
    E = LeastCost();
    if E is a leaf node then
        print();
        return;
    end
    for each child S of E do
        Add(S);
        S → parent = E;
    end
end
```

Here, M[][] is the input cost matrix that contains information like the number of available jobs, a list of available workers, and the associated cost for each job. The function MinCost()maintains a list of active nodes. The function LeastCost() calculates the minimum cost of the active node at each level of the tree. After finding the node with minimum cost, we remove the node from the list of active nodes and return it.

We're using the Add() function in the pseudocode, which calculates the cost of a particular node and adds it to the list of active nodes. In the search space tree, each node contains some information, such as cost, a total number of jobs, as well as a total number of workers.

Now let's run the algorithm on the sample example we've created:

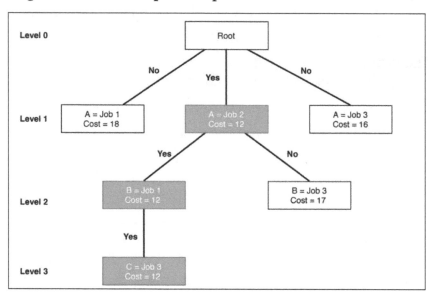

Initially, we've 3 jobs available. The worker A has the option to take any of the available jobs. So at level 1, we assigned all the available jobs to the worker A and calculated the cost. We can see that when we assigned jobs 2 to the worker A, it gives the lowest cost in level 1 of the search space tree. So we assign the job 2 to worker A and continue the algorithm. "Yes" indicates that this is currently optimal cost.

After assigning the job 2 to worker A, we still have two open jobs. Let's consider worker B now. We're trying to assign either job 1 or 3 to worker B to obtain optimal cost. Either we can assign the job 1 or 3 to worker B. Again we check the cost and assign job 1 to worker B as it is the lowest in level 2. Finally, we assign the job 3 to worker C, and the optimal cost is 12.

Advantages

In a branch and bound algorithm, we don't explore all the nodes in the tree. That's why the time complexity of the branch and bound algorithm is less when compared with other algorithms. If the problem is not large and if we can do the branching in a reasonable amount of time, it finds an optimal solution for a given problem. The branch and bound algorithm find a minimal path to reach the optimal solution for a given problem. It doesn't repeat nodes while exploring the tree.

Disadvantages

The branch and bound algorithm are time-consuming. Depending on the size of the given problem, the number of nodes in the tree can be too large in the worst case. Also, parallelization is extremely difficult in the branch and bound algorithm.

Transform and Conquer

Transform and conquer is a design paradigm where a given problem is transformed to another domain. This can be done for familiarity of simplicity. The problem is solved in the new domain. Then, the solutions are converted back to the original domain. In short, transform and conquer proposes two stage solution:

- First stage involves the transformation to another problem that is more amenable for solution.

- Second stage involves solving the new problem where the transformed new problem is solved. Then the solutions are converted back to the original problem.

This is explained through the following simple examples:

Consider the problem of multiplying two simple numbers XII and IV. These numbers are in Roman number system. As many are not comfortable with Roman number system, this gets transformed to another problem where Arabic numerals are used instead of Roman system.

- In the first stage, the numbers XII and IV is transformed to another problem of 12 X 4.

- In the second stage, the actual multiplication is done as 48, then the result is converted to Roman number as XLVIII.

The advantage is the familiarity of the Arabic numeral system over Roman system.

Let us consider another problem of convolution of two signals in spatial domain. Convolution involves shifting and adding which is complex. This is equivalent to simple multiplication in frequency domain. The two stage solution is given as follows:

- In the first stage, the problem is transformed to another domain where spatial data is converted to frequency domain. This is done using FFT transform.

- In the second stage, the transformed problem is solved by multiplication and transformed back to spatial domain using Inverse transform.

Another good example of transform and conquer technique is finding LCM using GCD. For example, if GCD of two numbers is available, then LCM can be obtained as follows:

$$\text{lcm}(m, n) = \frac{m \times n}{\text{GCD}(m, n)}$$

Variations of Transform and Conquer

Three variants of transform and conquer are as follows:

- Instance simplification is one variant where the problem transformed to the same problem of simpler or convenient instance. The illustrated example of roman number to Arabic number system is an example of instance simplification.

- Representation Change is another variety where the strategy involves the transformation of an instance to a different representation. But this is done without affecting the instance. The illustrated example of roman number to Arabic number system is an example of instance simplification.

- Problem reduction is a strategy that involves a transformation of a problem A to another type of problem B. It is assumed that the solution of problem B already exists. The illustrated example of reduction of computing LCM (Last Common Multiple) in terms of GCD is an example of problem reduction. s GCD. Hypothetically, let us assume that an algorithm exists only for GCD.

Presorting

Sorting an array before processing is called presorting. Presorting is helpful in various applications such as search and in finding element uniqueness.

Finding Unique Elements in an Array

Consider a problem of finding element uniqueness in an array. The problem can be defined as follows: Example: Given a random list of numbers, determine if there are any duplicates.

Brute force Algorithm: A brute force algorithm involves checking ever pair of elements for duplicated. This means comparing an element with all other elements of an array. The informal brute force algorithm for element uniqueness is given as follows:

Algorithm Uniqueness

```
for each x ∈ A

    for each y ∈ {A-x}

        if x=y then

            return not unique

        endif

    return unique
```

The complexity of this approach is $\theta(n^2)$.

Transform and Conquer approach: One can apply the principle of instance simplification here. One can sort the array instead. The advantage of sorting here is that only the adjacent elements to be checked. So the algorithm can be stated informally as follows:

1. Sort the numbers.

2. Check the adjacent numbers. If the numbers are same then return uniqueness as false.

3. End.

The formal algorithm is given as follows:

Algorithm Elementuniqueness-Presorting(A[1..n])

%% Input: Array A

%% Output: Unique or not

```
Begin
Sort A
for i = 1 to n-1
        if A[i] = A[i+1] return not unique
End for
return unique
End
```

Complexity Analysis: Sorting requires θ (n log n) time. The second step requires at most n-1 comparisons. Therefore, the total complexity is,

$$\theta(n)+\theta(n \log n)$$
$$= \theta(n \log n)$$

Search using Presorting

Presorting can be done for search also. The order in the array allows the usage of binary search. The informal algorithm for binary search is given as follows:

- Stage 1: Sort the array by Merge sort.

- Stage 2: Apply binary search.

Complexity Analysis: Sorting requires θ (n log n) time. The second step requires at most log(n) time. Therefore the total complexity is $\theta(n)+\theta(n \log n)$. Therefore, the efficiency of the procedure is $\Theta(n \log n) + O(\log n) = \Theta(n\log n)$.

Mode

Mode is defined as the element that occurs most often in a given array. For example, consider the following array of elements, A = [5, 1, 5, 5, 5, 7, 6, 5, 7, 5]. The mode of array A is 5 as 5 is the most common element that appear most. If several and different values occur most often any of them can be considered the mode.

Brute force Algorithm: The brute force algorithm is to scan the array repeatedly to find the frequencies of all elements. Informally, the frequency based approach is given below:

- Step 1: Find length of List A

  ```
  max ← max(A)
  ```

- Step 2: Set `freq[1..max] ← 0`

- Step 3: for each $x \in A$

  ```
  freq[x] = freq[x] + 1
  ```

- Step 4: mode ← freq[1]

- Step 5: for i ← 2 to max

  ```
  if freq[i] > freq[mode] mode ← i
  ```

- Step 6: return mode

Complexity Analysis: The complexity analysis of frequency based mode finding algorithm is $\theta(n^2)$.

Transform and conquer approach: Instead, the array can be sorted and run length of an element can be calculated on the sorted array. Informally, mode finding using presorting is given as follows:

- Sort the element of an array.

- Calculate the run length of an element.

- Print the element having longest length.

- Exit.

Formal algorithm is given as follows:

```
Sort A
i ← 0
frequency ← 0
while i ≤ n-1
       runlength ← 1; runvalue ← A[i]
       while i+runlength ≤ n-1 and A[i+runlength] = runvalue
            runlength = runlength + 1
       if runlength > frequency
            frequency ← runlength
            modevalue ← runvalue
    i = i + runlength
    return modevalue
```

Complexity Analysis: Sorting requires $\theta(n \log n)$ time. The finding of a run length requires only linear time as the array is already sorted. Therefore the worst case performance of the algorithm would be less than the brute-force method.

Matrix Operations

A matrix is a rectangular table of numbers. In scientific domain, matrices have many uses. Matrix addition and subtractions are relatively easy. Most of the scientific applications use matrix operations like matrix inverse and matrix determinant. So there is a need to solve these problems. As the computational complexity of these algorithms are high, transform and conquer approach can be used. Gaussian elimination uses transform and conquer approach to solve set of equations. Additionally, it can be used to decompose matrices also. Matrix decomposition is useful for find inverse of a matrix and matrix determinant.

Gaussian Elimination Method

Solving an equation means finding the values of the unknown. A simplest equation is of the form:

$$Ax = y$$

A solution of this equation is $x = y/A$. but this is true only when ($y \neq 0$ and A is not zero). All values of x satisfies the equation when $y = 0$. This logic can be extended for two unknowns. Let us consider the following set of equations:

$$A_{11}x + A_{12}y = B_1$$
$$A_{21}x + A_{22}y = B_2$$

The equations can be solved first by finding x as,

$$x = (B_1 - A_{12}y)/A_{11}$$

Substituting this in the second equation gives y.

In general, if one plots these two equations as lines, then the intersection of two lines in a single point, then the system of linear equations has a unique solution. If the lines are parallel, then there is no solution. If the lines coincide, then there would be infinite number of solutions.

In many applications, one may have to solve 'n' equations with 'n' unknowns. The set of linear equations are as below:

$$A_{11}x_1 + A_{12}x_2 + \ldots + A_{1n}x_n = B_1$$
$$A_{21}x_1 + A_{22}x_2 + \ldots + A_{2n}x_n = B_2$$
$$\ldots$$
$$A_{n1}x_1 + A_{n2}x_2 + \ldots + A_{nn}x_n = B_n$$

In matrix form, the above can be represented as $Ax = B$.

Gaussian elimination, names after Gauss, uses transform and conquer approach to transform this set of equations with 'n' unknowns,

$$a'_{11}x_1 + a'_{12}x_2 + \ldots + a'_{1n}x_n = B'_1$$
$$a'_{22}x_2 + \ldots + a'_{2n}x_n = B'_2$$
$$\vdots$$
$$a'_{nn}x_n = B'_n$$

The transformation can be represented as follows:

$$Ax = B \rightarrow A'x = B'$$

Here,

$$A = \begin{bmatrix} A_{11} & A_{12} & \cdots & A_{1n} \\ A_{21} & A_{22} & \cdots & A_{2n} \\ \cdots & & & \\ A_{n1} & A_{n2} & \cdots & A_{nn} \end{bmatrix} \quad B = \begin{bmatrix} B_1 \\ B_2 \\ \cdots \\ B_n \end{bmatrix}$$

Gaussian elimination aims to create a matrix with zeros in the lower triangle. This is called upper triangular matrix. This is done by elimination a variable at every stage in all equations. The advantage is that One can solve the last equation first, substitute into the second to last, and can proceed to solve the first one. To do the manipulations, Gaussian elimination uses some elementary steps. The following elementary steps are used by Gaussian elimination.

1. Exchanging two equations of the system: In this, two equations are exchanged. For example, consider the following equations:

$$x + y = 3$$
$$2x + y = 4$$

These equations can be exchanged as,

$$2x + y = 4$$
$$x + y = 3$$

2. Exchanging an equation with non-zero multiples:

Say,

$$x + y = 2 \text{ can be replaced as}$$

$$2x + 2y = 4.$$

3. Replacing the multiple of one equation to another equation. For example, row 2, R2, can be expressed as a multiple of row 1, R1, and row 3, R3.

The informal algorithm for Gaussian elimination is given as follows:

- Step 1: Write matrix A for a given set of equations.

- Step 2: Append a vector b to matrix A; this is called an augmentation matrix.

- Step 3: Apply the elementary operation to reduce the augmented matrix to a triangular form, called an echelon matrix. This is done as follows:

  - Keep a_{11} as a pivot (reference point) and elimination all a_{11}'s in other rows of matrix A. A pivot element is the coefficient in a set of equations that is used as a reference point to make all other coefficients in the column equal to zero. For example, in the second row, a_{11} can be eliminated by the factor $row_2 - (a_{11}/a_{11})$. Here, (a_{21}/a_{11}) is called a multiplier. This operation is applied throughout the row. Using the same logic, a_{11} is eliminated in all other equations.

- ◦ Similarly, using the multiples of (a_{31}/a_{11}), (a_{41}/a_{11}),..., (a_{n1}/a_{11}), matrix A can be reduced to an upper-triangular matrix A'.

Example: Solve the set of equations using Gaussian Elimination method,

$$3x_1 + x_2 + x_3 = 11$$

$$6x_1 + 4x_2 + x_3 = 29$$

$$x_1 + x_2 + x_3 = 7$$

In matrix notation, this can be written it as Ax = b. Augment the equation as below and apply the elementary operations as shown below:

$$\begin{vmatrix} 3 & 1 & 1 & 11 \\ 6 & 4 & 1 & 2 \\ 1 & 1 & 1 & 7 \end{vmatrix} \begin{matrix} \\ \text{row}\,2 - \dfrac{6}{3}\text{row}\,1 \\ \text{row}\,3 - \dfrac{1}{3}\text{row}\,1 \end{matrix}$$

$$\begin{vmatrix} 3 & 1 & 1 & 11 \\ 0 & 2 & -1 & 7 \\ 0 & 2/3 & 2/3 & 2/3 \end{vmatrix} \begin{matrix} \\ \text{row}\,2 - 2\,\text{row}\,1 \\ \text{row}\,3 - \dfrac{1}{3}\,\text{row}\,1 \end{matrix}$$

$$\begin{vmatrix} 3 & 1 & 1 & 11 \\ 0 & 2 & -1 & 7 \\ 0 & 0 & 1 & 1 \end{vmatrix} \begin{matrix} \\ \text{row}\,3 - \dfrac{1}{3}\text{row}\,2 \end{matrix}$$

$\therefore x_3 = 1$ from the last equation. Using this, one can substitute in the second equation to get,

$$2x_2 - x_3 = 7$$
$$2x_2 = 8$$
$$x_2 = 4$$

Using these two variables, the remaining variable can be obtained as follows:

$$3x_1 + x_2 + x_3 = 11$$
$$3x_2 + 5 = 11$$
$$x_2 = 11 - 5/3 = 6/3 = 2$$

Apply the elementary operation to reduce the augmented matrix to a triangular form called echelon matrix. So the idea is to keep a_{11} as pivot and eliminate all a_{11} in other equations. For example, in the second equation, a_{11} can be eliminated by the factor R2-(a_{21}/a_{11}). This operation is applied throughout the equation. Using the same logic, a11 is eliminated in all other equations. Similarly, using the multiple of (a_{31}/a_{11}), (a_{41}/a_{11}), ..., (a_{n1}/a_{11}), the matrix A can be reduced to a upper triangular matrix A'. Then, the solution can be obtained by back substitution. The algorithm for forward elimination is given as follows:

Thus the reduction is shown formally as follows:

```
for i ← 1 to n do A[i,n+1] ← B[i]

for i ← 1 to n - 1

        for j ← i+1 to n do

                for k ← i to n+1 do

                        A[j,k] ← A[j,k] ← A[i,k]* A[j,i]/ A[i,i]
```

The backward substitution is given as follows:

```
for j ← n to 1 step-1 do

        t ← 0

        for k ← j+1 to n do

                t ← t + A[j, k]* x[k]

        x[j] ← (A[j, n+1] - t) / A[j, j]
```

Complexity Analysis: How many operations are required for Gaussian elimination? One division and n multiplication/division is required. So (n+1) operations for (n -1) rows, requires (n - 1)(n + 1) = n^2 - 1 operations to eliminate the first column of matrix A. Similarly the second row involves (n - 1)^2 - 1 operations. So all n rows, the numbers of operations are:

$$\sum_{k=1}^{n} k^2 - 1 = \frac{n(n+1)(2n+1)}{6} - 1$$
$$= \frac{n(n-1)(2n+5)}{6}$$
$$\approx O(n^3)$$

So Gaussian elimination method time complexity is $O(n^3)$.

LU decomposition is an example of instance simplification. In LU decomposition, the given matrix is split or decomposed to two matrices L and U. Why? This splitting helps to solve a set of simultaneous equations faster. In other words, LU Decomposition is another method to solve a set of simultaneous linear equations effectively. Thus, the non-singular matrix [A], can be written as [A] = [L][U], Here,

[L] = lower triangular matrix

[U] = upper triangular matrix

Let the set of simultaneous equations are represented as follows in matrix form as:

$$Ax = b$$

Substituting A = LU gives,

$$LUx = b$$

First, let y = Ux. So by keeping

$$Ly = b$$

One can solve for y. Then, by solving Ux = y. One can solve for the unknown x in the set of linear equations. By matrix decomposition, the process of computing becomes faster.

Gaussian Elimination Method for LU Decomposition

It can be noted that the matrix U is the same as the coefficient matrix at the end of the forward elimination step and the matrix L is obtained using the multipliers that were used in the forward elimination process. One has to know the limitations of LU decomposition. They are listed below:

- Not all the matrices have LU decomposition.

- Rows or columns can be swapped to make LU decomposition feasible.

- LU decomposition is guaranteed if the leading submatrices have non-zero determinants. to make LU decomposition. A matrix Ak is called a leading submatrix of matrix A, if it is k x k matrix whose elements are top k rows and k left-most columns.

The example below illustrates the Gaussian elimination method for solving a set of equations and to find LU decomposition.

Example: Solve the set of equations using Gaussian Elimination method and find LU decomposition.

$$3x_1 + x_2 + x_3 = 11$$

$$6x_1 + 4x_2 + x_3 = 29$$

$$x_1 + x_2 + x_3 = 7$$

Solution: The first step is to augment the matrix. The above matrix can be augmented as follows:

$$A = \begin{bmatrix} 3 & 1 & 1 & 11 \\ 6 & 4 & 1 & 29 \\ 1 & 1 & 1 & 7 \end{bmatrix}$$

Gaussian elimination can be applied now to get upper triangular matrix.

$$\begin{vmatrix} 3 & 1 & 1 & 11 \\ 6 & 4 & 1 & 2 \\ 1 & 1 & 1 & 7 \end{vmatrix} \quad \begin{matrix} \\ \text{row}\,2 - \dfrac{6}{3}\text{row}\,1 \\ \text{row}\,3 - \dfrac{1}{3}\text{row}\,1 \end{matrix}$$

$$\begin{vmatrix} 3 & 1 & 1 & 11 \\ 0 & 2 & -1 & 7 \\ 0 & 2/3 & 2/3 & 2/3 \end{vmatrix} \quad \begin{matrix} \\ \text{row}\,2 - 2 \times \text{row}\,1 \\ \text{row}\,3 - \dfrac{1}{3} \times \text{row}\,1 \end{matrix}$$

$$\begin{vmatrix} 3 & 1 & 1 & 11 \\ 0 & 2 & -1 & 7 \\ 0 & 0 & 1 & 1 \end{vmatrix} \quad \begin{matrix} \\ \\ \text{row}\,3 - \dfrac{1}{3}\text{row}\,2 \end{matrix}$$

The lower-triangular matrix is obtained L is made up of 1's in the diagonal and the multipliers used for row reduction in the Gaussian elimination. It can be observed that the multipliers used in the above Gaussian elimination process is used to give matrix L.

$$L = \begin{bmatrix} 1 & 0 & 0 \\ 2 & 1 & 0 \\ 1/3 & 1/3 & 1 \end{bmatrix}$$

The upper triangular matrix is made up of elements that are the resultant of the Gaussian elimination process. It can be seen that, the resultant of the Gaussian elimination matrix with the diagonal 1's give the following matrix U:

$$U = \begin{bmatrix} 3 & 1 & 1 \\ 0 & 2 & -1 \\ 0 & 0 & 1 \end{bmatrix}$$

Using the matrices L and U, one can easily solve the simultaneous linear set of equations. The equation Ax = b is equivalent to LUx = b.

Let y = Ux

$$\therefore Ly = b$$

$$\Rightarrow \begin{bmatrix} 1 & 0 & 0 \\ 2 & 1 & 0 \\ 1/3 & 1/3 & 1 \end{bmatrix} \begin{bmatrix} y_1 \\ y_2 \\ y_3 \end{bmatrix} = \begin{bmatrix} 11 \\ 29 \\ 7 \end{bmatrix}$$

This yield the solutions as follows:

$$y_1 = 11, \ 2y_1 + y_2 = 29 \ \Rightarrow \ y_2 = 29 - 2y_1 = 7 \text{ and finally,}$$

$$\tfrac{1}{3}y_1 + \tfrac{1}{3}y_2 + y_3 = 7$$

$$\tfrac{11}{3} + \tfrac{7}{3} + y_3 = 7$$

$$y_3 = 7 - \tfrac{11}{3} - \tfrac{7}{3} = 1$$

having obtained y's, now the unknown x's can be obtained as follows:

Solving Ux = y implies,

$$\begin{bmatrix} 3 & 1 & 1 \\ 0 & 2 & -1 \\ 0 & 0 & 1 \end{bmatrix} \begin{bmatrix} x_1 \\ x_2 \\ x_3 \end{bmatrix} = \begin{bmatrix} 11 \\ 7 \\ 1 \end{bmatrix}$$

$\therefore$ The final solution is,

$$x_3 = 1; \ 2x_2 - x_3 = 7, \ 2x_2 = 7 + 1 \ \Rightarrow \ x_2 = 4 \ ; \text{ and finally,}$$

$$3x_1 + x_2 + x_3 = 11$$

$$3x_1 + 4 + 1 = 11$$

$$3x_1 = 6 \ \Rightarrow \ x_1 = 2$$

Therefore, the unknowns x_1, x_2 and x_3 are respectively 2, 4 and 1. It can be observed that the LU decomposition simplifies the computational effort.

Recursive Procedure

One can automate the above using a recursive procedure. The idea is to automate the above said procedure using matrix decomposition as shown below. Let us assume that A = LU; matrices A, L, and U can be partitioned as follows:

$$\begin{pmatrix} \alpha_{11} & \alpha_{12}^T \\ a_{21} & A_{22} \end{pmatrix} = \begin{pmatrix} 1 & 0 \\ \ell_{21} & L_{22} \end{pmatrix} \times \begin{pmatrix} v_{11} & u_{12}^T \\ 0 & v_{22} \end{pmatrix} = \begin{pmatrix} v_{11} & u_{12}^T \\ \ell_{21} \times v_{11} & \ell_{21} \times u_{12}^T + L_{22} U_{22} \end{pmatrix}$$

The informal algorithm is:

- Find α_{11},

- Update the value for a_{21} by dividing it with pivot value,

- $\alpha_{12}^T = u_{12}^T$,

- Update the value of A_{22} recursively.

This is illustrated in the following example:

Example: Find Gaussian Elimination for the given matrix using recursive procedure.

$$A = \begin{pmatrix} 3 & 1 & 1 \\ 6 & 4 & 1 \\ 1 & 1 & 1 \end{pmatrix}$$

Solution: Using $a_{11} = 3$, divide the entire column by 3. This gives the column $\begin{pmatrix} 2 \\ 1 \\ \frac{1}{3} \end{pmatrix}$. The matrix

$A_{22} = \ell_{21} \times u_{12}^T + L_{22} U_{22}$ can be updated as $\begin{pmatrix} 4 & 1 \\ 1 & 1 \end{pmatrix} - \begin{pmatrix} 2 \\ 1 \\ \frac{1}{3} \end{pmatrix} \times \begin{pmatrix} 1 & 1 \end{pmatrix} = \begin{pmatrix} 2 & -1 \\ 2 & 2 \\ \frac{2}{3} & \frac{2}{3} \end{pmatrix}$. This results in a matrix.

$$\begin{pmatrix} 3 & 1 & 1 \\ 2 & 2 & -1 \\ \frac{1}{3} & \frac{2}{3} & \frac{2}{3} \end{pmatrix}$$

Now, by choosing 2 as the pivot element and diving that by the entire column and computing A_{22},

$A_{22} = \left(\frac{2}{3}\right) - \left(\frac{1}{3}\right) \times (-1) = 3$, gives the matrix,

$$\begin{pmatrix} 3 & 1 & 1 \\ 2 & 2 & -1 \\ \frac{1}{3} & \frac{1}{3} & 1 \end{pmatrix}$$

This yields, the following matrices L and U,

$$L = \begin{pmatrix} 1 & 0 & 0 \\ 2 & 1 & 0 \\ \frac{1}{3} & \frac{1}{3} & 1 \end{pmatrix} \text{ and } U = \begin{pmatrix} 3 & 1 & 1 \\ 0 & 2 & -1 \\ 0 & 0 & 1 \end{pmatrix}$$

One can easily verify the LU decomposition as follows:

$$A = L \times U$$

$$\begin{pmatrix} 3 & 1 & 1 \\ 6 & 4 & 1 \\ 1 & 1 & 1 \end{pmatrix} = \begin{pmatrix} 1 & 0 & 0 \\ 2 & 1 & 0 \\ \frac{1}{3} & \frac{1}{3} & 1 \end{pmatrix} \times \begin{pmatrix} 3 & 1 & 1 \\ 0 & 2 & -1 \\ 0 & 0 & 1 \end{pmatrix}$$

It can be observed that the product of L and U gives the original matrix as it is. Therefore, the LU decomposition is correct.

LUP Decomposition

LUP is an extension of LU decomposition. Here the matrix A is decomposed to three matrices L, U and P. P is a permutation matrix. So,

$P A = L U$

P is a permutation matrix. In case, if rows or columns need to be swapped, then this can be avoided by the usage of permutation matrix. In that case, the orderings can be recorded using matrix P. Hence, $Ax = b$ can be written as,

$P Ax = Pb$

A can be decomposed as LU. P is just a permutation matrix used for swapping rows and columns. So, one can write,

$LUx = Pb$

Now the above equation is solved as previous methods:

- Define y=Ux and solve for Solve $Ly = Pb$ for unknown y. This process is called forward substation.

- Solve the unknown x by using the equation $Ux = y$. This is called backward substitution.

In the absence of partial pivoting, LUP decomposition is almost similar to LU decomposition.

Crout's Method of Decomposition

Crout's method is another method of LU decomposition similar to Gaussian elimination based LU decomposition. The formula for crout procedure can directly be derived. Let us consider a following 3×3 matrices as follows:

$$\begin{bmatrix} a_{11} & a_{12} & a_{13} \\ a_{21} & a_{22} & a_{23} \\ a_{31} & a_{32} & a_{33} \end{bmatrix} = \begin{bmatrix} l_{11} & 0 & 0 \\ l_{21} & l_{22} & 0 \\ l_{31} & l_{32} & l_{33} \end{bmatrix} \begin{bmatrix} 1 & u_{12} & u_{13} \\ 0 & 1 & u_{23} \\ 0 & 0 & 1 \end{bmatrix}$$

It can be observed that 3 X 3 matrix is expressed as a product of a lower triangular and upper triangular matrix. Perform the normal multiplication of LU. This yields the following expression:

$$\begin{bmatrix} a_{11} & a_{12} & a_{13} \\ a_{21} & a_{22} & a_{23} \\ a_{31} & a_{32} & a_{33} \end{bmatrix} = \begin{bmatrix} l_{11} & (l_{11}u_{12}) & (l_{11}u_{13}) \\ l_{21} & (l_{21}u_{12}+l_{22}) & (l_{21}u_{13}+l_{23}u_{23}) \\ l_{31} & (l_{31}u_{12}+l_{32}) & (l_{31}u_{13}+l_{32}u_{23}+l_{33}) \end{bmatrix}$$

Equating these two matrices, one can directly compute the first columns.

$l_{11} = a_{11}; \; l_{21} = a_{21}; \; l_{31} = a_{31};$

Then using these values, one can compute the second column as follows;

$$l_{11}u_{12} = a_{12}$$

$$\therefore u_{12} = \frac{a_{12}}{l_{11}} = \frac{a_{12}}{a_{11}}$$

$$l_{21}u_{12} + l_{22} = a_{22}$$

$$\therefore l_{22} = a_{22} - l_{21}u_{12}$$

$$l_{31}u_{12} + l_{32} = a_{32}$$

$$\therefore l_{32} = a_{32} - l_{31}u_{12}$$

From the above values, one can easily compute the third column:

$$l_{11}u_{13} = a_{13}$$

$$\therefore u_{13} = \frac{a_{13}}{l_{11}} = \frac{a_{13}}{a_{11}}$$

$$l_{21}u_{13} + l_{22}u_{23} = a_{23}$$

$$\therefore u_{23} = \frac{a_{23} - l_{21}u_{13}}{l_{22}}$$

$$l_{31}u_{13} + l_{32}u_{23} + l_{33} = a_{33}$$

$$\therefore l_{33} = a_{33} - l_{31}u_{13} - l_{32}u_{23}$$

Using these values, one can find matrices L and U respectively. This is illustrated in the following Example:

Example: Perform LU decomposition of the following matrix using Crout method,

$$\begin{pmatrix} 3 & 1 & 1 \\ 6 & 4 & 1 \\ 1 & 1 & 1 \end{pmatrix}$$

Solution: This is a 3 X 3 matrix. So comparing this matrix with,

$$\begin{bmatrix} a_{11} & a_{12} & a_{13} \\ a_{21} & a_{22} & a_{23} \\ a_{31} & a_{32} & a_{33} \end{bmatrix} = \begin{bmatrix} l_{11} & 0 & 0 \\ l_{21} & l_{22} & 0 \\ l_{31} & l_{32} & l_{33} \end{bmatrix} \begin{bmatrix} 1 & u_{12} & u_{13} \\ 0 & 1 & u_{23} \\ 0 & 0 & 1 \end{bmatrix}$$

Once can easily derive the values as below:

$$l_{11} = a_{11} = 3, \; l_{21} = a_{21} = 6 \text{ and } l_{31} = a_{31} = 1$$

$$u_{12} = \frac{a_{12}}{a_{11}} = \frac{1}{3}; \; l_{22} = a_{22} - l_{21}u_{12} = 4 - 6 \times \frac{1}{3} = 2; \; l_{32} = a_{32} - l_{31}u_{12} = 1 - \frac{1}{3} = \frac{2}{3}$$

$$u_{13} = \frac{a_{13}}{a_{11}} = \frac{1}{3}; \; u_{23} = \frac{a_{23} - l_{21}u_{13}}{l_{22}} = \frac{1 - 6 \times \frac{1}{3}}{2} = -\frac{1}{2}; \; l_{33} = a_{33} - l_{31}u_{13} - l_{32}u_{23} = 1 - \frac{1}{3} + \frac{1}{3} = 1$$

So arranging this in lower and upper triangular matrix, one gets,

$$L = \begin{pmatrix} 3 & 0 & 0 \\ 6 & 2 & 0 \\ 1 & {}^{2}/_{3} & 1 \end{pmatrix} \text{ and } U = \begin{pmatrix} 1 & {}^{1}/_{3} & {}^{1}/_{3} \\ 0 & 1 & -{}^{1}/_{2} \\ 0 & 0 & 1 \end{pmatrix}$$

One can check that the above decomposition is true as by multiplying L and U, one gets the original matrix as it is.

Finding Inverse of a Matrix

What is an inverse matrix? A matrix A^{-1} is said to the inverse of matrix A, if the following condition holds good.

$$AA^{-1} = I$$

Here, the matrix I is identity matrix. In other words, the inverse [B] of a square matrix [A] is defined as,

$$[A][B] = [I] = [B][A]$$

There is no guarantee that the inverse matrix exists for all matrices. If the inverse matrix does not exist for a matrix A, then A is called singular. It must be noted that matrix inverse does not exist for all matrices and not all square matrices have matrix inverse. Matrix inverse is useful for finding the unknown x of the equation Ax=y as,

$$x = A^{-1} \times b \text{ if } A^{-1} \text{ exists.}$$

To find the inverse of a matrix, one can write,

$$\begin{pmatrix} a_{11} & a_{12} & \cdots & a_{1n} \\ a_{21} & a_{22} & \cdots & a_{2n} \\ & & \vdots & \\ a_{n1} & a_{n2} & & a_{nn} \end{pmatrix} \begin{pmatrix} x_{11} & x_{12} & \cdots & x_{1n} \\ x_{21} & x_{22} & \cdots & a_{2n} \\ & & \vdots & \\ x_{n1} & x_{n2} & & x_{nn} \end{pmatrix} = \begin{pmatrix} 1 & 0 & \cdots & 0 \\ 0 & 1 & \cdots & 0 \\ & & \vdots & \\ 0 & 0 & & 1 \end{pmatrix}$$

This can be written as,

$$Ax_j = e_j$$

Where x_j and e_j are the vectors of unknowns in the jth column of the matrix inverse.

One can also use Gaussian process for decomposing the matrix A as A = LU and solving the equations. This will be useful for finding unknowns faster. The following Example illustrates the use of Gaussian elimination in the process of finding the determinant.

Example: Find the inverse matrix for the following matrix using Gaussian elimination method.

$$\begin{pmatrix} 3 & 2 \\ 2 & 7 \end{pmatrix}$$

Solution:

Let $A = \begin{pmatrix} 3 & 2 \\ 2 & 7 \end{pmatrix}$

Augment this matrix with,

$$\left[A \mid I \right] = \begin{bmatrix} 3 & 2 & 1 & 0 \\ 2 & 7 & 0 & 1 \end{bmatrix}$$

Apply Gaussian Elimination method as follows:

$$\left[A \mid I \right] = \begin{bmatrix} 3 & 2 & 1 & 0 \\ 0 & \dfrac{17}{3} & \dfrac{-2}{3} & 1 \end{bmatrix} R_1 \rightarrow R_2 - \dfrac{2R_1}{3}$$

Since the matrix is of order 2 x 2, the matrix inverse would be,

$$A^{-1} = \begin{pmatrix} X_{11} & X_{12} \\ X_{21} & X_{22} \end{pmatrix}$$

The first column of the matrix inverse is obtained as follows:

$$\begin{bmatrix} 3 & 2 \\ 0 & \dfrac{17}{3} \end{bmatrix} \begin{bmatrix} X_{11} \\ X_{21} \end{bmatrix} = \begin{bmatrix} 1 \\ \dfrac{-2}{3} \end{bmatrix}$$

$$\dfrac{17}{3} X_{21} = \dfrac{-2}{3}$$

$$X_{21} = \dfrac{-2}{17}$$

and,

$$3X_1 + 2X_{21} = 1$$

$$3X_{11} + \dfrac{2 \times -2}{17} = 1$$

$$3x_{11} = 1 + \frac{4}{17} = \frac{21}{17}$$

$$x_{11} = \frac{21}{17} \times \frac{1}{3} = \frac{7}{17}$$

Similarly the second column of the matrix inverse is obtained as follows:

$$\begin{bmatrix} 3 & 2 \\ 0 & \dfrac{17}{3} \end{bmatrix} \begin{bmatrix} x_{12} \\ x_{22} \end{bmatrix} = \begin{bmatrix} 0 \\ 1 \end{bmatrix}$$

$$\frac{17}{3} x_{22} = 1$$

$$x_{22} = \frac{3}{17}$$

$$3x_{12} + 2x_{22} = 0$$

$$3x_{12} = \frac{-2 \times 3}{17}$$

$$x_{12} = \frac{-2}{17}$$

By substituting these values in the matrix inverse, one can get the inverse matrix as follows:

$$\therefore A^{-1} \begin{bmatrix} \dfrac{7}{17} & \dfrac{-2}{17} \\ \dfrac{-2}{17} & \dfrac{3}{17} \end{bmatrix} = \frac{1}{17} \begin{bmatrix} 7 & -2 \\ -2 & 3 \end{bmatrix}$$

One can verify that the matrix inverse is correct by multiplying the matrix and the matrix inverse obtained. It is equal to matrix.

Finding Determinant of a Matrix

Finding determinant is one of the most frequently encountered operation in scientific applications. For a matrix A, such as this,

$$A = \begin{bmatrix} a_{11} & a_{12} & a_{13} \\ a_{21} & a_{22} & a_{23} \\ a_{31} & a_{32} & a_{33} \end{bmatrix}$$

The determinant D is denoted as,

$$D = \begin{vmatrix} a_{11} & a_{12} & a_{13} \\ a_{21} & a_{22} & a_{23} \\ a_{31} & a_{32} & a_{33} \end{vmatrix}$$

and is computed as follows:

$$D = a_{11}\begin{vmatrix} a_{22} & a_{23} \\ a_{32} & a_{33} \end{vmatrix} - a_{12}\begin{vmatrix} a_{21} & a_{23} \\ a_{31} & a_{33} \end{vmatrix} + a_{13}\begin{vmatrix} a_{21} & a_{22} \\ a_{31} & a_{32} \end{vmatrix}$$

As order of the matrix increases, finding determinant is very difficult. The method of finding determinant can be converted to another problem of finding the determinant using Gaussian elimination. The process of finding the determinant using Gaussian elimination is as follows:

- Decompose A = LU.

- Find the determinant, $As|A| = |LU|$
$$= |L||U|.$$

- The determinant of L is 1. The determinant of the matrix U is the product of its diagonals.

This is illustrated in the following Example:

Example: Find determinant of the following matrix,

$$\begin{bmatrix} 3 & 1 & 1 \\ 6 & 4 & 1 \\ 1 & 1 & 1 \end{bmatrix}$$

Solution: Using previous Example, one can find L and U as follows:

$$L = \begin{bmatrix} 1 & 0 & 0 \\ 2 & 1 & 0 \\ 1/3 & 1/3 & 1 \end{bmatrix}$$

and,

$$U = \begin{bmatrix} 3 & 1 & 1 \\ 0 & 2 & -1 \\ 0 & 0 & 1 \end{bmatrix}$$

Thus, Determinant of matrix A is given as follows:

$$|A| = |LU| = |L||U|$$
$$|L| = 1$$
$$|U| = \text{product of diagonal elements}$$
$$= 3 \times 2 \times 1 = 6$$

Therefore, the determinant of the matrix is 6.

Backtracking

Backtracking is a technique based on algorithm to solve problem. It uses recursive calling to find the solution by building a solution step by step increasing values with time. It removes the solution that doesn't give rise to the solution of the problem based on the constraints given to solve the problem. Backtracking algorithm is applied to some specific types of problems:

- Decision problem used to find a feasible solution of the problem.

- Optimisation problem used to find the best solution that can be applied.

- Enumeration problem used to find the set of all feasible solutions of the problem.

In backtracking problem, the algorithm tries to find a sequence path to the solution which has some small checkpoints from where the problem can backtrack if no feasible solution is found for the problem.

Example:

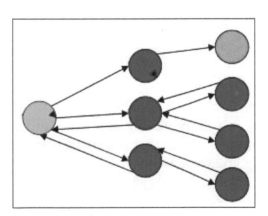

Here, Green is the start point, blue is the intermediate point, red are points with no feasible solution, dark green is end solution.

Here, when the algorithm propagates to an end to check if it is a solution or not, if it is then returns the solution otherwise backtracks to the point one step behind it to find track to the next point to find solution.

Algorithm:

```
Step 1 - if current_position is goal, return success

Step 2 - else,

Step 3 - if current_position is an end point, return failed.

Step 4 - else, if current_position is not end point, explore and repeat
above steps.
```

Let's use this backtracking problem to find the solution to N-Queen Problem. In N-Queen problem, we are given an N×N chessboard and we have to place n queens on the board in such a way that no two queens attack each other. A queen will attack another queen if it is placed in horizontal, vertical or diagonal points in its way. Here, we will do 4-Queen problem.

Here, the solution is:

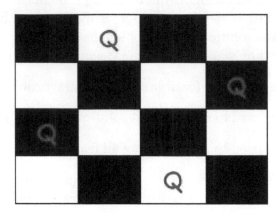

Here, the binary output for n queen problem with 1's as queens to the positions are placed.

```
{0 , 1 , 0 , 0}

{0 , 0 , 0 , 1}

{1 , 0 , 0 , 0}

{0 , 0 , 1 , 0}
```

For solving n queens problem, we will try placing queen into different positions of one row. And checks if it clashes with other queens. If current positioning of queens if there are any two queens attacking each other. If they are attacking, we will backtrack to previous location of the queen and change its positions. And check clash of queen again.

Algorithm:

Step 1 – Start from 1st position in the array.

Step 2 – Place queens in the board and check. Do,

   Step 2.1 – After placing the queen, mark the position as a part of the solution and then recursively check if this will lead to a solution.

   Step 2.2 – Now, if placing the queen doesn't lead to a solution and trackback and go to step (a) and place queens to other rows.

   Step 2.3 – If placing queen returns a lead to solution return TRUE.

Step 3 – If all queens are placed return TRUE.

Step 4 – If all rows are tried and no solution is found, return FALSE.

Now, Let's use backtracking to solve the Rat in a Maze problem: In rat in a maze problem, we are with an NxN maze the first position of the maze i.e [0][0] and will end at position [n-1][n-1] of the array. In this path there are some dead roads which do not lead to a solution. Using backtracking in this problem we will go down step by step to reach the final goal position in the maze.

Randomized Algorithms

Randomness is a state of the system whose behaviour follows no deterministic or predictable pattern. Some of the daily encounters like gambling, puzzles, decision making process and heuristics are examples of randomness.

Randomness is used as a computing tool by randomized algorithms for algorithm design. Randomized algorithms are also called probabilistic algorithms. An algorithm takes an input, process it and generates an output. This is shown in figure.

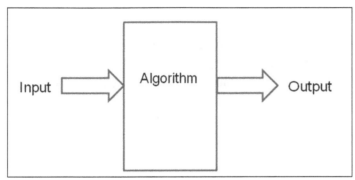

Algorithm Environment.

Algorithms can be classified into deterministic algorithms and randomized algorithms. The output is always fixed for deterministic algorithms. Randomized algorithms are on the other hand [1,2,3] is as shown in figure.

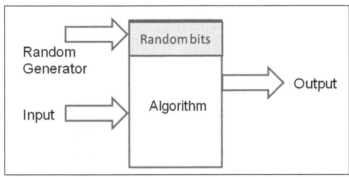

A Randomized algorithm.

It should be noted that randomized algorithms output is based on random decisions and its output is based on probability. There would be negligible errors on the long run. In short, Randomized Algorithms are dependent on inputs and use random choices as part of the logic itself. What are the advantages of randomized algorithms? Some of the advantages of randomized algorithms are given below:

- Known for its simplicity.

- Very Efficient.

- Computational complexity is better than deterministic algorithms.

Some of the disadvantages of randomized algorithms are as given below:

- Reliability is an issue.

- Quality is dependent on quality of random number generator used as part of the algorithm.

But randomized algorithms are very popular and are useful to solve many problems in computer science domain effectively. Let us discuss some of the design principles that are useful for randomized algorithm design.

Concept of Witness

This is one of the important design principles for randomized algorithms. The concept of witness is about checking whether given input X has property Y or not. The core idea is the concept of witness that gives a guarantee. Some of the problems like random trials and Primality testing can be solved using this concept of witness.

Fingerprinting

Fingerprinting is the concept of using a shorter message representative of a larger object. This representative is called fingerprinting. If two large strings need to be checked, then instead of comparing two larger strings, two fingerprints can be compared. The problem of comparing larger strings can be done using this design principle.

Randomized Sampling and Ordering

Some problems can be solved by random sampling and ordering. This is done by randomizing the input distribution or order or by partitioning or sampling randomly. Some of the problems that use this principle are hiring problem and randomized quicksort.

Foiling Adversary

This is another useful principle. This can be viewed as a game between a person and an adversary with both are attempting to maximize their gains. This can be view as a selection of algorithm from a large set of algorithms.

Types of Randomized Algorithms

There are two types of algorithms. One is called Las Vegas Algorithms and another is called Monte Carlo Algorithms. Las Vegas Algorithms have the following characteristics:

- Always correct

- Probably fast

Randomized quicksort is an example of Las Vegas algorithm. It is faster than the traditional quicksort algorithm and its results are always correct. Monte Carlo algorithms were designed by Nicholas Metropolis in 1949. Unlike Las Vegas algorithms, Monte Carlo algorithms give results that are mostly or probably correct. These algorithms have guaranteed running time unlike Las Vegas algorithms. Primality testing problem can be solved using Monte Carlo algorithms.

Complexity Class

Like P and NP classes for deterministic algorithms, randomized algorithms also can be grouped together as class of problems. Some of the classes are given below:

RP Class

RP class is a set of decision problems solvable with one-sided error in polynomial time. It is an abbreviation of Random Polynomial algorithms. What is a one sided error? If the correct answer is 'NO', then the algorithm always returns 'NO' as the answer. But, if the correct answer is 'YES', return algorithm result is associated with a probability. In other words, the algorithm output would be 'YES' with probability $\geq \frac{1}{2}$. Monte Carlo algorithms belong to class RP.

ZPP Class

ZPP is a class of decision problems that are solvable in expected polynomial time. Las Vegas algorithms are examples of ZPP class. There is a theorem that defines the hierarchies as follows:

$$P \subseteq ZPP \subseteq RP \subseteq NP$$

Random Numbers

One of the primary requirements of good quality randomized algorithms is the quality of its random number generator. The quality of the random number generator determines the reliability of the randomized algorithm.

A random number generator generates a random number. The true random numbers are based on radioactive decay; flip of coins, shot noise, radiations. One of the characteristic of the "true" random number generator is that the generated number should not appear again. But, based on the memory and processor limitations, generation of such number is often difficult. So, Pseudo random numbers are generated. Pseudo-random numbers are as good as true random numbers in most of the situations.

Pseudo-random numbers are generated using software applications and can be recreated if formula is known. But, Pseudo-random numbers are sufficient for most of the purposes. Some of the characteristics of "Good" random numbers are:

- Efficiency,

- Deterministic Property,

- Uniformity,

- Independence,

- Long cycle.

There are many algorithms are available for generating pseudorandom numbers. One simplest algorithm is called Linear Congruential Generator (LCG). The formula of LCG is given below:

$$X_{i+1} = (a* + b)\% \ m$$

Here, a and b are large prime numbers, and m is 2^{32} or 2^{64}. The initial value of is called a seed.

Often a permutation array is created by generating random numbers and storing it as an array. The array of random numbers is called permutation array. The steps of creating a permutation array are given as follows:

- Let index = 1.

- Generate random number.

- Swap A[index] and random number.

- Fill the array.

The formal algorithm based on [1,2,3] is given as follows:

```
Algorithm random-array(A)

Begin

     for index = 1 to N

     k = random();

     Exchange A[index] and A[k]

     End for

End
```

Hiring Problem

Hiring problem is a problem of hiring a secretary among a group of secretaries. This problem can be solved using deterministic and randomized algorithm. Informally, the steps of hiring problem is given as follows:

- Initial candidate is best candidate.

- Interview new candidate.

- If new candidate is better, then hire new candidate and old candidate is fired.

What is the complexity analysis? Conducting interview and hiring costs something. If n candidates interviewed and m candidates hired. In that case, the total cost of the algorithm would be $O(m \times C_{hire} + n \times C_{Interview})$.

The computational complexity can be improved by randomized hiring algorithm. The improvement comes because of shuffling the input. By random order of the input, the algorithm becomes randomized algorithm. The steps of the randomized hiring problem are given as follows:

- Randomly permute array A.

- Let Initial candidate is best candidate.

- Interview new candidate.

- If new candidate is better, then hire new candidate and old candidate is fired.

Primality Testing

Primality testing is one of the most important randomized algorithms. Primality testing problem can be formally given as follows: Given a number, how to check whether it is prime or not?

A number N is a prime number only if it is divisible by 1 and N. A brute force method of testing a number whether it is prime or not is to check divisibility from 2 to sqrt(N). Obviously, the problem becomes hard when N is very large.

A randomized algorithm can be written for Primality testing using the principles of concept of witness. Concept of witness is checking whether given input X has property Y or not. Obviously, the idea is to select a witness to guarantee the prime of the given number. If the reliability is an issue, then the number of random trials can be increased.

Fermat stated that a number n is prime if and only if the congruence $x^{n-1} \equiv 1 \pmod{n}$ is satisfied for every integer x between 0 and n. based on this, a randomized algorithm can be given as follows:

- Read number n.

- Pick a witness x uniformly in the range 1 to n.

- Check for Fermat Criteria.

- If number is composite, it is always true. If number is prime, it is probably correct.

The formal algorithm is given as follows:

```
Algorithm FermatTest(n)

Begin

        Choose x ∈ {1, 2, . . . , n - 1} uniformly at random.

        If x^(n-1) ≢ 1 (mod n), return composite

                Else return probably prime

            End if

End
```

Complexity Analysis: The algorithm involves k trials for picking x randomly. The algorithm involves squaring/ multiplication and modulo operations. Therefore, the algorithm has at most $O(\log n)$ steps.

Randomized Large String Comparison

This is another useful algorithm. The aim of this algorithm is to compare very large strings. A brute force approach is to check every bit of the message. Obviously, the conventional algorithm is tedious for larger strings. A better randomized algorithm can be designed for this problem. The idea is to use the concept of fingerprinting. Fingerprint is a representative of larger message. So, the problem of comparing larger strings is reduced to the comparison of fingerprints of larger strings.

The informal algorithm for comparing two larger strings a and b is given as follows:

- Choose a prime uniformly from n to n^k where k is a constant > 2.

- Find fingerprint for message a and b.

- Check for equality using fingerprint.

The formal algorithm is given as follows:

```
Algorithm Random-Equal(a,b)

Begin

      Choose p ∈ {2, . . . , nᵏ} uniformly at random.

      m = Fingerprint of message a

       n = Fingerprint of message b

       if m = n then

            return true

       else

       return false

End
```

Complexity Analysis: It can be observed that the fingerprints of two larger strings a and b, m, n respectively and p requires only $O(\log n)$ bits. Therefore, the algorithm rrequires at most $O(\log n)$ steps. The reliability if required can be extended to k trials. Even then, the complexity of this algorithm is better than quadratic complexity of the traditional algorithm.

Randomized Quicksort

The concept of randomized quicksort is based on randomize input distribution or order. Randomized quicksort is based on this concept. Traditional quicksort uses a partitioning algorithm to pick pivotal element. A randomized algorithm can be written by randomly picking the pivot element. The informal algorithm can be given as follows:

- Pick a pivot element randomly.

- Recursively perform sort on subarrays.

The formal algorithm for choosing the pivotal element is given as follows:

```
Algorithm Randomized-Partition(A, p, r)

Begin

     i ← Random(p, r)

     Exchange A[r] ↔ A[i]

     Return Partition(A, p, r)

End
```

The complete algorithm is given as follows:

```
Algorithm Randomized-Quicksort(A, p, r)

Begin

if p < r

     then q ← Randomized-Partition(A, p, r)

          Randomized-Quicksort(A, p , q-1)

          Randomized-Quicksort(A, q+1, r)

End if

End
```

Complexity Analysis: The behavior of Randomized Quick Sort is determined not only by the input but also by the random choices of the pivot. The randomized analysis for randomized quicksort is done as follows:

Rename the elements of A as $z_1, z_2, \ldots, z_n$, with z_i being the ith smallest element (Rank "i"). Define the set $Z_{ij} = \{z_i, zi+1, \ldots, z_j\}$ be the set of elements between z_i and z_j, inclusive. The indicator variable for randomized quicksort is given as follows:

$$\text{Let } X_{ij} = I\left\{z_i \text{ is compared to } z_j\right\}$$

Let X be the total number of comparisons performed by the algorithm. Then,

$$\left[X = \sum_{i=1}^{n-1} \sum_{j=i+1}^{n} X_{ij}\right]$$

Therefore, the expected number of comparisons performed by the algorithm is,

$$E[X] = E\left[\sum_{i=1}^{n-1} \sum_{j=i+1}^{n} X_{ij}\right] = \sum_{i=1}^{n-1} \sum_{j=i+1}^{n} E[X_{ij}]$$

by linearity
of expectation

$$= \sum_{i=1}^{n-1} \sum_{j=i+1}^{n} \Pr\left\{ z_i \text{ iscompared to } z_j \right\}$$

Then, one can observe that there are only two cases as shown below:

- Case 1: Pivot chosen such as: $z_i < x < z_j$. In this case, z_i and z_j will never be compared.

- Case 2: z_i or z_j is the pivot. In that case, z_i and z_j will be compared only if one of them is chosen as pivot before any other element in range z_i to z_j.

Therefore, $\Pr\{Z_i$ is compared with $Z_j\} = \Pr\{Z_i$ or Z_j is chosen as pivot before other elements in $Z_{i,j}\}$ = 2 / (j-i+1). Finally, the Expectation of the random variable is given as,

$$E[X] = \sum_{i=1}^{n-1} \sum_{j=i+1}^{n} \Pr\left\{ z_i \text{ iscompared to } z_j \right\}$$

Therefore,

$$E[X] = \sum_{i=1}^{n-1} \sum_{j=i+1}^{n} \frac{2}{j-i+1} = \sum_{i=1}^{n-1} \sum_{k=1}^{n-i} \frac{2}{k+1} < \sum_{i=1}^{n-1} \sum_{k=1}^{n} \frac{2}{k} = \sum_{i=1}^{n-1} O(\log n)$$

Therefore, the complexity analysis of randomized quicksort is same as the traditional quicksort algorithm.

Dynamic Programming

The method of solving problems in which a complex problem is split into simpler steps to find a solution to the complex problem is termed as dynamic programming. Some of the areas of study within dynamic programming are shortest path algorithm, and knapsack problem and flow scheduling. This chapter has been carefully written to provide an easy understanding about dynamic programming.

Dynamic programming is useful for solving multistage optimization problems, especially sequential decision problems. Richard Bellman is widely considered as the father of dynamic programming. He was an American mathematician. Richard Bellman is also credited with the coining of the word "Dynamic programming". Here, the word "dynamic" refers to some sort of time reference and "programming" is interpreted as planning or tabulation rather than programming that is encountered in computer programs.

Dynamic programming is used in variety of applications. Dynamic programming (DP) is used to solve discrete optimization problems such as scheduling, string-editing, packaging, and inventory management. Dynamic programming employs the following steps as shown below:

- Step 1: The given problem is divided into a number of subproblems as in "divide and conquer" strategy. But in divide and conquer, the subproblems are independent of each other but in dynamic programming case, there are all overlapping subproblems. A recursive formulation is formed of the given problem.

- Step 2: The problem, usually solved in the bottom-up manner. To avoid, repeated computation of multiple overlapping subproblems, a table is created. Whenever a subproblem is solved, then its solution is stored in the table so that in future its solutions can be reused. Then the solutions are combined to solve the overall problem.

There are certain rules that govern dynamic programming. One is called Principle of optimality:

- Rule 1: Bellman's principle of optimality states that at a current state, the optimal policy depends only on the current state and independent of the decisions that are taken in the previous stages. This is called the principle of optimality. In simple words, the optimal solution to the given problem has optimal solution for all the subproblems that are contained in the given problem.

- Rule 2: Dynamic programming problems have overlapping subproblems. So, the idea is to solve smaller instances once and records solutions in a table. This is called memoization, a corrupted word of memorization.

- Rule 3: Dynamic programming computes in bottom-up fashion. Thus, the solutions of the subproblems are extracted and combined to give solution to the original problem.

Fibonacci Problem

The Fibonacci sequence is given as (0, 1, 2, 3, 5, 8, 13. . .). It was given by Leonardo of Pisa. The Fibonacci recurrence equation is given below:

$$F_0 = 0$$
$$F_1 = 1$$
$$F_n = F_{n-1} + F_{n-2} \text{ for } n \geq 2.$$

Conventional Algorithm

The conventional pseudocode for implementing the recursive equation is given below:

```
Fib1(N)

{       if (N =< 1)

                return 1;

        else

                return Fib(N-1) + Fib(N-2)

}
```

This straight forward implementation is inefficient. This is illustrated in the following Figure:

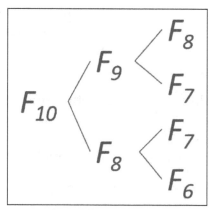

A portion of the Recurrence Tree.

Complexity Analysis: It can be observed that there are multiple overlapping subproblems. As 'n' becomes large, the number of subproblems also would increase exponentially. This leads to repeated computation and thus the algorithm becomes ineffective. The complexity analysis of this algorithm yields $T(n) = \Omega(\phi^n)$. Here ϕ is called golden ratio whose value is given approximately as 1.62.

Dynamic Programming Approach

The best way to solve this problem is to use dynamic programming approach. The dynamic programming approach uses an approach of storing the results of the intermediate problems. Hence the key is to reuse the results of the previously computed subproblems rather than recomputing the subproblems repeatedly. As a subproblem is computed only once, this exponential algorithm is reduced to a polynomial algorithm. To store the intermediate results, a table is created and its values are reused. This table is shown in table.

Table: Fibonacci Table.

F_0	F_1	F_2	F_3	F_4	F_5	F_6	F_7	F_8	F_9	F_{10}
0	1	1	2	3	5	8	13	21	34	55

The tabular computation can avoid recomputation as the intermediate results can be used instead of recomputed. The algorithm based on this approach is given below:

An iterative version of this algorithm can be given as follows:

```
Fib2(n)

{       int Fn = 1, Fn1 = 1, Fn2 = 1

        for(I = 2; I <= n; I++)

        {       Fn = Fn1 + Fn2

                Fn2 = Fn1

                Fn1 = Fn

        }

        return Fn

}
```

Complexity Analysis: It can be observed that two variables 'Fn1' and 'Fn2' track Fibonacci(n-1) and Fibonacci(n) to compute Fibonacci(n+1). As repeat condition spans only n-1 times, the complexity analysis of this algorithm is $\cong$ O(n). This is far better than exponential conventional algorithm.

Binomial Coefficient

Binomial coefficient can be obtained using this formula,

$$\begin{bmatrix} n \\ k \end{bmatrix} = \frac{n!}{k!(n-k)!} \text{ for } 0 \le k \le n.$$

The conventional algorithm to implement the above formula is given as below:

```
Int bin(int n, int k)

{

        if (k = 0 or n = k )

                return 1;

        else

                return(bin(n-1, k-1) + bin(n-1, k))

}
```

But, the difficulty with this formula is that the factorial of a number can be very large. For example, the factorial, Of 49! = 608,281,864,034,267,560,872,252,163,321,295,376,887,552,831,379,210,240,000,000,000. Therefore, the application of conventional formula is difficult for large value of 'n'.

Dynamic Programming Approach

The dynamic programming approach can be applied for this problem. The recursive formulation of binomial coefficient is given as follows:

$$\begin{bmatrix} n \\ k \end{bmatrix} = \begin{cases} \begin{bmatrix} n-1 \\ k-1 \end{bmatrix} + \begin{bmatrix} n-1 \\ k \end{bmatrix} & 0 < k < n \\ 1 & k = 0 \text{ or } k = n \end{cases}$$

The Dynamic Programming approach for this problem would be:

- Divide the problem $\binom{n}{k}$ into many sub problems like $\binom{0}{0}, \binom{1}{0}, \binom{1}{1}, ..., \binom{n}{n}$. A bottom-up approach can be used to solve the problem from scratch.

- To avoid recomputation of the subproblems, a table can be used where the results of the subproblems can be stored.

This would be similar to Pascal triangle as given below in figure:

$$c(0,0)$$
$$c(1,0) \quad c(1,1)$$
$$c(2,0) \quad c(2,1) \quad c(2,2)$$
$$c(3,0) \quad c(3,1) \quad c(3,2) \quad c(3,3)$$
$$c(4,0) \quad c(4,1) \quad c(4,2) \quad c(4,3) \quad c(4,4)$$

Pascal Triangle.

It can be observed that, each row depends only on the preceding row. Therefore, only linear space and quadratic time are needed. The Table for computation is given below:

	0	1	2	...	k-1	k
0	1					
1	1	1				
.						
.						
.						
n-1					$C(n-1,k-1)$	$C(n-1,k)$
n						$C(n,k)$

This algorithm is known as Pascal's Triangle. The formal algorithm is given below:

```
Int bin(int n, int k)

    {

    int i, j;

    int B[0..n, 0..k];

    for i = 0 to n

            for j = 0 to minimum(i, k)

                    if( j = 0 or j = i)

                            B[i, j] = 1;

                    else

                            B[i, j] = B[i-1, j-1] + B[i-1, j];

    return B[n, k]

}
```

Complexity Analysis: The complexity analysis of this algorithm can be observed as O(nk) as the algorithm has two loops that spans from 1 to n. Hence the algorithm body gets executed at most n^2 times. ∴ The complexity of the algorithm is O(nk) and the space complexity is also O(nk).

Shortest Path Algorithm

Shortest Path Problem is usually associated with a weighted graph that has two vertices u and v, and we want to find a path of minimum total weight between u and v. Length of a path is the sum of the weights of its edges.

Example: Shortest path between Bangalore and Madurai. An example of a graph for shortest path is given in figure. Applications of shortest path problem include Internet packet routing, Flight reservations and Driving directions.

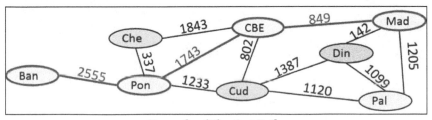

Example of Shortest Path.

The shortest path algorithm is associated with a directed weighted graph and the path length is sum of weights of the edges on the path. The source vertex is the place where the path begins and the destination vertex is the vertex where the path ends. Once the source and destination are finalized the vertices in the increasing order is reported from the source vertex. We construct the shortest path edge by edge; at each step adding one new edge, corresponding to construction of shortest path to the current new vertex.

Shortest Path Notations

For each vertex $v \in V$ where V is the set of vertices. $\delta(s, v)$ is shortest-path weight and $d[v]$ is the shortest-path weight estimate. Initially, $d[v] = \infty$ and $d[v] \to \delta(s,v)$ as algorithm progresses. $\pi[v] = $ predecessor of v on a shortest path from s and if no predecessor exists, $\pi[v] = $ NIL. π induces a tree called the shortest-path tree as shown in figure.

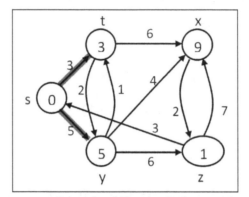

Example of Shortest Path.

The input to the algorithm is the Directed graph G = (V, E), with V being the set of vertices and E being the edges. A weight function $w : E \to R$ is associated with each edge of the graph. A path is denoted by a sequence of vertices. The weight of path $p = \langle v_0, v_1, \ldots, v_k \rangle$, is the weight of the edges between the vertices in the path. The Shortest path weight from u to v: $d(u, v) = \min w(p)$: if there exists a path p or p from u to v ∞ otherwise. Note that there might be multiple shortest paths from u to v. There may be many types of shortest path algorithms.

Initialization

All the shortest-paths algorithms start with INITIALIZE-SINGLE-SOURCE. Initially for every vertex v in G, $d[v]$ the shortest path estimate is set to ∞ and the $\pi[v]$, the predecessor of every vertex v is set to Nil. $d[s]$, the shortest path estimate of source node is set to 0.

```
Alg.: INITIALIZE-SINGLE-SOURCE (V, s)

for each v ∈ V

      do d[v] ← ∞

      π[v] ← NIL

d[s] ← 0
```

Shortest Path Tree

For every node $v \in V$, $\pi[v]$ is the predecessor of v in shortest path from source s to v. This value is set to Nil if does not exist. All our algorithms will output a shortest-path tree whose root is the source s and the edges are (π[v],v). The shortest path between s and v is the unique tree path from root s to v. Consider Source node 1 and destination node 7, a direct path between the nodes will cost 14, however a shorter path through two other nodes costs only 11.

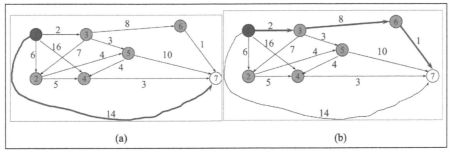

(a)   (b)

Shortest Path.

Shortest Path Variants

There are many variants of the shortest path algorithms. They are:

- Single-source single-destination (1-1): Find the shortest path from source s to destination v.

- Single-source all-destination(1-Many): Find the shortest path from s to each vertex v.

- Single-destination shortest-paths (Many-1): Find a shortest path to a given destination vertex t from each vertex v.

- All-pairs shortest-paths problem (Many-Many): Find a shortest path from u to v for every pair of vertices u and v.

- Single source/All destinations: nonnegative edge cost.

- Need to solve: Determine a shortest path from v to each of the remaining vertices of G.

Single-destination Shortest Paths

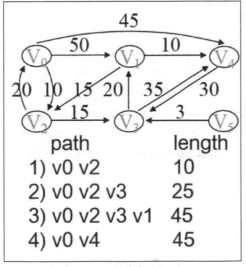

Single source/All destinations.

Among the shortest path algorithms given above the single destination shortest paths is about finding a shortest path to a given destination vertex t from each vertex v. Here we reverse the direction of each edge and finding the distances between every pair of vertices in a weighted directed graph G. Figure below shows the example of the Single source/All destinations -nonnegative edge cost where we need to determine a shortest path from v to each of the remaining vertices of G.

Shortest Path Properties

If some path from s to v contains a negative cost cycle, there does not exist a shortest path. Otherwise, there exists a shortest s-v that is simple. A negative cycle can produce arbitrarily long negative paths by traversing cycle a number of times. The negative-weight edges may form negative-weight cycle. If such cycles are reachable from the source, then $\delta(s, v)$ the shortest-path weight is not properly defined.

Relaxation Process

For each vertex v, we maintain an upper bound d[v] on the weight of shortest path from s to v and d[v] initialized to infinity. Relaxing an edge (u, v) = testing whether we can improve the shortest path to v found so far by going through u. d[v] is the weight of the path to vertex v, d[u] is the weight of the path to vertex u, w[u,v] is weight of edge [u,v] and π[v] indicates the predecessor of v in the shortest path to it.

If $d[v] > d[u] + w(u, v)$ and we can improve the shortest path to v. The updated $d[v] \Rightarrow d[v] = d[u] + w(u,v)$ and π[v] is updated as $\Rightarrow \pi[v] \leftarrow u$.

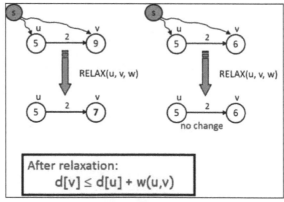

Relaxation Step.

Relaxing an edge (u, v) consists of testing whether we can improve the shortest path to v found so far by going through u, then updating d[v] and π[v] accordingly. A relaxation step may either decrease the value of the shortest-path estimate d[v] and update v's predecessor π [v], or cause no change.

Triangle Inequality

For any edge (u, v), we have (s; v) (s; u)+w(u; v). The weight of the shortest path from s to v is no greater than the weight of the shortest path from s to u plus the weight of the edge from u to v. For all $(u, v) \in E$, we have:

$$\delta(s, v) \le \delta(s, u) + w(u, v)$$

If u is on the shortest path to v we have the equality sign.

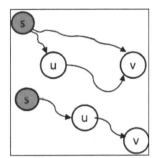

Triangular Property.

Optimal Substructure Property

All sub-paths of shortest paths are also shortest paths. The shortest path problem has the following optimal substructure property. If a node x lies in the shortest path from a source node u to destination node v then the shortest path from u to v is combination of shortest path from u to x and shortest path from x to v.

Upper-bound Property

We always have $d[v] \ge \delta(s, v)$ for all v. The estimate never rises since the relaxation process is so defined that it only lowers the estimate.

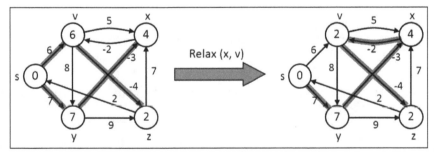

Upper-bound Property and Relaxation step.

Convergence Property

If s u → v is a shortest path, and if $d[u] = \delta(s, u)$ at any time prior to relaxing edge (u, v), then $d[v] = \delta(s, v)$ at all times after relaxing (u, v). As shown in figure, If $d[v] > \delta(s, v) \Rightarrow$ after relaxation:

$$d[v] = d[u] + w(u, v) \text{ and } d[v] = 5 + 2 = 7$$

Otherwise, the value remains unchanged, because it must have already been the shortest path value.

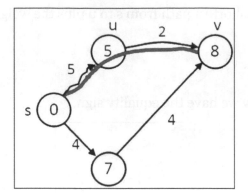

Path Relaxation Property

Let $p = \langle v_0, v_1, \ldots, v_k \rangle$ be a shortest path from $s = v_0$ to v_k. If we relax, in order, (v_0, v_1), (v_1, v_2), $\ldots$, (v_{k-1}, v_k), even intermixed with other relaxations, then $d[v_k] = \delta(s, v_k)$.

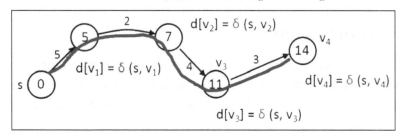

Predecessor-subgraph Property

Once $d[v] = \delta(s, v)$ for all $v \in V$, the predecessor sub-graph is a shortest-paths tree rooted at s. The Predecessor subgraph $G_\pi = (V_\pi, E_\pi)$, is defined where,

$$V_\pi = \{v \in V : \pi[v] \neq \text{Nil}\} \cup \{s\}$$

$$E_\pi = \{(\pi[v], v) \in E : v \in V_\pi - \{s\}\}$$

The No-path property of course says that if there is no path from s to v, then we always have $d[v] = \delta(s, v) = \infty$.

Applications

Some of the general types of applications of shortest path algorithms include minimization of the total distance traveled, minimization of the total cost of a sequence of activities, minimization of the total time of a sequence of activities. Application areas include network optimization, packet routing, image segmentation, computer-assisted surgery, computer games, DNA analysis, injection molding, operator scheduling, production planning, re-allocation of resources, approximation of piecewise linear functions and VLSI physical design. As discussed the shortest path algorithms find applications in many diverse areas.

Relaxation is the only means by which shortest-path estimates and predecessors change. The shortest path algorithms differ in how many times they relax each edge and the order in which they relax edges. Bellman-Ford algorithm relaxes each edge many times, while Dijkstra's algorithm for directed acyclic graphs relaxes each edge exactly once.

Algorithms

Dijkstra's algorithm and Bellman-Ford algorithm both use the common operations of Initialization and Relaxation. In Dijkstra's algorithm negative weights are not allowed. In the Bellman-Ford algorithm negative weights are allowed but negative cycles reachable from the source are not allowed.

Dijkstra's Algorithm

The steps and assumptions of the Dijkstra's algorithm are as follows:

- The distance of a vertex v from a vertex s is the length of a shortest path between s and v.

- Dijkstra's algorithm computes the distances of all the vertices from a given start vertex s.

- Assumptions are made that:

  ○ The graph is connected.

  ○ The edges are undirected.

  ○ The edge weights are nonnegative.

- Grow a "cloud" of vertices, beginning with s eventually covering all the vertices.

- We store with each vertex v a label d(v) representing the distance of v from s in the subgraph consisting of the cloud and its adjacent vertices.

- At each step:

  ○ We add to the cloud the vertex u outside the cloud with the smallest distance label, d(u).

  ○ We update the labels of the vertices adjacent to u.

Edge Relaxation

Now let us discuss the edge relaxation procedure in detail. Consider an edge e = (u,z) such that, u is the vertex most recently added to the cloud and z is not in the cloud. The relaxation of edge e updates distance d(z) as follows: d(z) ← min{d(z),d(u) + weight(e)}. In other words we consider the edge from u to z that is the minimum.

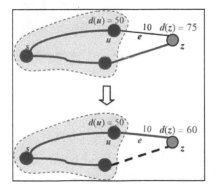

We start with node A and d[A] at this point is 0 Figure. Now we add to the cloud the vertex u outside the cloud with the smallest distance label, d(u) which here is vertex C and d[C] = 2 (A-C). We then update the labels of the vertices adjacent to u, here note that label of vertex D is updated from 4 to 3 (A-C-D), and label of vertex F (A-C-F) is updated to 11. Note that the path to B from A through C (C-B) and path to D from A (A-D) are not the shortest and are marked (in dotted lines) shown in figure.

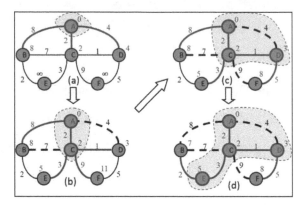

Now we add to the cloud the vertex D outside the cloud with the smallest distance label, d[D] =3 (A-C-D). We then update the labels of the vertices adjacent to u, here note that label of vertex F is updated from 11 to 8 (A-C-D-F), and the path that is not the shortest (C-F) is marked (in dotted lines) shown in Figure (c).

Now we add to the cloud the vertex E outside the cloud with the smallest distance label, d[E] =5 (A-C-E). We then update the labels of the vertices adjacent to u, here note that label of vertex B is updated from 8 to 7 (A-C-E-B), and the path that is not the shortest (C-F) is marked (in dotted lines) shown in figure (d).

Now we add to the cloud the vertex B outside the cloud with the smallest distance label, d[B] =7(A-C-E-B). We then update the labels of the vertices adjacent to u, here no updation occurs. Finally we add the node F to the cloud:

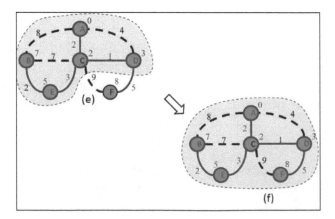

Dijkstra's Algorithm

A priority queue stores the vertices outside the cloud where Key is distance for the element which is the vertex. Locator-based methods are used to insert - insert(k,e) which returns a locator and replaceKey(l,k) which changes the key of an item. We store two labels with each vertex, Distance (d(v) label) and locator in the priority queue.

Dijkstra's algorithm assumes that $w(e) \geq 0$ for each e in the graph. We maintain a set S of vertices such that, every vertex $v \in S$, $d[v]=\delta(s, v)$, i.e., the shortest-path from s to v has been found. (Initial values: S=empty, d[s]=0 and $d[v]=\infty$).

- Select the vertex $u \in V-S$ such that:

  $d[u]=\min \{d[x]|x \in V-S\}$. Set $S=S \cup \{u\}$

- For each node v adjacent to u do RELAX(u, v, w).

- Repeat step the above steps until S=V.

The pseudo code for the algorithm is shown below:

```
dist[s] ←0          (distance to source vertex is zero)

for all v ∈ V-{s}

     do dist[v] ←∞     (set all other distances to infinity)

S←Ø                     (S, the set of visited vertices is initially empty) \
Q←V

(Q, the queue initially contains all vertices)

while Q ≠Ø          (while the queue is not empty)

 do u ← mindistance(Q,dist)    (select the element of Q with the min. distance)

 S←S∪{u}    (add u to list of visited vertices)

 for all v ∈ neighbors[u]

     do if dist[v] > dist[u] + w(u, v) (if new shortest path found)

          then d[v] ←d[u] + w(u, v) (set new value of shortest path)

return dist
```

Features of Dijkstra's Algorithm

The Dijkstra's algorithm is a greedy algorithm. It "Visits" every vertex only once, when it becomes the vertex with minimal distance amongst those still in the priority queue. However distances may be revised multiple times since the current values represent only the 'best guess' based on our observations so far. Once a vertex is visited we are guaranteed to have found the shortest path to that vertex.

Analysis of the Algorithm

The Graph operation is the method incidentEdges which is called once for each vertex. The Label operations are the ones where we set/get the distance and locator labels of vertex z that is of the order O(deg(z)) times and setting/getting a label takes O(1) time. The Priority queue operations include insertion where each vertex is inserted once into the priority queue and removed once from the priority queue, where each insertion or removal takes O(log n) time. The key of a vertex in the priority queue is modified at most deg(w) times, where each key change takes O(log n) time.

Thus the Dijkstra's algorithm runs in O((n + m) log n) time provided the graph is represented by the adjacency list structure - Recall that $S_v deg(v) = 2m$. The running time can also be expressed as O(m log n) since the graph is connected.

Dijkstra's Algorithm – Walkthrough

Let us use the graph in figure to find the shortest path using Dijkstra's algorithm.

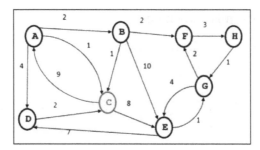

Initially the distance to all vertices except the source vertex is initialized to ∞. Let us assume that C is the source vertex d[C] = 0 and C is added to the cloud. Now we update labels of neighbors of C – here A is updated to 9 and E to 8. Since distance to E is the shortest from C that will be the next node to be considered.

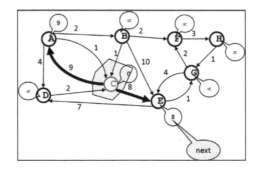

Now vertex E is added to the cloud and we update labels of neighbors of E – here D is updated to 15 (C-E-D that is 8+7=15) and G to 9 (C-E-G that is 8+1=9). Since distance to A is the shortest from C that will be the next node to be considered.

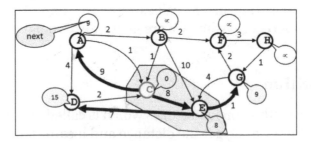

Now vertex A is added to the cloud and we update labels of neighbors of A – here B is updated to 11 (C-A-B that is 9+2=11) and D's label is revised from 15 to 13 through new path (C-A-D that is 9+4=13). Since distance to G is the shortest from C that will be the next node to be considered.

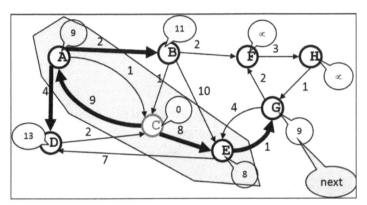

Now vertex G is added to the cloud and we update labels of neighbors of G – here F is updated to 11 (C-E-G-F that is 8+1+2=11). Since distance to B is one of the shortest from C that will be the next node to be considered.

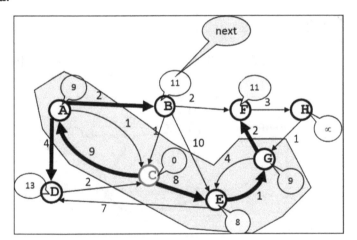

Now vertex B is added to the cloud but no updating takes place. Since distance to F is the shortest from C that will be the next node to be considered.

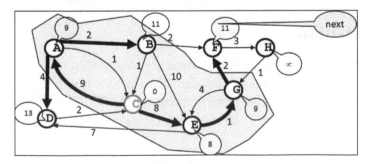

Now vertex F is added to the cloud and we update labels of neighbors of F – here H is updated to 14 (C-E-G-F-H that is 8+1+2+3=14). Since distance to D is the shortest from C that will be the next node to be considered.

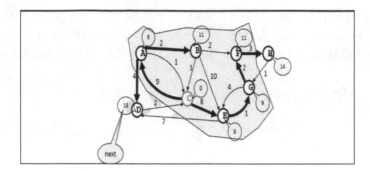

Now vertex D is added to the cloud but no updating takes place. Since distance to H is the shortest from C that will be the next node to be considered.

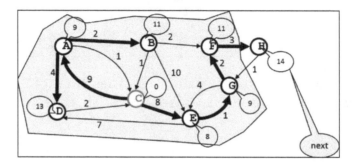

Now vertex H is added to the cloud and since all the vertices of the graph have been visited the algorithm completes.

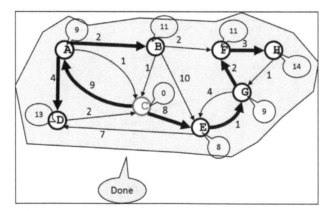

Bellman-Ford Algorithm

Bellman-Ford algorithm is a dynamic programming algorithm that solves the single source shortest path problem. The main advantage of the algorithm is that it works even when some weights are negative. Single-source shortest path problem computes $\delta(s, v)$ and $\pi[v]$ for all $v \in V$. The algorithm allows negative edge weights - can detect negative cycles. The basic idea of this algorithm is as follows.

- Each edge is relaxed $|V-1|$ times by making $|V-1|$ passes over the whole edge set.

- To make sure that each edge is relaxed exactly $|V - 1|$ times, it puts the edges in an unordered list and goes over the list $|V - 1|$ times.

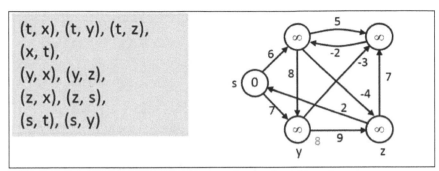

Example of a negative weight graph and its edges.

The algorithm works even with negative-weight edges. We will assume that the edges are directed edges otherwise we would have negative-weight cycles. Iteration i finds all shortest paths that use i edges. The algorithm can be extended to detect a negative-weight cycle if it exists.

The input to the algorithm is the graph G with set of vertex V and set of Edges E and the starting vertex s. Then, it computes computes $\delta(s, v)$ and $\pi[v]$ for all $v \in V$. The output is TRUE if no negative-weight cycles are reachable from the source s. Else the output is FALSE indicating that the solution doesn't exist. The variable $d_{s,v}$ is used to store the shortest path weight from vertex s to v and $\pi_{s,v}$ is used to store the predecessor of v on a shortest path from s.

In the first step, $d_{s,v}$ is set to 0 if vertex v is a source node and to infinity otherwise. $\pi_{s,v}$ is initialized to Nil initially. In the second step, relax function is carried out which is repeated for V-1 iterations. In each iteration, an edge (u,v) is considered and checked whether the shortest path weight of v to s (i.e. $d_{s,v}$) can be made lesser by adding u as the intermediate vertex in the shortest path of v to s. If the $d_{s,v}$ can be reduced, then the corresponding $\pi_{s,v}$ is updated as u. The same is repeated for all the edges in the graph. By the end of this step, each $d_{s,v}$ will have the shortest path weight between s to $v \in V[G]$. The final step is used to identify for the presence of negative weight cycle in the graph. If there still exists a shortest path with $d_{s,v}$ weight which can be further reduced by adding an intermediate edge u, then it indicates that there exist a negative cycle in the graph and hence no solution exists. The time complexity of this algorithm is $T(n) = O(VE) = O(V^3)$.

Algorithm: Bellman-Ford(G, s)

```
1. for each v in G.V {//Initialize 0-edge shortest paths

   if (v==s) d_{s,v} =0; else = d_{s,v}=∞//set the 0-edge shortest distance from s to v

        π_{s,v} = NIL; //set the predecessor of v on the shortest path}

2. Repeat |G.V|-1 times {//bottom-up construct 0-to-(|V|-1)-edges shortest paths

        for each edge (u, v) in G.E{

            if(d_{s,v} > d_{s,u} + w_{(u,v)}){

                d_{s,v} = d_{s,u} + w_{(u,v)};

                π_{s,v} = u; } }
```

```
3. for each edge (u, v) in G.E {//test negative cycle

      If (d_{s,v} > d_{s,u} + w_{(u,v)}) return false; // there is no solution

   }

return true;
```

Example of Bellman-Ford Algorithm

Let us consider the same example graph shown now in figure below. It consists of vertex set V= {z, u, x, v, y}. In accordance with the first step all $d_{s,v}$ and $\pi_{s,v}$ are initialized to be infinity and NIL respectively. The next step is to identify the shortest path weight. First, it starts with vertex z (the source vertex). Using the step 2 of the algorithm, the shortest path from z to u is identified as the single edge (z,u). Hence $d_{z,u}$ is set to 6 and $\pi_{z,u}$ to NIL. Similarly $d_{z,x}$ is set to 7 and $\pi_{z,x}$ to NIL since these are the only paths from z to u and x respectively. Next to identify the shortest path between the vertex z and v, the two possible paths (z,u,v) and (z,x,v) are tested. The corresponding values and predecessors of these paths are used to find distances $(d_{z,v} = 11(6+5), \pi_{z,v} = u)$ and $(d_{z,v} = 4(7-3), \pi_{z,v} = x)$ for the two paths respectively. Since the second path (z,x,v) has less weight it is chosen as the shortest path between z and v. Similarly the shortest path between z and y is identified to be (z,u,y) with $d_{z,y} = 2, \pi_{z,y} = u$. As the iteration goes on, a new shortest path from z to u is identified through z and v. Now $d_{z,u}$ is reset to 2, $\pi_{z,u} = v$. At this stage of the algorithm all the shortest paths are identified. Now the check for negative cycle is performed. There exist a shortest path (z,x,v,u,y) whose $d_{z,y}$ = -2 is less than the already computed $d_{z,y}$ = 2. This indicates that, there exist a negative cycle (u,v,y) in the graph.

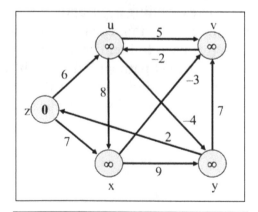

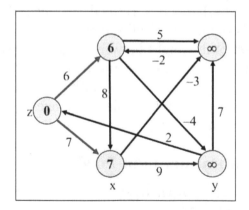

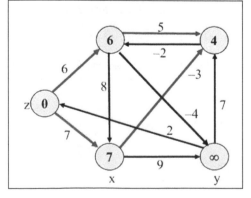

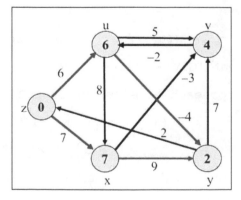

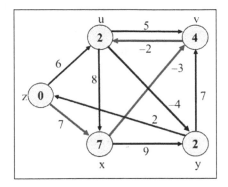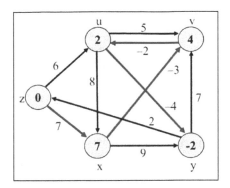

Illustration of Bellman-Ford algorithm.

Bellman-ford Algorithm: Dynamic Programming

For each node v, find the length of the shortest path to any node t that uses at most 1 edge, or write down ∞ if there is no such path. If v = t we get 0; if (v, t) ∈ E then we get len(v, t); else just put down ∞. Now, suppose for all v we have solved for length of the shortest path to t that uses i – 1 or fewer edges.

We can use the above to solve for the shortest path that uses i or fewer edges. The shortest path from v to t that uses i or fewer edges will first go to some neighbor x of v, and then take the shortest path from x to t that uses i−1 or fewer edges, which we've already solved for. So, we just need to take the minimum over all neighbors x of v. At most i = n – 1 edges need to be processed to obtain the answer. The main observation made here are as follows: (i) If there is a negative cycle, then there is no solution. Because adding this cycle again can always produces a less weighted path. (ii) If there is no negative cycle, a shortest path has at most |V|-1 edges. The basic idea behind solving this algorithm using dynamic programming is that for all the paths have at most 0 edge, find all the shortest paths, for all the paths have at most 1 edge, find all the shortest paths and so on and finally for all the paths have at most |V|-1 edge, find all the shortest paths. The algorithm for the above is given below:

Bellman-Ford pseudocode:

```
initialize d[v][0] = infinity for v != t. d[t][i]=0 for all i.

for i=1 to n-1:

for each v != t:

d[v][i] = min

(v,x) 2E

(len(v,x) + d[x][i-1])

For each v, output d[v][n-1].
```

Example: Based on the above idea, the shortest path from node 1 to other nodes of figure below is discovered. The total number of nodes is 3 and hence the process repeats 3 times. First the shortest paths with 0-edge are discovered from vertex 1 to 1, 1 to 2 and 1 to 3. The path weights for 1 to 1, 1 to 2 and 1 to 3 are 0, ∞ and ∞ respectively.

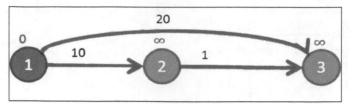

Shortest paths with 0-edge.

Next, the shortest paths with 1-edge are discovered from vertex 1 to 1, 1 to 2 and 1 to 3. The path weights for 1 to 1, 1 to 2 and 1 to 3 are 0, 10 and 20 respectively.

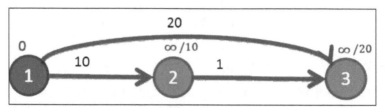

Shortest paths with 1-edge.

Finally, the shortest paths with 2-edges are discovered from vertex 1 to 1, 1 to 2 and 1 to 3. The path weights for 1 to 1, 1 to 2 and 1 to 3 are 0, 10 and 11 respectively. The path from 1 to 3 changes from 20 to 10 since the 2-edge path is shorter than the 1-edge path.

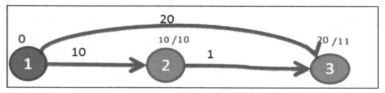

Shortest paths with 2-edges.

Bellman-Ford Algorithm — Walkthrough

Let us consider one more example for the graph given in figure below. The same procedure mentioned above is repeated to find the shortest path from vertex 1.

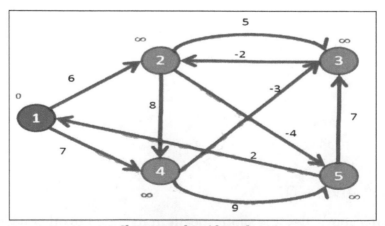

Shortest paths with 0-edge.

Now we find the shortest path from 1 with 1 edge which is 1-2 and 1-4. Hence the d value of 2 changes from ∞ to 6 and that of 4 changes from ∞ to 7.

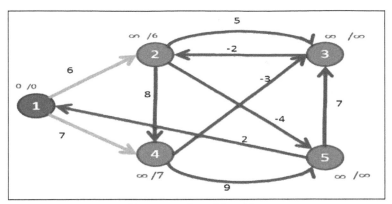

Shortest paths with 1-edge.

Now we find the shortest path from 1 with 2 edges which is 1-2-3 (d =11) and 1-4-3 (d=4). Hence the d value of 3 is 11/4. The 2 edge path to 5 is 1-2-5 and so d value of 5 is ∞/2.

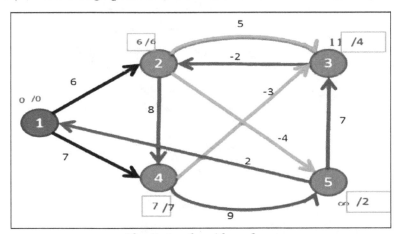

Shortest paths with 2-edges.

Now we find the shortest path from 1 with 3 edges such as 1-4-3-2(d =2) Hence the d value of 2 is 6/2.

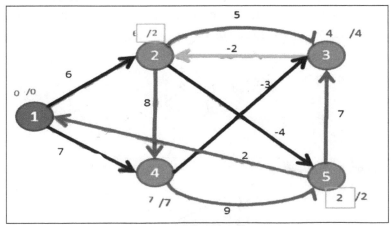

Shortest paths with 3-edges.

Now we find the shortest path from 1 with 4 edges such as 1-4-3-2-5 (d =-2) Hence the d value of 5 is 2/-2.

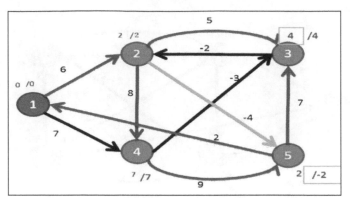

Shortest paths with 4-edges.

The shortest paths with negative cycle is shown in figure below. The shortest path from 1 to 5 is 1-4-3-2-5 and its weight is -2.

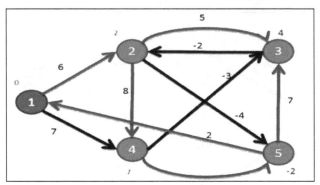

Shortest paths with negative cycle.

All-pair Shortest Path Algorithm

It aims at computing the shortest paths between all pairs of vertices in a directed graph G = (V, E). Each edge e (u, v) has a weight w which is a real number (i.e. Weight function w : E → R). The output is an n× n matrix of shortest-path distances $\delta(u, v)$. For example, let us consider graph in figure. The all-pair shortest path algorithm finds the shortest path from vertex 1 to all the other vertices, vertex 2 to all other vertices and so on.

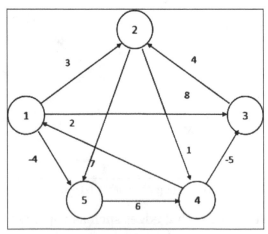

Directed Graph.

The possible solutions for All-Pairs Shortest Paths is to run BELLMAN-FORD once from each vertex. The time complexity is $O(V^2E)$, which is $O(V^4)$ if the graph is dense ($E = \Theta(V^2)$). If there are no negative-weight edges, we could run Dijkstra's algorithm once from each vertex. The time complexity is then $O(VElogV)$ with binary heap and $O(V^3logV)$ if the graph is dense. Assume $G=(V,E)$ is a graph such that $c[v,w] \geq 0$, where C is the matrix of edge costs. Find for each pair (v,w), the shortest path from v to w. In other words we need to find the matrix of shortest paths. Certainly this is a generalization of Dijkstra's. A dedicated All-Pairs Shortest Paths algorithm is called Floyd-Warshall Algorithm.

Floyd-Warshall Algorithm

Floyd-Warshall Algorithm uses nxn matrix A to compute the lengths of the shortest paths using a dynamic programming technique. Initially, let Let $A[i,j] = c[i,j]$ for all i,j & $i \neq j$ where $c[i, j]$ is the cost matrix of the edges, i and j are vertices.

If (i,j) is not an edge, set $A[i,j]=$infinity and $A[i,i]=0$. The main idea is to find $A_k[i,j] = \min (A_{k-1}[i,j], A_{k-1}[i,k] + A_{k-1}[k,j])$ where A_k is the matrix after k-th iteration and path from i to j does not pass through a vertex higher than k.

To find the shortest paths that uses 2 or fewer edges find A^2, where multiplication is defined as minimum of sums instead sum of products. That is $(A^2)_{ij} = \min\{A_{ik} + A_{kj} | k =1..n\}$. This operation is $O(n^3)$. Using A^2 you can find A^4 and then A^8 and so on. Therefore to find A^n we need log n operations. Hence the time complexity of this algorithm is $O(\log n * n^3)$. The following is the pseudo code of Floyd-Warshall Implementation:

```
Initialize A[i,j] = C[i,j]

Initialize all A[i,i] = 0

    for k from 1 to n

        for i from 1 to n

        for j from 1 to n

            if (A[i,j] > A[i,k]+A[k,j])

                A[i,j] = A[i,k]+A[k,j];
```

Knapsack Problem and Flow Scheduling

Given a set of items, each with a weight and a value, determine a subset of items to include in a collection so that the total weight is less than or equal to a given limit and the total value is as large as possible. The knapsack problem is in combinatorial optimization problem. It appears as a subproblem in many, more complex mathematical models of real-world problems. One general approach to difficult problems is to identify the most restrictive constraint, ignore the others, solve a knapsack problem, and somehow adjust the solution to satisfy the ignored constraints.

Applications

In many cases of resource allocation along with some constraint, the problem can be derived in a similar way of Knapsack problem. Following is a set of example:

- Finding the least wasteful way to cut raw materials.

- Portfolio optimization.

- Cutting stock problems.

Problem Scenario

A thief is robbing a store and can carry a maximal weight of W into his knapsack. There are n items available in the store and weight of ith item is w_i and its profit is p_i. What items should the thief take? In this context, the items should be selected in such a way that the thief will carry those items for which he will gain maximum profit. Hence, the objective of the thief is to maximize the profit. Based on the nature of the items, Knapsack problems are categorized as: Fractional Knapsack and Knapsack.

Fractional Knapsack

In this case, items can be broken into smaller pieces; hence the thief can select fractions of items. According to the problem statement:

- There are n items in the store.

- Weight of ith item $w_i > 0$.

- Profit for i^{th} item $p_i > 0$.

- Capacity of the Knapsack is W.

In this version of Knapsack problem, items can be broken into smaller pieces. So, the thief may take only a fraction x_i of ith item.

$$0 \leqslant x_i \leqslant 1$$

The ith item contributes the weight $x_i.w_i$ to the total weight in the knapsack and profit $x_i.p_i$ to the total profit. Hence, the objective of this algorithm is to,

$$\text{maximize} \sum_{n=1}^{n} (x_i.pi)$$

subject to constraint,

$$\sum_{n=1}^{n} (x_i.wi) \leqslant W$$

It is clear that an optimal solution must fill the knapsack exactly, otherwise we could add a fraction of one of the remaining items and increase the overall profit. Thus, an optimal solution can be obtained by,

$$\sum_{n=1}^{n} (x_i . wi) = W$$

In this context, first we need to sort those items according to the value of $\frac{p_i}{w_i}$, so that $\frac{p_i+1}{w_i+1} \leq \frac{p_i}{w_i}$. Here, x is an array to store the fraction of items.

```
Algorithm: Greedy-Fractional-Knapsack (w[1..n], p[1..n], W)

for i = 1 to n

   do x[i] = 0

weight = 0

for i = 1 to n

   if weight + w[i] ≤ W then

      x[i] = 1

      weight = weight + w[i]

   else

      x[i] = (W - weight) / w[i]

      weight = W

      break

return x
```

Analysis

If the provided items are already sorted into a decreasing order of $\frac{p_i}{w_i}$, then the whileloop takes a time in O(n); Therefore, the total time including the sort is in O(n logn).

Example: Let us consider that the capacity of the knapsack W = 60 and the list of provided items are shown in the following table:

Item	A	B	C	D
Profit	280	100	120	120
Weight	40	10	20	24
Ratio $\left(\dfrac{p_i}{w_i}\right)$	7	10	6	5

As the provided items are not sorted based on $\frac{p_i}{w_i}$. After sorting, the items are as shown in the following table:

Item	B	A	C	D
Profit	100	280	120	120
Weight	10	40	20	24
Ratio $\left(\dfrac{p_i}{w_i}\right)$	10	7	6	5

Solution: After sorting all the items according to $\frac{p_i}{w_i}$. First all of B is chosen as weight of B is less than the capacity of the knapsack. Next, item A is chosen, as the available capacity of the knapsack is greater than the weight of A. Now, C is chosen as the next item. However, the whole item cannot be chosen as the remaining capacity of the knapsack is less than the weight of C.

Hence, fraction of C (i.e. (60 – 50)/20) is chosen. Now, the capacity of the Knapsack is equal to the selected items. Hence, no more items can be selected.

- The total weight of the selected items is 10 + 40 + 20 * (10/20) = 60.

- And the total profit is 100 + 280 + 120 * (10/20) = 380 + 60 = 440.

This is the optimal solution. We cannot gain more profit selecting any different combination of items.

0-1 Knapsack

In 0-1 Knapsack, items cannot be broken which means the thief should take the item as a whole or should leave it. This is reason behind calling it as 0-1 Knapsack. Hence, in case of 0-1 Knapsack, the value of x_i can be either 0 or 1, where other constraints remain the same.

0-1 Knapsack cannot be solved by Greedy approach. Greedy approach does not ensure an optimal solution. In many instances, Greedy approach may give an optimal solution. The following examples will establish our statement:

Example: Let us consider that the capacity of the knapsack is W = 25 and the items are as shown in the following table:

Item	A	B	C	D
Profit	24	18	18	10
Weight	24	10	10	7

Without considering the profit per unit weight (p_i/w_i), if we apply Greedy approach to solve this problem, first item A will be selected as it will contribute maximum profit among all the elements.

After selecting item A, no more items will be selected. Hence, for this given set of items total profit is 24. Whereas, the optimal solution can be achieved by selecting items, B and C, where the total profit is 18 + 18 = 36.

Example: Instead of selecting the items based on the overall benefit, in this example the items are selected based on ratio p_i/w_i. Let us consider that the capacity of the knapsack is W = 60 and the items are as shown in the following table:

Item	A	B	C
Price	100	280	120
Weight	10	40	20
Ratio	10	7	6

Using the Greedy approach, first item A is selected. Then, the next item B is chosen. Hence, the total profit is 100 + 280 = 380. However, the optimal solution of this instance can be achieved by selecting items, B and C, where the total profit is 280 + 120 = 400. Hence, it can be concluded that Greedy approach may not give an optimal solution. To solve 0-1 Knapsack, Dynamic Programming approach is required.

Problem Statement

A thief is robbing a store and can carry a maximal weight of W into his knapsack. There are n items and weight of ith item is w_i and the profit of selecting this item is p_i. What items should the thief take?

Dynamic-programming Approach

Let i be the highest-numbered item in an optimal solution S for W dollars. Then S' = S - {i} is an optimal solution for W - w_i dollars and the value to the solution S is V_i plus the value of the sub-problem. We can express this fact in the following formula: define c[i, w] to be the solution for items 1,2, ... , i and the maximum weight w. The algorithm takes the following inputs:

- The maximum weight W.

- The number of items n.

- The two sequences v = <v_1, v_2, ..., v_n> and w = <w_1, w_2, ..., w_n>.

```
Dynamic-0-1-knapsack (v, w, n, W)

for w = 0 to W do

    c[0, w] = 0

for i = 1 to n do

    c[i, 0] = 0

    for w = 1 to W do

        if w_i ≤ w then
```

```
if v  + c[i-1, w-w ] then
     i             i

    c[i, w] = v  + c[i-1, w-w ]
               i              i

    else c[i, w] = c[i-1, w]

else

    c[i, w] = c[i-1, w]
```

The set of items to take can be deduced from the table, starting at c[n, w] and tracing backwards where the optimal values came from. If c[i, w] = c[i-1, w], then item i is not part of the solution, and we continue tracing with c[i-1, w]. Otherwise, item i is part of the solution, and we continue tracing with c[i-1, w-W].

Analysis

This algorithm takes $\theta(n, w)$ times as table c has $(n + 1).(w + 1)$ entries, where each entry requires $\theta(1)$ time to compute.

Transitive Closure and Shortest Path Algorithms

A binary relation R is said exists between two vertices, say u and v, can be mathematically represented as u R v. A binary relation that is considered here is a path relation and hence a relation u R v indicates that, there is a path from u to v.

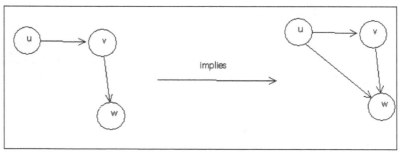

Transitive Closure.

A transitive relation states that if there is a binary relation between u to v and v to w, then there exists a relation from u to w. If R is a set of transitive relations, then the adjacency matrix of R is called reachability matrix, connectivity matrix pr path matrix.

In other words, the matrix B can be said as,

$$B = A + A^2 + A^3 + \cdots + A^n$$

And path matrix P is denoted as,

$$P_{ij} = \begin{cases} 1 & \text{if } ij^{th} \text{ entry of matrix B is not zero} \\ 0 & \text{otherwise} \end{cases}$$

If the entry value of Path matrix is 1, then it indicates that there exists a path and if the value is zero, it indicates that the path is absent. This is given mathematically as follows:

$$P_{ij} = \begin{cases} 1 & \text{if there is an edges between } V_i \text{ and } V_j \\ 0 & \text{if there is no edge vertices } V_i \text{ and } V_j \end{cases}$$

Warshall Algorithm

Warshall algorithm is used to construct transitive closure of a matrix. This is done as transitive closure T as the last matrix in the sequence of n-by-n matrices,

$P^{(0)}, \dots, P^{(k)}, \dots, P^{(n)}$, where $P^{(0)} = A$. Here A is adjacency matrix.

The key idea of this algorithm is $P^{(0)}, \dots, P^{(k)}, \dots, P^{(n)}$, on the k-th iteration, the algorithm determines for every pair of vertices i, j if a path exists from i and j with just vertices 1,...,k allowed as intermediate vertices. The recurrence equation of this algorithm is given as below:

$$P^{(k)}[i,j] = P^{(k-1)}[i,j] \text{ or } \left(P^{(k-1)}[i,k] \text{ and } P^{(k-1)}[k,j] \right)$$

The rules of constructing $P^{(k)}$ from $P^{(k-1)}$ is given below:

- Rule 1: If an element in row i and column j is 1 in $P^{(k-1)}$, it remains 1 in $P^{(k)}$.

- Rule 2: If an element in row i and column j is 0 in $P^{(k-1)}$, it has to be changed to 1 in $P^{(k)}$ if and only if the element in its row i and column k and the element in its column j and row k are both 1's in $P^{(k-1)}$.

This algorithm is illustrated in the following Example:

Example - Find the transitive closure of the following graph shown in figure:

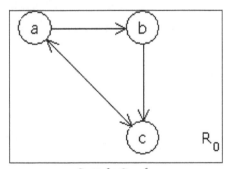

Sample Graph.

Solution - The initial adjacency matrix is given as follows:

	a	b	c
a	0	1	0
b	0	0	1
c	1	0	0

It can be observed that, the entry 1 indicates the presence of edge and 0 indicates the absence of edge. With R1 node as intermediate node, the adjacency matrix is changed as follows:

	a	b	c
a	0	1	0
b	0	0	1
c	1	1	0

It can be observed that now path between c to b is possible with the availability of node 'a'. Now node R2 is made available, that is nodes 1 and 2, the adjacency matrix is changed as follows:

	a	b	c
a	0	1	1
b	0	0	1
c	1	0	0

It can be seen, the path between nodes a and c is possible. Now node R3 is made available. This means, all the nodes are available. The adjacency matrix is changed as follows:

	a	b	c
a	1	1	1
b	1	1	1
c	1	1	1

Thus one can observe that there is connectivity between all the nodes.

The formal Warshall algorithm based on [1,2] is given as follows:

```
Algorithm warshall(G,A)

Begin

    for i = 1 to n

            for j = 1 to n      %% Initialize

            P[i,j] = A[i,j]

            End for

    End for

     for k = 1 to n

     for i = 1 to n
```

```
   for j = 1 to n     %% Initialize

     P[i,j,k] = P[i,j,k-1]  v (P[i,k,k-1]  ^ P[k,j,k-1]) %%

   End for

       End for

   End for

  return P

 End
```

Complexity Analysis: It can be seen, the algorithm is reduced to filling the table. If both number of rows and columns are same, the algorithm complexity is reduced to $\Theta(n^3)$ as there are three loops involved. The space complexity is given as $\Theta(n^2)$.

Floyd Algorithm

Floyd algorithm finds shortest paths in a graph. It is known as all pair shortest path algorithm as the algorithm finds shortest path from any vertex to any other vertex. The problem can be formulated as follows: Given a graph and edges with weights, compute the weight of the shortest path between pairs of vertices. Can the transitive closure algorithm be applied here? Yes. Floyd algorithm is a variant of this algorithm. In a weighted digraph, Floyd algorithm finds shortest paths between every pair of vertices. There is only one restriction as no negative edge allowed in Floyd algorithm. This is illustrated in the following figure:

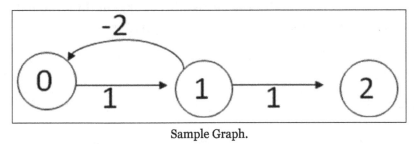

Sample Graph.

It can be observed that the shortest path from vertex 0 vertex 2 tends to be $-\infty$. In reality, the distance cannot be negative and there exists a positive path of 2 from vertex 0 to vertex 2. This is the reason why Floyd algorithm fails when edge weight is negative.

One way to solve this problem is to apply shortest path algorithms like Djikstra's algorithm 'n' times between all possible combinations of vertices with every path takes $\Theta(n^3)$.

Instead, Floyd algorithm can be tried. Floyd algorithm have the following initial conditions: It represent the graph G by its cost adjacency matrix with cost[i][j]. If the edge <i,j> is not in G, the cost[i][j] is set to some sufficiently large number. D[i][j] is the cost of the shortest path form i to j, using only those intermediate vertices with an index <= k.

The recursive relation of the algorithm is given as follows:

$$D^k(i,j) = \min\left\{D^{k-1}(i,j), D^{k-1}(i,k) + D^{k-1}(k,j)\right\}, k \geq 1$$

Example: Find the shortest path for the following graph as shown in figure:

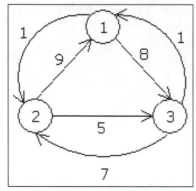

Sample graph.

The edge weights are given in the following adjacency matrix:

	1	2	3
1	0	1	8
2	9	0	5
3	1	7	0

Solution: D[0] is same as the adjacency matrix. Therefore, The given adjacency matrix is D[0]. Vertex 1 is made intermediate node. With the availability of this node 1, the path between vertex 3 and vertex 2 is possible. This results in the modified path matrix.

$$D[1] = \begin{bmatrix} 0 & 1 & 8 \\ 9 & 0 & 5 \\ 1 & 2 & 0 \end{bmatrix}$$

In the next iteration, nodes 1 and 2 are made temporary. Therefore, the modified path matrix is given as follows:

$$D[2] = \begin{bmatrix} 0 & 1 & 6 \\ 9 & 0 & 5 \\ 1 & 2 & 0 \end{bmatrix}$$

In the next iteration, all the three nodes are available. This results in the modified path matrix as given below:

$$D[3] = \begin{bmatrix} 0 & 1 & 6 \\ 6 & 0 & 5 \\ 1 & 2 & 0 \end{bmatrix}$$

This is the final path matrix.

The formal Floyd algorithm is given as follows:

```
Algorithm Floyd-Marshall (G,s,t)
          begin
           for i = 1 to n
                for j = 1 to n
                     D[i,j] = A[i,j] %% Initialize
                  endfor
              endfor
D[0] = aij
          for k = 1 to n
              for i = 1 to n
              for j = 1 to n
                     D[i,j] = min{D[i,j] , D[i,k] + D[k,j]}
                  endfor
              endfor
        endfor
      end
```

Complexity Analysis: The complexity analysis of Floyd algorithm is same as Warshall algorithm. Time complexity of this algorithm is $\Theta(n^3)$ as there are three loops involved. The space complexity is given as $\Theta(n^2)$ similar to Warshall algorithm.

Multistage Graphs and TSP Problem

Travelling salesman problem (TSP) is an interesting problem. It can be stated as follows: Given a set of n cities and distances between the cities in the form a graph. TSP finds a tour that starts and terminates in the source city. The restriction is that, every other city should be visited exactly once and the focus is to find the tour of shortest length.

It can be said as a function, f(i,s), shortest sub-tour given that we are at city i and still have to visit the cities in s (and return to home city). In other words, we move from city I to city j and focus is that all cities needs to be visited except city j and should be back to city i.

Let g(i, S) be the length of a shortest path starting at vertex i, going through all vertices in S and terminating at vertex 1. This can be stated formulated as follows:

$$g(1, V - \{1\}) = \min_{2 \le k \le n} \{c_{1k} + g(k, V - \{1, k\})\}$$

This represents the optimal tour. In general, the recursive function is given as follows:

$$g(i,S) = \min_{j \in S} \left\{ c_{ij} + g\left(j, S - \{J\}\right) \right\}$$

This concept is illustrated through this numerical example:

Example: Apply dynamic programming for the following graph as shown in figure and find the optimal TSP tour.

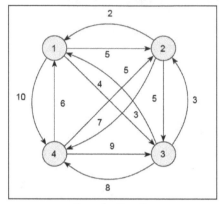

Sample Graph.

Solution: Assuming that the starting city 1, let us find the optimal tour.

Let us initialize s = null and find the cost as follows:

$$g\left(2, \varnothing\right) = C_{21} = 2$$
$$g\left(3, \varnothing\right) = C_{31} = 4$$
$$g\left(4, \varnothing\right) = C_{41} = 6$$

Let us consider size =1, then the possible values are {1}, {2}, {3}.

$$g\left(2, \{3\}\right) = C_{23} + g\left(3, \varnothing\right)$$
$$= 5 + 4 = 9$$
$$g\left(2, \{4\}\right) = C_{24} + g\left(4, \varnothing\right)$$
$$= 7 + 6 = 13$$
$$g\left(3, \{2\}\right) = C_{32} + g\left(2, \varnothing\right)$$
$$= 3 + 2 = 5$$
$$g\left(3, \{4\}\right) = C_{34} + g\left(4, \varnothing\right)$$
$$= 8 + 6 = 14$$
$$g\left(4, \{2\}\right) = C_{42} + g\left(2, \varnothing\right)$$
$$= 5 + 2 = 7$$
$$g\left(4, \{3\}\right) = C_{43} + g\left(3, \varnothing\right)$$
$$= 9 + 4 = 13$$

Let the size s increased by 1, that is, $|s| = 2$.

Now, $g(1,s)$ is computed with $|s| = 2$, $i \neq 1$, $1 \notin s$, $i \notin n$, i.e, involves two intermediate nodes.

$$g(2,\{3,4\}) = \min\{C_{23} + g(3,\{4\}), C_{24} + g(4,\{3\})\}$$
$$= \min\{5+14, \; 7+13\}$$
$$= \min\{19, 20\} = 19.$$

$$g(3,\{2,4\}) = \min\{C_{32} + g(2,\{4\}), C_{34} + g(4,\{2\})\}$$
$$= \min\{3+13, \; 8+7\}$$
$$= \min\{16,15\} = 15.$$

$$g(4,\{2,3\}) = \min\{C_{42} + g(2,\{3\}), C_{43} + g(3,\{2\})\}$$
$$= \min\{5+9, \; 9+5\}$$
$$= \min\{14,14\} = 14.$$

Let the size is increased by 1, that is, $|s| = 3$.

Finally, the total cost is calculated involving three intermediate nodes. That is $|s| = 3$. As $|s| = n-1$, where n is the number of nodes, the process terminates.

$$g(1,\{2,3,4\}) = \min\{C_{12} + g(2,\{3,4\}), C_{13} + g(3,\{2,4\}), C_{14} + g(4,\{2,3\})\}$$
$$= \min\{5+19, \; 3+15, \; 10+14\}$$
$$= \min\{24, 18, 24\}$$
$$= 18.$$

Hence, the minimum cost tour is 18. The path can be constructed by noting down the 'k' that yielded the minimum value. It can be seen that the minimum was possible via route 3.

$\therefore$ $P(1,\{2,3,4\}) = 3$. Thus tour goes from $1 \rightarrow 3$. It can be seen that $C(3,\{2,4\}) \wedge$ minimum.

$\therefore$ $P(3,\{2,4\}) = 2$

Hence the path goes like $1 \rightarrow 3 \rightarrow 2$ and the final TSP tour is given as $1 \rightarrow 3 \rightarrow 2 \rightarrow 1$.

Complexity Analysis:

$$n + \sum_{k=2}^{n}(n-1)\binom{n-2}{n-k}(n-k)$$
$$= O(n^2 2^n)$$

Multistage Graphs

The idea for Stagecoach problem is that a salesman is travelling from one town to another town, in the old west. His means of travel is a stagecoach. Each leg of his trip cost a certain amount and he wants to find the minimum cost of his trip, given multiple paths. A sample multistage graph is shown in Figure.

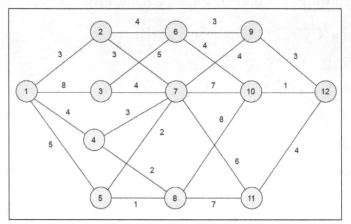

Sample Multistage Graph.

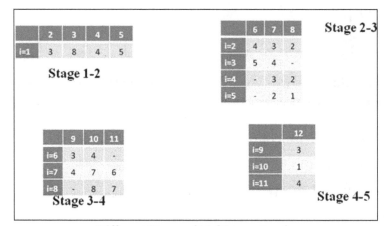

Different Stages of Multistage Graph.

Solution:

Stage 4-5: There are three possibilities for going to destination given that one is at points 9, 10 or 11.

$$\text{cost}(4,9)=3$$
$$\text{cost}(4,10)=1$$
$$\text{cost}(4,11)=4$$

$$\cos t(3,6)=\min\begin{cases}3+\cos t(4,9)=3+3=6\\4+\cos t(4,10)=4+1=5^*\end{cases}$$

$$\cos t(3,7)=\min\begin{cases}4+\cos t(4,9)=4+3=7^*\\7+\cos t(4,10)=7+1=8\\6+\cos t(4,11)=6+4=10\end{cases}$$

$$cost(3,8) = \min \begin{cases} 8 + cost(4,10) = 8 + 1 = 9^* \\ 7 + cost(4,11) = 7 + 4 = 11 \end{cases}$$

Stage 2-3: The optimal choices at stages 2 can be given as follows:

$$cost(2,2) = \min \begin{cases} 4 + cost(3,6) = 4 + 5 = 9^* \\ 3 + cost(3,7) = 3 + 7 = 10 \end{cases}$$

$$cost(2,3) = \min \begin{cases} 5 + cost(3,6) = 5 + 5 = 10^* \\ 4 + cost(3,7) - 4 + 7 - 11 \end{cases}$$

$$cost(2,4) = \min \begin{cases} 3 + cost(3,7) = 3 + 7 = 10^* \\ 4 + cost(3,8) = 4 + 9 = 13 \end{cases}$$

$$cost(2,5) = \min \begin{cases} 2 + cost(3,7) = 2 + 7 = 9^* \\ 2 + cost(3,8) = 2 + 9 = 11 \end{cases}$$

$$cost(1,5) = \min \begin{cases} 3 + cost(2,2) = 3 + 9 = 12^* \\ 8 + cost(2,3) = 8 + 10 = 18 \\ 4 + cost(2,4) = 4 + 10 = 14 \\ 5 = cost(2,5) = 5 + 9 = 14 \end{cases}$$

The formal algorithm is given as follows:

```
Algorithm Fgraph(G)
     Begin
     cost = 0
     n = |V|
     stage = n-1
     while (j <= stage) do
     Choose a vertex k such that C[j,k] + cost k is minimum.
     cost[j] = c[j,k]+cost(k)
      j = j-1
     Add the cost of C(j,r) to record k.
     d[j] = k
     End while
```

```
        return cost[j]

    end
```

The path recovery is done as follows:

```
Algorithm path(G,d,n,k)

        Begin

        n = |V|

        stage = n-1

                for j = 2 to stage

                path[j] = d[path[j-1]]

                End for

        End
```

Complexity Analysis:

- Time efficiency: $\Theta(n^3)$

- Space efficiency: $\Theta(n^2)$

Backward Reasoning

A sample graph is shown in figure below. Let us solve this problem using backward reasoning.

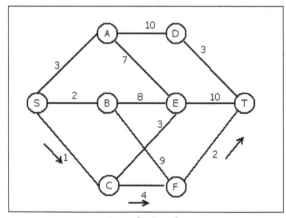

Sample Graph.

Backward approach starts like this:

$$C(S, A) = 3$$
$$C(S, B) = 2$$
$$C(S, C) = 1$$
$$C(S, D) = \min\{10 + C(S, A)\}$$
$$= \min\{10 + 3\} = 13.$$

$$C(S, E) = \min\{7 + C(S, A), 8 + C(S, B), 3 + C(S,C)\}$$
$$= \min\{7+3, 8+2, 3+1\}$$
$$= \min\{10, 10, 4\} = 4$$

$$C(S, F) = \min\{9 + \text{Cost}(S, B), 4 + \text{Cost}(S, C)\}$$
$$= \min\{9+3, 4+1\} = 5$$

$$D(S, T) = \min\{3 + C(S, D), 10 + C(S, E), 2 + C(S,F)\}$$
$$= \min\{3+13, 10+4, 2+5\} = 7$$

The path can be recovered as follows: $T \to F \to C \to S$.

Chained Matrix Multiplication

Chained matrix multiplication is an interesting problem. It can be formally stated as follows: Given a sequence or chain $A_1, A_2, ..., A_n$ of n matrices to be multiplied, then How to compute the product $A_1 A_2 ... A_n$. It must be observed that Matrix Multiplication is not commutative. That is $AB \neq BA$. On the other hand, matrix multiplication follows associative law, i.e., $(AB)C = A(BC)$. Hence, given 'n' matrices, there are many orders in which matrix multiplication can be carried out. In other words, there are many possible ways of placing parenthesis. Chained matrix multiplication is a problem of multiplying matrix multiplications such that it is low cost.

Example: Consider the chain A_1, A_2, A_3, A_4 of 4 matrices. Show some of the ways in which the matrix multiplication can be carried out?

Solution: Some of the ways the matrices can be multiplied are as follows:

$$1. \left(A_1\left(A_2\left(A_3 A_4\right)\right)\right) \quad 2. \left(A_1\left(\left(A_2 A_3\right)A_4\right)\right) \quad 3. \left(\left(A_1 A_2\right)\left(A_3 A_4\right)\right),$$

$$4. \left(\left(A_1\left(A_2 A_3\right)\right)A_4\right) \quad 5. \left(\left(\left(A_1 A_2\right)A_3\right)A_4\right)$$

The ordering seems to follow Catalan sequence. It follows the following recursive relationship.

$$C_0 = 1 \text{ and } C_{n+1} = \sum_{i=0}^{n} C_i C_{n-1} \text{ for } n \geq 0;$$

The first few Catalan numbers for n = 0, 1, 2, 3, ... are 1, 1, 2, 5, 14, 42, 132, 429, 1430, 4862, ...

Brute Force Algorithm

One way to solve this problem is to use brute force method by listing out all the possible ways and choosing the best possible way. The following algorithm segment shows how the matrix multiplication is carried out in a traditional manner:

Input: Matrices $A_{m \times n}$ and $B_{n \times r}$ (with dimensions m×n and n×r)

Output: Matrix $C_{m \times r}$ resulting from the product A·B

```
for i ← 1 to m

    for j ← 1 to r

        C[i, j] ← 0

        for k ← 1 to n

            C[i, j] ← C[i, j] + A[i, k] · B[k, j]

return C
```

Complexity analysis: The cost of multiplication is mnr where m,n and r are dimensions of matrices A and B. By changing the order of the matrices, the optimization can be carried out. The following example illustrates the advantages of changing the order of the matrices.

Example: Consider three matrices $A_{2\times3}$, $B_{3\times4}$, and $C_{4\times5}$. Show two different orders and find the optimal way of multiplying these matrices.

Solution: There are 2 ways to parenthesize. One way is to multiply these three matrices as - ((AB) C) = $D_{2\times4} \cdot C_{4\times5}$. This is done as follows:

- AB $\Rightarrow 2 \times 3 \times 4 = 24$ scalar multiplications,

- DC $\Rightarrow 2 \times 4 \times 5 = 40$ scalar multiplications,

- Total = 24 + 40 = 64 multiplications.

Another way is to multiply this as follows: (A(BC)) = $A_{2\times4} \cdot E_{3\times5}$

- BC $\Rightarrow 3 \times 4 \times 5 = 60$ scalar multiplications,

- AE $\Rightarrow 2 \times 3 \times 5 = 30$ scalar multiplications,

- Total = 60 + 30 = 90 scalar multiplications.

So, it can be observed that the optimal way of matrix multiplication is ((AB)C).

From this example, it can be noted that cost and order matters. The optimal matrix multiplication reduces the cost. In other words, Given a chain A_1, A_2, ..., A_n of n matrices, where for i=1, 2, ..., n, matrix Ai has dimension $p_{i-1} \times p_i$. It is necessary to parenthesize the product $A_1A_2...An$ such that the total number of scalar multiplications is minimized.

Dynamic Programming Idea

The idea is to apply dynamic programming to find chained matrix multiplication. An optimal parenthesization of the product $A_1A_2...A_n$ splits the product between A_1 and A_k for some integer k where $1 \leq k < n$.

First compute matrices $A_{1..k}$ and $A_{k+1..n}$; then multiply them to get the final matrix $A_{1..n}$. Dynamic programming solution requires formulation of the recursive formula. The recursive formula can be formulated as follows:

- Let C[i, j] be the minimum number of scalar multiplications necessary to compute $A_{i..j}$.

- Minimum cost to compute $A_{1..n}$ is $C[1, n]$.

- Suppose the optimal parenthesization of $A_{i..j}$ splits the product between A_k and A_{k+1} for some integer k where $i \leq k < j$.

The recursive formulation is given as follows:

$$C[i, j] = C[i, k] + C[k+1, j] + p_{i-1}p_k p_j \quad \text{for } i \leq k < j$$
$$\text{With } C[i, i] = 0 \text{ for } i = 1, 2, \dots, n \text{ (Initial Condition)}$$

The informal algorithm for chained matrix multiplication is given as follows:

- Read n chain of matrices.

- Compute C[i,j] recursively and fill the table.

- Compute R[i,j] to keep track of k that yields minimum cost.

- Return C[1,n] as minimum cost.

The formal algorithm is given as follows:

```
Algorithm dp_chainmult(p,n)

Begin

     for i = 1 to n do

         C[ i, j ] = 0

     end for

     for diagonal = 1 to n-1

         for i = 1 to n-diagonal

             j = i + diagonal

                 C[ i, j ] = ∞

                 for k = 1 to j-1 do

                 if C[ i, j ] < C[ i, k ]+C[ k+1, j]+ p_{i-1} × p_k × p_j   then

                 C[i,j]= C[ i, k ]+C[ k+1, j]+ p_{i-1} × p_k × p_j

                     R[i,j] = k

                 else

                     C[i,j] = C[i,j]

                 R[i,j] = k

                 End if

             End for
```

```
        End for
    end for
 return C[1,n]
```

Complexity Analysis: The algorithm has three loops ranging from 1 to n. Therefore, the complexity analysis of this algorithm is $O(n^3)$ and the algorithm just needs to fill up the table. If the rows and columns are assumed to be equal, the space complexity of this algorithm is $O(n^2)$.

Example: Apply dynamic programming algorithm and apply for this for the following four matrices with the dimension given as below as in Table.

Table: Initial matrices with dimensions given.

A	B	C	D
4×5	5×3	3×2	2×7
$P_0 P_1$	$P_1 P_2$	$P_2 P_3$	$P_3 P_4$

Solution: Based on the recurrence equation, one can observe that $C[1,1] = 0$; $C[2,2] = 0$; $C[3,3] = 0$; $C[4,4] = 0$.

Table: Initial Table.

0			
	0		
		0	
			0

Using the recursive formula, the table entries can be computed as follows:

$$C[1,2] = C[1,1] + C[2,2] + P_0 \cdot P_1 \cdot P_2$$
$$= 0 + 0 + 4 \times 5 \times 3 = 60$$
$$C[2,3] = C[2,2] + C[3,3] + P_1 \cdot P_2 \cdot P_3$$
$$= 0 + 0 + 5 \times 3 \times 2 = 30$$
$$C[3,4] = C[3,3] + C[4,4] + P_2 \cdot P_3 \cdot P_4$$
$$= 0 + 0 + 3 \times 2 \times 7 = 42$$

Table: After First Diagonal.

0	60		
	0	30	
		0	42
			0

$$C[1,3] = C[1,1] + C[2,3] + P_0 \cdot P_1 \cdot P_3$$
$$= 0 + 30 + 4 \times 5 \times 2$$
$$= 30 + 40 = 70 \quad (k = 1)$$
$$C[1,3] = C[1,2] + C[3,3] + P_0 \cdot P_2 \cdot P_3$$
$$= 60 + 0 + 4 \times 3 \times 2$$
$$= 84 \quad\quad\quad (k = 2)$$

The minimum is 70 when k = 1.

$$C[2,4] = C[2,2] + C[3,4] + P_1 \cdot P_2 \cdot P_4$$
$$= 0 + 42 + 5 \times 3 \times 7$$
$$= 42 + 105 = 147 \quad (k = 2)$$
$$C[2,4] = C[2,3] + C[4,4] + P_1 \cdot P_3 \cdot P_4$$
$$= 30 + 0 + 5 \times 2 \times 7$$
$$= 30 + 70 = 100 \quad\quad (k = 3)$$

The minimum is 100 when k = 3. The matrix is shown in table.

Table: After second diagonal computation.

0	60	70	
	0	30	100
		0	42
			0

Now, C[1,4] is computed.

$$C[1,4] = C[1,1] + C[2,4] + P_0 \cdot P_1 \cdot P_4$$
$$= 0 + 100 + 4 \times 5 \times 7$$
$$= 100 + 140 = 200 \quad (k = 1)$$
$$C[1,4] = C[1,2] + C[3,4] + P_0 \cdot P_2 \cdot P_4$$
$$= 60 + 42 + 4 \times 3 \times 7$$
$$= 60 + 42 + 84 = 186 \quad (k = 2)$$
$$C[1,4] = C[1,3] + C[4,4] + P_0 \cdot P_3 \cdot P_4$$
$$= 70 + 0 + 4 \times 2 \times 7$$
$$= 70 + 56 = 126 \quad\quad (k = 3)$$

The minimum is 126 and this happens when k = 3.

The resulting matrix is shown in table.

Table: Final Table.

0	60	70	126
	0	30	100
		0	42
			0

The order can be obtained by finding minimum k that yielded the least cost. A table can be created and filled up with this minimum k. this is given as shown in table.

Table: Table of minimum k.

0	1	1	3
	0	2	3
		0	3
			0

From the table, one can reconstruct the matrix order as follows: [A (B C) D].

Optimal Binary Search Tree

Given a sorted array keys[0.. n-1] of search keys and an array freq[0.. n-1] of frequency counts, where freq[i] is the number of searches to keys[i]. Construct a binary search tree of all keys such that the total cost of all the searches is as small as possible. Let us first define the cost of a BST. The cost of a BST node is level of that node multiplied by its frequency. Level of root is 1.

Examples:

```
Input:   keys[] = {10, 12}, freq[] = {34, 50}

There can be following two possible BSTs

        10                        12

           \                     /

             12                10

          I                       II
```

Frequency of searches of 10 and 12 are 34 and 50 respectively.

The cost of tree I is 34*1 + 50*2 = 134

```
The cost of tree II is 50*1 + 34*2 = 118

Input:  keys[] = {10, 12, 20}, freq[] = {34, 8, 50}
```

There can be following possible BSTs:

```
    10              12              20        10            20
      \            /  \            /            \          /
      12         10    20         12            20        10
        \                        /              /           \
        20                     10             12            12
     I              II             III           IV            V
```

```
Among all possible BSTs, cost of the fifth BST is minimum.

Cost of the fifth BST is 1*50 + 2*34 + 3*8 = 142
```

Optimal Substructure

The optimal cost for freq[i..j] can be recursively calculated using following formula:

$$optcost(i,j) = \sum_{k=1}^{j} freq[k] + \min_{r=i}^{j} \left[optcost(i,r-1) + optcost(r+1,j) \right]$$

We need to calculate optCost(0, n-1) to find the result.

The idea of above formula is simple, we one by one try all nodes as root (r varies from i to j in second term). When we make rth node as root, we recursively calculate optimal cost from i to r-1 and r+1 to j. We add sum of frequencies from i to j, this is added because every search will go through root and one comparison will be done for every search.

Overlapping Subproblems

Following is recursive implementation that simply follows the recursive structure mentioned above:

```cpp
// A naive recursive implementation of
// optimal binary search tree problem
#include <bits/stdc++.h>
using namespace std;


// A utility function to get sum of
// array elements freq[i] to freq[j]
int sum(int freq[], int i, int j);
```

```c
// A recursive function to calculate
// cost of optimal binary search tree
int optCost(int freq[], int i, int j)
{
    // Base cases
    if (j < i)  // no elements in this subarray
        return 0;
    if (j == i) // one element in this subarray
        return freq[i];


    // Get sum of freq[i], freq[i+1], ... freq[j]
    int fsum = sum(freq, i, j);


    // Initialize minimum value
    int min = INT_MAX;
    // One by one consider all elements
    // as root and recursively find cost
    // of the BST, compare the cost with
    // min and update min if needed
    for (int r = i; r <= j; ++r)
    {
        int cost = optCost(freq, i, r - 1) +
                   optCost(freq, r + 1, j);
        if (cost < min)
            min = cost;
    }


    // Return minimum value
    return min + fsum;
}
// The main function that calculates
```

```cpp
// minimum cost of a Binary Search Tree.
// It mainly uses optCost() to find
// the optimal cost.
int optimalSearchTree(int keys[],
                      int freq[], int n)
{
    // Here array keys[] is assumed to be
    // sorted in increasing order. If keys[]
    // is not sorted, then add code to sort
    // keys, and rearrange freq[] accordingly.
    return optCost(freq, 0, n - 1);
}


// A utility function to get sum of
// array elements freq[i] to freq[j]
int sum(int freq[], int i, int j)
{
    int s = 0;
    for (int k = i; k <= j; k++)
    s += freq[k];
    return s;
}


// Driver Code
int main()
{
    int keys[] = {10, 12, 20};
    int freq[] = {34, 8, 50};
    int n = sizeof(keys) / sizeof(keys[0]);
    cout << "Cost of Optimal BST is "
         << optimalSearchTree(keys, freq, n);
```

```
    return 0;

}

// This is code is contributed

// by rathbhupendra
```

Output: Cost of Optimal BST is 142.

Time complexity of the above naive recursive approach is exponential. It should be noted that the above function computes the same subproblems again and again. We can see many subproblems being repeated in the following recursion tree for freq[1..4].

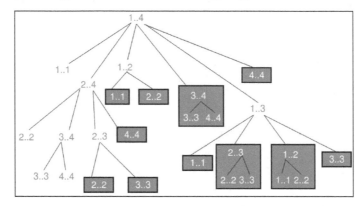

Since same suproblems are called again, this problem has Overlapping Subprolems property. So optimal BST problem has both properties of a dynamic programming problem. Like other typical Dynamic Programming(DP) problems, recomputations of same subproblems can be avoided by constructing a temporary array cost[][] in bottom up manner.

Dynamic Programming Solution

Following is C/C++ implementation for optimal BST problem using Dynamic Programming. We use an auxiliary array cost[n][n] to store the solutions of subproblems. cost[0][n-1] will hold the final result. The challenge in implementation is, all diagonal values must be filled first, then the values which lie on the line just above the diagonal. In other words, we must first fill all cost[i][i] values, then all cost[i][i+1] values, then all cost[i][i+2] values. So how to fill the 2D array in such manner> The idea used in the implementation is same as Matrix Chain Multiplication problem, we use a variable 'L' for chain length and increment 'L', one by one. We calculate column number 'j' using the values of 'i' and 'L'.

```
// Dynamic Programming code for Optimal Binary Search

// Tree Problem

#include <bits/stdc++.h>

using namespace std;


// A utility function to get sum of array elements
```

```
// freq[i] to freq[j]
int sum(int freq[], int i, int j);


/* A Dynamic Programming based function that calculates
minimum cost of a Binary Search Tree. */
int optimalSearchTree(int keys[], int freq[], int n)
{
    /* Create an auxiliary 2D matrix to store results
    of subproblems */
    int cost[n][n];


    /* cost[i][j] = Optimal cost of binary search tree
    that can be formed from keys[i] to keys[j].
    cost[0][n-1] will store the resultant cost */


    // For a single key, cost is equal to frequency of the key
    for (int i = 0; i < n; i++)
        cost[i][i] = freq[i];


    // Now we need to consider chains of length 2, 3, ... .
    // L is chain length.
    for (int L = 2; L <= n; L++)
    {
        // i is row number in cost[][]
        for (int i = 0; i <= n-L+1; i++)
        {
            // Get column number j from row number i and
            // chain length L
            int j = i+L-1;
            cost[i][j] = INT_MAX;
```

```
            // Try making all keys in interval keys[i..j] as root
            for (int r = i; r <= j; r++)
            {
            // c = cost when keys[r] becomes root of this subtree
            int c = ((r > i)? cost[i][r-1]:0) +
                    ((r < j)? cost[r+1][j]:0) +
                    sum(freq, i, j);
            if (c < cost[i][j])
                cost[i][j] = c;
            }
        }
    }
    return cost[0][n-1];
}


// A utility function to get sum of array elements
// freq[i] to freq[j]
int sum(int freq[], int i, int j)
{
    int s = 0;
    for (int k = i; k <= j; k++)
    s += freq[k];
    return s;
}


// Driver code
int main()
{
    int keys[] = {10, 12, 20};
    int freq[] = {34, 8, 50};
    int n = sizeof(keys)/sizeof(keys[0]);
```

```
cout << "Cost of Optimal BST is " << optimalSearchTree(keys, freq, n);

return 0;
}
```

Output: Cost of Optimal BST is 142.

The time complexity of the above solution is $O(n^4)$. The time complexity can be easily reduced to $O(n^3)$ by pre-calculating sum of frequencies instead of calling sum() again and again. In the above solutions, we have computed optimal cost only. The solutions can be easily modified to store the structure of BSTs also. We can create another auxiliary array of size n to store the structure of tree. All we need to do is, store the chosen 'r' in the innermost loop.

Understanding Sorting Algorithms

Sequencing the elements of a list in a certain order is known as sorting algorithms. Some of the major types of sorting algorithms are comparison sort, comb sort, insertion sort, shell sort, selection sort, hybrid sorting algorithm, etc. This chapter closely examines these sorting algorithms to provide an extensive understanding of the subject.

A sorting algorithm is a method for reorganizing a large number of items into a specific order, such as alphabetical, highest-to-lowest value or shortest-to-longest distance. Sorting algorithms take lists of items as input data, perform specific operations on those lists and deliver ordered arrays as output. The many applications of sorting algorithms include organizing items by price on a retail website and determining the order of sites on a search engine results page.

In other words, a sorted array is an array that is in a particular order. For example, $[a,b,c,d]$ is sorted alphabetically, $[1,2,3,4,5]$ is a list of integers sorted in increasing order, and $[5,4,3,2,1]$ is a list of integers sorted in decreasing order.

A sorting algorithm takes an array as input and outputs a permutation of that array that is sorted.

There are two broad types of sorting algorithms: integer sorts and comparison sorts.

Comparison Sort

Comparison sorts compare elements at each step of the algorithm to determine if one element should be to the left or right of another element.

Comparison sorts are usually more straightforward to implement than integer sorts, but comparison sorts are limited by a lower bound of $O(n \log n)$, meaning that, on average, comparison sorts cannot be faster than $O(n \log n)$, A lower bound for an algorithm is the *worst-case* running time of the *best* possible algorithm for a given problem. The "on average" part here is important: there are many algorithms that run in very fast time if the inputted list is *already* sorted, or has some very particular (and overall unlikely) property. There is only one permutation of a list that is sorted, but $n!$ possible lists, so the chances that the input is already sorted is very unlikely, and on average, the list will not be very sorted.

The running time of comparison-based sorting algorithms is bounded by $\Omega(n \log n)$.

A comparison sort can be modeled as a large binary tree called a decision tree where each node represents a single comparison. Because the sorted list is some permutation of the input list, for an input list of length n there are $n!$ possible permutations of that list. This is a decision tree because each of the $n!$ is represented by a leaf, and the path the algorithm must take to get to each leaf is the series of comparisons and outcomes that yield that particular ordering.

At each level of the tree, a comparison is made. Comparisons happen, and we keep traveling down the tree; until the algorithm reaches the leaves of the tree, there will be a leaf for each permutation, so there are $n!$ leaves.

Each comparison halves the number of future comparisons the algorithm must do (since if the algorithm selects the right edge out of a node at a given step, it will not search the nodes and paths connected to the left edge). Therefore, the algorithm performs $O(n \log n)$, comparisons. Any binary tree, with height h, has a number of leaves that is less than or equal to 2^h.

From this,

$$2^h \geq n!.$$

Taking the logarithm results in,

$$h \geq \log(n!).$$

From Stirling's approximation,

$$n! > \left(\frac{n}{e}\right)^n.$$

Therefore,

$$h \geq \log\left(\frac{n}{e}\right)^n$$
$$= n \log\left(\frac{n}{e}\right)^n$$
$$= n \log n - n \log e$$
$$= \Omega(n \log n).$$

Integer Sort

Integer sorts are sometimes called counting sorts (though there is a specific integer sort algorithm called counting sort). Integer sorts do not make comparisons, so they are not bounded by $\Omega(n \log n)$. Integer sorts determine for each element x how many elements are less than x If there are 14 elements that are less than x then x will be placed in the 15th slot. This information is used to place each element into the correct slot immediately—no need to rearrange lists.

Properties of Sorting Algorithms

All sorting algorithms share the goal of outputting a sorted list, but the way that each algorithm goes about this task can vary. When working with any kind of algorithm, it is important to know how fast it runs and in how much space it operates—in other words, its time complexity and space complexity. Comparison-based sorting algorithms have a time complexity of $\Omega(n \log n)$, meaning the algorithm can't be faster than $n \log n$. However, usually, the running time of algorithms is discussed in terms of big O, and not Omega. For example, if an algorithm had a worst-case running time of $\Omega(n \log n)$, then it is guaranteed that the algorithm will never be slower than $\Omega(n \log n)$, and if an algorithm has an average-case running time of $O(n^2)$, then on average, it will not be slower than $O(n^2)$.

The running time describes how many operations an algorithm must carry out before it completes. The space complexity describes how much space must be allocated to run a particular algorithm. For example, if an algorithm takes in a list of size n and for some reason makes a new list of size n for each element in n the algorithm needs n^2 space.

Additionally, for sorting algorithms, it is sometimes useful to know if a sorting algorithm is stable.

Stability

A sorting algorithm is stable if it preserves the original order of elements with equal key values (where the key is the value the algorithm sorts by). For example,

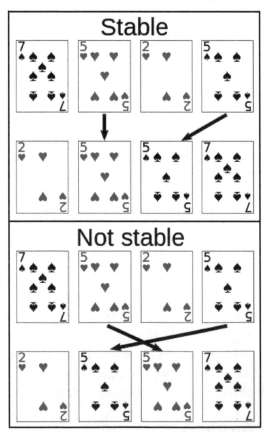

When the cards are sorted by value with a stable sort, the two 5s must remain in the same order in the sorted output that they were originally in. When they are sorted with a non-stable sort, the 5s may end up in the opposite order in the sorted output.

Common Sorting Algorithms

There are many different sorting algorithms, with various pros and cons. Here are a few examples of common sorting algorithms.

Merge Sort

Mergesort is a comparison-based algorithm that focuses on how to merge together two pre-sorted arrays such that the resulting array is also sorted.

Insertion Sort

Insertion sort is a comparison-based algorithm that builds a final sorted array one element at a time. It iterates through an input array and removes one element per iteration, finds the place the element belongs in the array, and then places it there.

Bubble Sort

Bubble sort is a comparison-based algorithm that compares each pair of elements in an array and swaps them if they are out of order until the entire array is sorted. For each element in the list, the algorithm compares every pair of elements.

Quicksort

Quicksort is a comparison-based algorithm that uses divide-and-conquer to sort an array. The algorithm picks a pivot element, $A[q]$, and then rearranges the array into two subarrays $A[p...q-1]$, such that all elements are less than $A[q]$, and $A[q+1...r]$, such that all elements are greater than or equal to $A[q]$.

Heapsort

Heapsort is a comparison-based algorithm that uses a binary heap data structure to sort elements. It divides its input into a sorted and an unsorted region, and it iteratively shrinks the unsorted region by extracting the largest element and moving that to the sorted region.

Counting Sort

Counting sort is an integer sorting algorithm that assumes that each of the n input elements in a list has a key value ranging from 0 to k for some integer k. For each element in the list, counting sort determines the number of elements that are less than it. Counting sort can use this information to place the element directly into the correct slot of the output array.

Choosing a Sorting Algorithm

To choose a sorting algorithm for a particular problem, consider the running time, space complexity, and the expected format of the input list.

Algorithm	Best-case	Worst-case	Average-case	Space Complexity	Stable?
Merge Sort	$O(n \log n)$	$O(n \log n)$	$O(n \log n)$	$O(n)$	Yes
Insertion Sort	$O(n)$	$O(n^2)$	$O(n^2)$	$O(1)$	Yes
Bubble Sort	$O(n)$	$O(n^2)$	$O(n^2)$	$O(1)$	Yes
Quicksort	$O(n \log n)$	$O(n^2)$	$O(n \log n)$	$\log n$ best, n avg	Usually not*
Heapsort	$O(n \log n)$	$O(n \log n)$	$O(n \log n)$	$O(1)$	No
Counting Sort	$O(k+n)$	$O(k+n)$	$O(k+n)$	$O(k+n)$	Yes

*Most quicksort implementations are not stable, though stable implementations do exist.

When choosing a sorting algorithm to use, weigh these factors. For example, quicksort is a very fast algorithm but can be pretty tricky to implement; bubble sort is a slow algorithm but is very easy to implement. To sort small sets of data, bubble sort may be a better option since it can be implemented quickly, but for larger datasets, the speedup from quicksort might be worth the trouble implementing the algorithm.

Comparison Sort

A Comparison Sort is a sorting algorithm where the final order is determined only by comparisons between the input elements. In this there are three sorting algorithms: merge-sort, quicksort, and heap-sort.

Each of these algorithms takes an input array a and sorts the elements of a into non-decreasing order in $O(n \log n)$ (expected) time. These algorithms are all comparison-based. Their second argument, c, is a Comparator that implements the compare(a,b) method. These algorithms don't care what type of data is being sorted; the only operation they do on the data is comparisons using the compare(a,b) method. compare(a,b) returns a negative value if $a < b$, a positive value if $a > b$, and zero if $a = b$.

Merge Sort

The merge-sort algorithm is a classic example of recursive divide and conquer: If the length of a is at most 1, then a is already sorted, so we do nothing. Otherwise, we split a into two halves, $a0 = a[0],...,a[\ /2-1]$ and $a1 = a[n/2],...,a[n-1]$. We recursively sort $a0$ and $a1$, and then we merge (the now sorted) $a0$ and $a1$ to get our fully sorted array a:

```
<T> void mergeSort(T[] a, Comparator<T> c) {
```

```
    if (a.length <= 1) return;

    T[] a0 = Arrays.copyOfRange(a, 0, a.length/2);

    T[] a1 = Arrays.copyOfRange(a, a.length/2, a.length);

    mergeSort(a0, c);

    mergeSort(a1, c);

    merge(a0, a1, a, c);

}
```

An example is shown in Figure below.

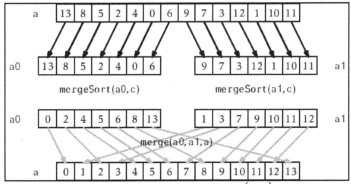

The execution of $\text{mergeSort}(a,c)$.

Compared to sorting, merging the two sorted arrays a0 and a1 is fairly easy We add elements to a one at a time. If a0 or a1 is empty, then we add the next elements from the other (non-empty) array. Otherwise, we take the minimum of the next element in a0 and the next element in a1 and add it to a:

```
    <T> void merge(T[] a0, T[] a1, T[] a, Comparator<T> c) {


int i0 = 0, i1 = 0;

    for (int i = 0; i < a.length; i++) {

        if (i0 == a0.length)

            a[i] = a1[i1++];

        else if (i1 == a1.length)

            a[i] = a0[i0++];

        else if (compare(a0[i0], a1[i1]) < 0)

            a[i] = a0[i0++];

        else
```

```
        a[i] = a1[i1++];

}
```

Notice that the merge$(a0,a1,a,c)$ algorithm performs at most n-1 comparisons before running out of elements in one of a0 or a1.

To understand the running-time of merge-sort, it is easiest to think of it in terms of its recursion tree. Suppose for now that n is a power of two, so that $n = 2^{\log n}$, and $\log n$ is an integer. Merge-sort turns the problem of sorting n elements into two problems, each of sorting n/2 elements. These two subproblem are then turned into two problems each, for a total of four subproblems, each of size n/4. These four subproblems become eight subproblems, each of size n/8, and so on. At the bottom of this process, n/2 subproblems, each of size two, are converted into n problems, each of size one. For each subproblem of size $n/2^i$, the time spent merging and copying data is $O(n/2^i)$. Since there are 2^i subproblems of size $n/2^i$, the total time spent working on problems of size 2^i, not counting recursive calls is,

$$2^i \times O(n/2^i) = O(n)$$

Therefore, the total amount of time taken by merge-sort is,

$$\sum_{i=0}^{\log n} O(n) = O(n \log n)$$

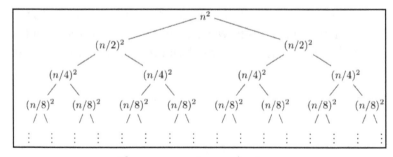

The merge-sort recursion tree.

The proof of the following theorem is based on preceding analysis, but has to be a little more careful to deal with the cases where n is not a power of 2.

Theorem: *The* mergeSort(a,c) *algorithm runs in* $O(n \log n)$ *time and performs at most* n logn *comparisons.*

Proof. The proof is by induction on n. The base case, in which $n = 1$, is trivial; when presented with an array of length 0 or 1 the algorithm simply returns without performing any comparisons.

Merging two sorted lists of total length n requires at most n−1 comparisons. Let $C(n)$ denote the maximum number of comparisons performed by mergeSort(a,c) on an array a of length n. If n is even, then we apply the inductive hypothesis to the two subproblems and obtain.

$$C(n) \le n\text{-}1 + 2C(n/2)$$
$$\le n\text{-}1 + 2\big((n/2)\log(n/2)\big)$$
$$= n\text{-}1 + n\log(n/2)$$
$$= n\text{-}1 + n\log n - n$$
$$< n\log n.$$

The case where n is odd is slightly more complicated. For this case, we use two inequalities that are easy to verify:

$$\log(x+1) \le \log(x)+1,$$

for all $x \ge 1$ and

$$\log(x+1/2)+\log(x-1/2) \le 2\log(x),$$

for all $x \ge 1/2$. Inequality $(\log(x+1) \le \log(x)+1,\ )$comes from the fact that $\log(x)+1 = \log(2x)$ while $(\log(x+1/2)+\log(x-1/2) \le 2\log(x),)$ follows from the fact that $\log$ is a concave function. With these tools in hand we have, for odd n,

$$C(n) \le n\text{-}1 + C(\lceil n/2 \rceil) + C(\lfloor n/2 \rfloor)$$
$$\le n\text{-}1 + \lceil n/2 \rceil \log\lceil n/2 \rceil + \lfloor n/2 \rfloor \log\lfloor n/2 \rfloor$$
$$= n\text{-}1 + n\log(n/2+1/2)\log(n/2+1/2) + (n/2-1/2)\log(n/2-1/2)$$
$$\le n\text{-}1 + n\log(n/2) + (1/2)\big(\log(n/2+1/2) - \log(n/2-1/2)\big)$$
$$\le n\text{-}1 + n\log(n/2) + 1/2$$
$$< n + n\log(n/2)$$
$$= n + n(\log n - 1)$$
$$= n\log n.$$

Quicksort

The quicksort algorithm is another classic divide and conquer algorithm. Unlike merge-sort, which does merging after solving the two subproblems, quicksort does all of its work upfront.

Quicksort is simple to describe: Pick a random pivot element, x, from a; partition a into the set of elements less than x, the set of elements equal to x, and the set of elements greater than x; and, finally, recursively sort the first and third sets in this partition.

```
<T> void quickSort(T[] a, Comparator<T> c) {

    quickSort(a, 0, a.length, c);

}
```

```
<T> void quickSort(T[] a, int i, int n, Comparator<T> c) {

    if (n <= 1) return;

    T x = a[i + rand.nextInt(n)];

    int p = i-1, j = i, q = i+n;

    // a[i..p]<x,   a[p+1..q-1]??x, a[q..i+n-1]>x

    while (j < q) {

        int comp = compare(a[j], x);

        if (comp < 0) {          // move to beginning of array

            swap(a, j++, ++p);

        } else if (comp > 0) {

            swap(a, j, --q);   // move to end of array

        } else {

            j++;                 // keep in the middle

        }

    }

    // a[i..p]<x,   a[p+1..q-1]=x, a[q..i+n-1]>x

    quickSort(a, i, p-i+1, c);

    quickSort(a, q, n-(q-i), c);
```

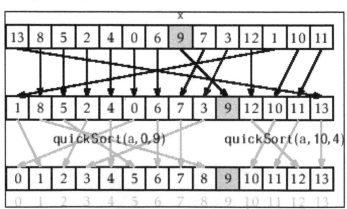

An example execution of quick Sort $(a, 0, 14, c)$.

All of this is done in place, so that instead of making copies of subarrays being sorted, the quick Sort (a, i, n, c) method only sorts the subarray $a[i], \ldots a[i+n-1]$. Initially, this method is invoked with the arguments quick Sort $(a, 0, a.length, c)$.

At the heart of the quicksort algorithm is the in-place partitioning algorithm. This algorithm, without using any extra space, swaps elements in a and computes indices p and q so that,

$$a[i] \begin{cases} < x & \text{if } 0 \le i \le p \\ = x & \text{if } p \le i \le q \\ > x & \text{if } q \le i \le n\text{-}1 \end{cases}$$

This partitioning, which is done by the while loop in the code, works by iteratively increasing p and decreasing q while maintaining the first and last of these conditions. At each step, the element at position j is either moved to the front, left where it is, or moved to the back. In the first two cases, j is incremented, while in the last case, j is not incremented since the new element at position j has not yet been processed.

Quicksort is very closely related to the random binary search trees. In fact, if the input to quicksort consists of n distinct elements, then the quicksort recursion tree is a random binary search tree. To see this, recall that when constructing a random binary search tree the first thing we do is pick a random element x and make it the root of the tree. After this, every element will eventually be compared to , with smaller elements going into the left subtree and larger elements into the right.

In quicksort, we select a random element x and immediately compare everything to x, putting the smaller elements at the beginning of the array and larger elements at the end of the array. Quicksort then recursively sorts the beginning of the array and the end of the array, while the random binary search tree recursively inserts smaller elements in the left subtree of the root and larger elements in the right subtree of the root.

The above correspondence between random binary search trees and quicksort means that we can translate Lemma below to a statement about quicksort:

Lemma: *When quicksort is called to sort an array containing the integers* $0,....,n-1$, *the expected number of times element* i *is compared to a pivot element is at most* H_{i+1} H_{n+1}.

A little summing up of harmonic numbers gives us the following theorem about the running time of quicksort:

Theorem: *When quicksort is called to sort an array containing* n *distinct elements, the expected number of comparisons performed is at most* $2n \ln n + O(n)$.

Proof. Let T be the number of comparisons performed by quicksort when sorting n distinct elements. Using Lemma above and linearity of expectation, we have:

$$E(T) = \sum_{i=0}^{n-1} \left(H_{i+1} + H_{n-1} \right)$$
$$= 2 \sum_{i=0}^{n} H_i$$
$$\le 2 \sum_{i=0}^{n} H_n$$
$$\le 2n \ln n + 2n = 2n \ln n + O(n)$$

Theorem below describes the case where the elements being sorted are all distinct. When the input array, a, contains duplicate elements, the expected running time of quicksort is no worse, and can be even better; any time a duplicate element x is chosen as a pivot, all occurrences of x get grouped together and do not take part in either of the two subproblems.

Theorem: *The* quick Sort(a,c) *method runs in* $O(n \log n)$ *expected time and the expected number of comparisons it performs is at most* $2n \ln n + O(n)$.

Heapsort

The heap-sort algorithm is another in-place sorting algorithm. Heap-sort uses the binary heaps. Recall that the BinaryHeap data structure represents a heap using a single array. The heap-sort algorithm converts the input array a into a heap and then repeatedly extracts the minimum value.

More specifically, a heap stores n elements in an array, a, at array locations $a[0],...a[n-1]$ with the smallest value stored at the root, $a[0]$. After transforming a into a BinaryHeap, the heap-sort algorithm repeatedly swaps a and $a[n-1]$, decrements n, and calls trick le Down(0) so that $a[0],...a[n-2]$ once again are a valid heap representation. When this process ends (because n−o) the elements of a are stored in decreasing order, so a is reversed to obtain the final sorted order. Figure below shows an example of the execution of heap Sort(a,c).

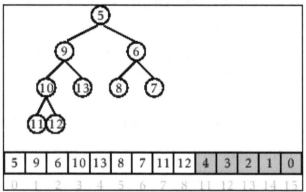

The shaded part of the array is already sorted. The unshaded part is a `BinaryHeap`.
During the next iteration, element 5 will be placed into array location.

```
<T> void sort(T[] a, Comparator<T> c) {

    BinaryHeap<T> h = new BinaryHeap<T>(a, c);

    while (h.n > 1) {

        h.swap(--h.n, 0);

        h.trickleDown(0);

    }

    Collections.reverse(Arrays.asList(a));

}
```

A key subroutine in heap sort is the constructor for turning an unsorted array a into a heap. It would be easy to do this in $O(n \log n)$ time by repeatedly calling the BinaryHeap add(x) method, but we can do better by using a bottom-up algorithm. Recall that, in a binary heap, the children of $a[i]$ are stored at positions $a[2i+1]$ and $a[2i+2]$. This implies that the elements $a[\lfloor n/2 \rfloor],\ldots a[n-1]$ have no children. In other words, each of $a[\lfloor n/2 \rfloor],\ldots a[n-1]$ is a sub-heap of size 1. Now, working backwards, we can call trickle Down(i) for each $i \in \{\lfloor n/2 \rfloor-1,\ldots,0\}$. This works, because by the time we call trickle Down(i), each of the two children of $a[i]$ are the root of a sub-heap, so calling trickle Down(i) makes $a[i]$ into the root of its own subheap.

```
BinaryHeap(T[] a, Comparator<T> c) {
    this.c = c;
    this.a = a;
    n = a.length;
    for (int i = n/2-1; i >= 0; i--) {
        trickleDown(i);
    }
}
```

The interesting thing about this bottom-up strategy is that it is more efficient than calling add(x) n times. To see this, notice that, for $n/2$ elements, we do no work at all, for $n/4$ elements, we call trickle Down(i) on a subheap rooted at $a[i]$ and whose height is one, for $n/8$ elements, we call trickle Down(i) on a subheap whose height is two, and so on. Since the work done by trickle Down(i) is proportional to the height of the sub-heap rooted at $a[i]$, this means that the total work done is at most,

$$\sum_{i=1}^{\log n} O\big((i-1)n/2^i\big) \le \sum_{i=1}^{\infty} O(n/2^i) = O(n)\sum_{i=1}^{\infty} i/2^i = O(2n) = O(n).$$

The second-last equality follows by recognizing that the sum $\sum_{i=1}^{\infty} i/2^i$ is equal, by definition of expected value, to the expected number of times we toss a coin up to and including the first time the coin comes up as heads and applying Lemma.

The following theorem describes the performance of heap Sort(a,c).

Theorem: *The* heap Sort(a,c) *method runs in* $O(n \log n)$ *time and performs at most* $2n \log n + O(n)$ *comparisons.*

Proof. The algorithm runs in three steps: (1) transforming a into a heap, (2) repeatedly extracting the minimum element from a, and (3) reversing the elements in a. We have just argued that step 1 takes $O(n)$ time and performs $O(n)$ comparisons. Step 3 takes $O(n)$ time and performs no comparisons. Step 2 performs n calls to trickle Down(0). The i th such call operates on a heap of size $n-i$ and performs at most $2 \log(n-i)$ comparisons. Summing this over i gives,

$$\sum_{i=0}^{n-i} 2\log(n-i) \le \sum_{i=0}^{n-i} 2\log n = 2n\log n$$

Adding the number of comparisons performed in each of the three steps completes the proof.

A Lower-Bound for Comparison-Based Sorting.

We have now seen three comparison-based sorting algorithms that each run in $O(n\log n)$ time. By now, we should be wondering if faster algorithms exist. The short answer to this question is no. If the only operations allowed on the elements of a are comparisons, then no algorithm can avoid doing roughly $n\log n$ comparisons. This is not difficult to prove, but requires a little imagination. Ultimately, it follows from the fact that

$$\log(n!) = \log n + \log(n-1) + ... + \log(1) = n\log n - O(n)$$

We will start by focusing our attention on deterministic algorithms like merge-sort and heap-sort and on a particular fixed value of n. Imagine such an algorithm is being used to sort n distinct elements. The key to proving the lower-bound is to observe that, for a deterministic algorithm with a fixed value of n, the first pair of elements that are compared is always the same. For example, in heap Sort(a,c), when n is even, the first call to trickle Down(i) is with $i = n/2-1$ and the first comparison is between elements $a[n/2-1]$ and $a[n-1]$.

Since all input elements are distinct, this first comparison has only two possible outcomes. The second comparison done by the algorithm may depend on the outcome of the first comparison. The third comparison may depend on the results of the first two, and so on. In this way, any deterministic comparison-based sorting algorithm can be viewed as a rooted binary comparison tree. Each internal node, u, of this tree is labeled with a pair of indices $u.i$ and $u.j$. If $a[u.i] < a[u.j]$ the algorithm proceeds to the left subtree, otherwise it proceeds to the right subtree. Each leaf w of this tree is labeled with a permutation $w.p[0],...,w.p[n-1]$ of $0,...n-1$. This permutation represents the one that is required to sort a if the comparison tree reaches this leaf. That is,

$$a[w.p[0]] < a[w.p[1]] < ... < a[w.p[n-1]]$$

An example of a comparison tree for an array of size $n = 3$ is shown in figure below.

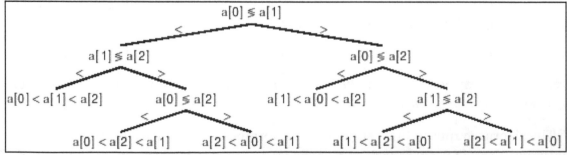

A comparison tree for sorting an array $a[0],a[1],a[2]$ of length $n = 3$.

The comparison tree for a sorting algorithm tells us everything about the algorithm. It tells us exactly the sequence of comparisons that will be performed for any input array, a, having n distinct elements and it tells us how the algorithm will reorder a in order to sort it. Consequently, the comparison tree must have at least n! leaves; if not, then there are two distinct permutations that lead to the same leaf; therefore, the algorithm does not correctly sort at least one of these permutations.

For example, the comparison tree in above figure has only $4 < 3! = 6$ leaves. Inspecting this tree, we see that the two input arrays $3,1,2$ and $3,2,1$ both lead to the rightmost leaf. On the input $3,1,2$ this leaf correctly outputs $a[1] = 1, a[2] = 2. a[0] = 3$. However, on the input $3,2,1$, this node incorrectly outputs $a[1] = 2, a[2] = 1. a[0] = 3$. This discussion leads to the primary lower-bound for comparison-based algorithms.

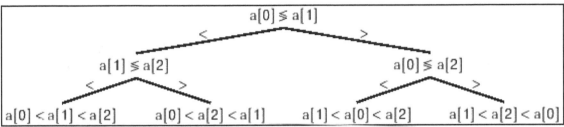

A comparison tree that does not correctly sort every input permutation.

Theorem: *For any deterministic comparison-based sorting algorithm A and any integer $n \geq 1$, there exists an input array a of length n such that A performs at least $\log(n!) = n \log n - O(n)$ comparisons when sorting a.*

Proof: By the preceding discussion, the comparison tree defined by A must have at least n! leaves. An easy inductive proof shows that any binary tree with k leaves has a height of at least $\log k$. Therefore, the comparison tree for A has a leaf, w, with a depth of at least $\log(n!)$ and there is an input array a that leads to this leaf. The input array a is an input for which A does at least $\log(n!)$ comparisons.

Above theorem deals with deterministic algorithms like merge-sort and heap-sort, but doesn't tell us anything about randomized algorithms like quicksort. Could a randomized algorithm beat the $\log(n!)$ lower bound on the number of comparisons? The answer, again, is no. Again, the way to prove it is to think differently about what a randomized algorithm is.

In the following discussion, we will assume that our decision trees have been "cleaned up" in the following way: Any node that cannot be reached by some input array a is removed. This cleaning up implies that the tree has exactly n! leaves. It has at least n! leaves because, otherwise, it could not sort correctly. It has at most n! leaves since each of the possible n! permutation of n distinct elements follows exactly one root to leaf path in the decision tree.

We can think of a randomized sorting algorithm, R, as a deterministic algorithm that takes two inputs: The input array a that should be sorted and a long sequence $b = b_1, b_2, b_3, \ldots, b_m$ of random real numbers in the range $[0,1]$. The random numbers provide the randomization for the algorithm. When the algorithm wants to toss a coin or make a random choice, it does so by using some element from b. For example, to compute the index of the first pivot in quicksort, the algorithm could use the formula $\lfloor nb_1 \rfloor$.

Now, notice that if we fix b to some particular sequence $\hat{b}$ then R becomes a deterministic sorting algorithm, $R(\hat{b})$, that has an associated comparison tree, $T(\hat{b})$. Next, notice that if we select a to be a random permutation of $\{1,...,n\}$, then this is equivalent to selecting a random leaf, w, from the n! leaves of $T(\hat{b})$.

If we select a random leaf from any binary tree with k leaves, then the expected depth of that leaf is at least $\log k$. Therefore, the expected number of comparisons performed by the (deterministic) algorithm $R(\hat{b})$ when given an input array containing a random permutation of $\{1,...,n\}$ is at least $\log(n!)$. Finally, notice that this is true for every choice of $\hat{b}$, therefore it holds even for R. This completes the proof of the lower-bound for randomized algorithms.

Theorem: *For any integer $n \geq 1$ and any (deterministic or randomized) comparison-based sorting algorithm A, the expected number of comparisons done by A when sorting a random permutation of $\{1,...,n\}$ is at least* $\log(n!) = n \log n - O(n)$.

Bubble Sort

Bubble sort is a simple sorting algorithm. This sorting algorithm is comparison-based algorithm in which each pair of adjacent elements is compared and the elements are swapped if they are not in order. This algorithm is not suitable for large data sets as its average and worst case complexity are of $O(n^2)$ where n is the number of items.

Working of Bubble sort

We take an unsorted array for our example. Bubble sort takes $O(n^2)$ time so we're keeping it short and precise.

Bubble sort starts with very first two elements, comparing them to check which one is greater.

In this case, value 33 is greater than 14, so it is already in sorted locations. Next, we compare 33 with 27.

We find that 27 is smaller than 33 and these two values must be swapped.

The new array should look like this –

Next we compare 33 and 35. We find that both are in already sorted positions.

Then we move to the next two values, 35 and 10.

We know then that 10 is smaller 35. Hence they are not sorted.

We swap these values. We find that we have reached the end of the array. After one iteration, the array should look like this –

To be precise, we are now showing how an array should look like after each iteration. After the second iteration, it should look like this –

Notice that after each iteration, at least one value moves at the end.

And when there's no swap required, bubble sorts learns that an array is completely sorted.

Now we should look into some practical aspects of bubble sort.

Algorithm

We assume list is an array of n elements. We further assume that swapfunction swaps the values of the given array elements.

```
begin BubbleSort(list)

   for all elements of list
      if list[i] > list[i+1]
         swap(list[i], list[i+1])
      end if
   end for


   return list


end BubbleSort
```

Pseudocode

We observe in algorithm that Bubble Sort compares each pair of array element unless the whole array is completely sorted in an ascending order. This may cause a few complexity issues like what if the array needs no more swapping as all the elements are already ascending.

To ease-out the issue, we use one flag variable swapped which will help us see if any swap has happened or not. If no swap has occurred, i.e. the array requires no more processing to be sorted, it will come out of the loop.

Pseudocode of BubbleSort algorithm can be written as follows –

```
procedure bubbleSort( list : array of items )


   loop = list.count;


   for i = 0 to loop-1 do:
      swapped = false
```

```
    for j = 0 to loop-1 do:


        /* compare the adjacent elements */

        if list[j] > list[j+1] then

            /* swap them */

            swap( list[j], list[j+1] )

            swapped = true

        end if


    end for


    /*if no number was swapped that means

    array is sorted now, break the loop.*/


    if(not swapped) then

        break

    end if


    end for


end procedure return list
```

Implementation

One more issue we did not address in our original algorithm and its improvised pseudocode, is that, after every iteration the highest values settles down at the end of the array. Hence, the next iteration need not include already sorted elements. For this purpose, in our implementation, we restrict the inner loop to avoid already sorted values.

Comb Sort

Comb sort is a simple sorting algorithm which improves on bubble sort. The main idea for this type of algorithm is to eliminate the small values near the end of the list, as these slow down the sorting process.

How it works:

In comb sort, the main usage is of gaps. For example, in bubble sort the gap between two elements was 1 whilst here the gap starts out as a large value and shrinks until it reaches the value 1, when it practically becomes bubble sort. The shrink factor determines how much the gap is lessened. The value is crucial, so an ideal value would be 1.3.

Step by Step Example

Having the following list, let's try to use comb sort to arrange the numbers from lowest to greatest:

Unsorted list:

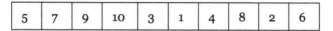

| 5 | 7 | 9 | 10 | 3 | 1 | 4 | 8 | 2 | 6 |

Iteration 1, gap = 8. The distance of 8 from the first element 5 to the next element, leads to the element of 2, these numbers are not in the right order so they have to swap. Also, the same distance is between 7 and 6 which also are not in the right order, so again a swap is required:

| 2 | 7 | 9 | 10 | 3 | 1 | 4 | 8 | 5 | 6 |
| 2 | 6 | 9 | 10 | 3 | 1 | 4 | 8 | 5 | 7 |

Iteration 2, gap =6, the elements that were compare on each line are 2 with 4, 6 with 8, 5 with 9 and 7 with 10:

2	7	9	10	3	1	4	8	5	7
2	6	9	10	3	1	4	8	5	7
2	6	5	10	3	1	4	8	9	7
2	6	5	7	2	1	4	8	9	10

Iteration 3, gap = 4:

2	7	9	10	3	1	4	8	5	10
2	1	9	10	3	6	4	8	5	10
2	1	4	10	3	6	5	8	9	10
2	1	4	7	3	6	5	8	9	10
2	1	4	7	3	6	5	8	9	10
2	1	4	7	3	6	5	8	9	10

Iteration 4, gap = 3:

2	1	4	7	3	6	5	8	9	10
2	1	4	7	3	6	5	8	9	10
2	1	4	7	3	6	5	8	9	10
2	1	4	5	3	6	7	8	9	10
2	1	4	5	3	6	5	8	9	10
2	1	4	5	3	6	5	8	9	10
2	1	4	5	3	6	7	8	9	10

Iteration 5, gap =2:

2	1	4	5	3	6	7	8	9	10
2	1	4	5	3	6	7	8	9	10
2	1	3	5	4	6	7	8	9	10
2	1	3	5	4	6	7	8	9	10
2	1	3	5	4	6	7	8	9	10
2	1	3	5	4	6	7	8	9	10
2	1	3	5	4	6	7	8	9	10
2	1	3	5	4	6	7	8	9	10

Iteration 6, gap =1:

1	2	3	5	4	6	7	8	9	10
1	2	3	5	4	6	7	8	9	10
1	2	3	4	5	6	7	8	9	10
1	2	3	4	5	6	7	8	9	10
1	2	3	4	5	6	7	8	9	10
2	2	3	4	5	6	7	8	9	10
1	2	3	4	5	6	7	8	9	10
1	2	3	4	5	6	7	8	9	10

Iteration: since the items are sorted, no swaps will be made and the algorithm ends its execution.

Sample Code

1. #include < iostream >

2. using namespace std;

```
3.  int newGap(int gap) {
4.     gap = (gap * 10) / 13;
5.     if (gap == 9 || gap == 10)
6.       gap = 11;
7.     if (gap < 1)
8.       gap = 1;
9.     return gap;
10. }
11. void combsort(int a[], int aSize) {
12.   int gap = aSize;
13.   for (;;) {
14.     gap = newGap(gap);
15.     bool swapped = false;
16.     for (int i = 0; i < aSize - gap; i++) {
17.       int j = i + gap;
18.       if (a[i] > a[j]) {
19.         std::swap(a[i], a[j]);
20.         swapped = true;
21.       }
22.     }
23.     if (gap == 1 && .swapped)
24.       break;
25.   }
26. }
27. int main ()
28. {
29.   int n;
30.   int *a;
31.   cout << "Please insert the number of elements to be sorted: ";
32.   cin >> n;      // The total number of elements
```

```
33.   a = (int *)calloc(n, sizeof(int));

34.   for(int i=0;i< n;i++)

35.   {

36.

37.          cout << "Input " << i << " element: ";

38.          cin >>a[i]; // Adding the elements to the array

39.   }

40.   cout << "Unsorted list:" << endl; // Displaying the unsorted
      array

41.   for(int i=0;i< n;i++)

42.   {

43.          cout << a[i] << " ";

44.   }

45.   combsort(a,n);

46.   cout << "nSorted list:" << endl;  // Display the sorted array

47.   for(int i=0;i < n;i++)

48.   {

49.          cout << a[i] << " ";

50.   }

51.   return 0;

52. }
```

Output

Code Explanation

At first, the method newGap calculates the size of the gap, based on the number of elements to be sorted. The combsort method is the one who sorts the numbers from the array, at first with the highest gap, which is calculated by calling the newGap method, then it passes through the array and checks the proper elements if they are in the right order, and if not, the library function swap is executed. This continues until the gap reaches the value 1 and no more swaps have been executed.

Complexity

This is quite surprising. Despite being based on the idea of a Bubble Sort the time complexity is just O(n log n), and space complexity for in-place sorting is O(1).

Advantages

- Is proper for data sets composed of either numbers or strings.
- Time complexity very good, could be compared to quick sort.
- No recursive function-calls.
- In-place-sorting, no extra memory needed.
- No worst-case-situation like in Quicksort.

Disadvantages

- You have to resize the gap with a division by 1.3, which is a fraction.

Insertion Sort

Insertion sort is based on the idea that one element from the input elements is consumed in each iteration to find its correct position i.e, the position to which it belongs in a sorted array.

It iterates the input elements by growing the sorted array at each iteration. It compares the current element with the largest value in the sorted array. If the current element is greater, then it leaves the element in its place and moves on to the next element else it finds its correct position in the sorted array and moves it to that position. This is done by shifting all the elements, which are larger than the current element, in the sorted array to one position ahead.

Implementation

```
void insertion_sort ( int A[ ] , int n)

{

    for( int i = 0 ;i < n ; i++ ) {
    /*storing current element whose left side is checked for its
         correct position .*/
```

```
    int temp = A[ i ];

    int j = i;


    /* check whether the adjacent element in left side is greater or
        less than the current element. */


    while(  j > 0  && temp < A[ j -1]) {


        // moving the left side element to one position forward.
            A[ j ] = A[ j-1];
            j= j - 1;


        }
    // moving current element to its  correct position.
        A[ j ] = temp;

    }

}
```

Take array $A[] = [7, 4, 5, 2]$.

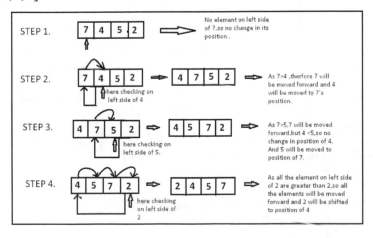

Since 7 is the first element has no other element to be compared with, it remains at its position. Now when on moving towards 4, 7 is the largest element in the sorted list and greater than 4. So, move 4 to its correct position i.e. before 7. Similarly with 5, as 7 (largest element in the sorted list) is greater than 5, we will move 5 to its correct position. Finally for 2, all the elements on the left side of 2 (sorted list) are moved one position forward as all are greater than 2 and then 2 is placed in the first position. Finally, the given array will result in a sorted array.

Time Complexity

In worst case,each element is compared with all the other elements in the sorted array. For N elements, there will be N2 comparisons. Therefore, the time complexity is O(N²).

Shell Sort

The shell sort, sometimes called the "diminishing increment sort," improves on the insertion sort by breaking the original list into a number of smaller sublists, each of which is sorted using an insertion sort. The unique way that these sublists are chosen is the key to the shell sort. Instead of breaking the list into sublists of contiguous items, the shell sort uses an increment i, sometimes called the gap, to create a sublist by choosing all items that are i items apart.

This can be seen in first figure below. This list has nine items. If we use an increment of three, there are three sublists, each of which can be sorted by an insertion sort. After completing these sorts, we get the list shown in second figure below. Although this list is not completely sorted, something very interesting has happened. By sorting the sublists, we have moved the items closer to where they actually belong.

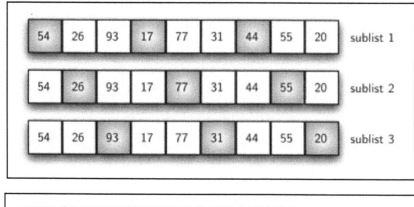

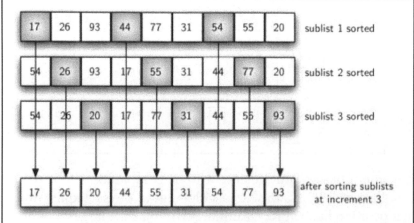

Figure above shows a final insertion sort using an increment of one; in other words, a standard insertion sort. Note that by performing the earlier sublist sorts, we have now reduced the total number of shifting operations necessary to put the list in its final order. For this case, we need only four more shifts to complete the process.

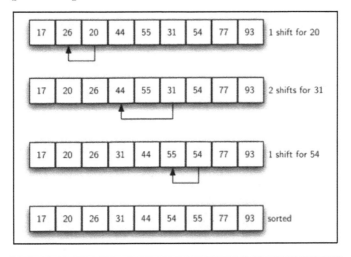

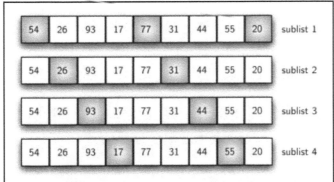

We said earlier that the way in which the increments are chosen is the unique feature of the shell sort. The function shown in ActiveCode 1 uses a different set of increments. In this case, we begin with $\frac{n}{2}$ sublists. On the next pass, $\frac{n}{4}$ sublists are sorted. Eventually, a single list is sorted with the basic insertion sort.

Following is the implementation of ShellSort.

```cpp
// C++ implementation of Shell Sort

#include  <iostream>

using namespace std;


/* function to sort arr using shellSort */

int shellSort(int arr[], int n)

{

    // Start with a big gap, then reduce the gap

    for (int gap = n/2; gap > 0; gap /= 2)
```

```
    {
        // Do a gapped insertion sort for this gap size.
        // The first gap elements a[0..gap-1] are already in gapped order
        // keep adding one more element until the entire array is
        // gap sorted
        for (int i = gap; i < n; i += 1)
        {
            // add a[i] to the elements that have been gap sorted
            // save a[i] in temp and make a hole at position i
            int temp = arr[i];

            // shift earlier gap-sorted elements up until the correct
            // location for a[i] is found
            int j;
            for (j = i; j >= gap && arr[j - gap] > temp; j -= gap)
                arr[j] = arr[j - gap];

            //  put temp (the original a[i]) in its correct location
            arr[j] = temp;
        }
    }
    return 0;
}


void printArray(int arr[], int n)
{
    for (int i=0; i<n; i++)
        cout << arr[i] << " ";
}
```

```
int main()

{

    int arr[] = {12, 34, 54, 2, 3}, i;

    int n = sizeof(arr)/sizeof(arr[0]);


    cout << "Array before sorting: \n";

    printArray(arr, n);


    shellSort(arr, n);


    cout << "\nArray after sorting: \n";

    printArray(arr, n);


    return 0;

}
```

Output:

Array before sorting:

12 34 54 2 3

Array after sorting:

2 3 12 34 54

Time Complexity: Time complexity of above implementation of shellsort is O(n²). In the above implementation gap is reduce by half in every iteration. There are many other ways to reduce gap which lead to better time complexity.

Selection Sort

Selection sort is conceptually the most simplest sorting algorithm. This algorithm will first find the smallest element in the array and swap it with the element in the first position, then it will find the second smallest element and swap it with the element in the second position, and it will keep on doing this until the entire array is sorted.

It is called selection sort because it repeatedly selects the next-smallest element and swaps it into the right place.

Working of Selection Sort

Following are the steps involved in selection sort(for sorting a given array in ascending order):

1. Starting from the first element, we search the smallest element in the array, and replace it with the element in the first position.

2. We then move on to the second position, and look for smallest element present in the sub-array, starting from index 1, till the last index.

3. We replace the element at the second position in the original array, or we can say at the first position in the subarray, with the second smallest element.

4. This is repeated, until the array is completely sorted.

Let's consider an array with values {3, 6, 1, 8, 4, 5}

Below, we have a pictorial representation of how selection sort will sort the given array.

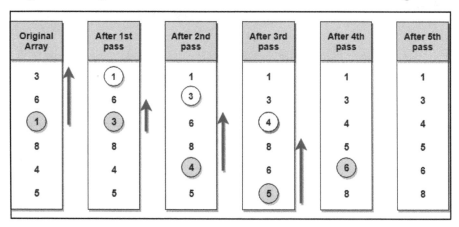

In the first pass, the smallest element will be 1, so it will be placed at the first position.

Then leaving the first element, next smallest element will be searched, from the remaining elements. We will get 3 as the smallest, so it will be then placed at the second position.

Then leaving 1 and 3(because they are at the correct position), we will search for the next smallest element from the rest of the elements and put it at third position and keep doing this until array is sorted.

Finding Smallest Element in a Subarray

In selection sort, in the first step, we look for the smallest element in the array and replace it with the element at the first position. This seems doable, isn't it?

Consider that you have an array with following values {3, 6, 1, 8, 4, 5}. Now as per selection sort, we will start from the first element and look for the smallest number in the array, which is **1** and we will find it at the index 2. Once the smallest number is found, it is swapped with the element at the first position.

Well, in the next iteration, we will have to look for the second smallest number in the array. How can we find the second smallest number? This one is tricky?

If you look closely, we already have the smallest number/element at the first position, which is the right position for it and we do not have to move it anywhere now. So we can say, that the first element is sorted, but the elements to the right, starting from index 1 are not.

So, we will now look for the smallest element in the subarray, starting from index 1, to the last index.

After we have found the second smallest element and replaced it with element on index 1(which is the second position in the array), we will have the first two positions of the array sorted.

Then we will work on the subarray, starting from index 2 now, and again looking for the smallest element in this subarray.

Implementing Selection Sort Algorithm

In the C program below, we have tried to divide the program into small functions, so that it's easier for you to understand which part is doing what.

There are many different ways to implement selection sort algorithm, here is the one that we like:

```c
// C program implementing Selection Sort

# include <stdio.h>


// function to swap elements at the given index values

void swap(int arr[], int firstIndex, int secondIndex)

{

    int temp;

    temp = arr[firstIndex];

    arr[firstIndex] = arr[secondIndex];

    arr[secondIndex] = temp;

}


// function to look for smallest element in the given subarray

int indexOfMinimum(int arr[], int startIndex, int n)

{
```

```
    int minValue = arr[startIndex];

    int minIndex = startIndex;


    for(int i = minIndex + 1; i < n; i++) {

        if(arr[i] < minValue)

        {

            minIndex = i;

            minValue = arr[i];

        }

    }

    return minIndex;

}


void selectionSort(int arr[], int n)

{

    for(int i = 0; i < n; i++)

    {

        int index = indexOfMinimum(arr, i, n);

        swap(arr, i, index);

    }


}


void printArray(int arr[], int size)

{

    int i;

    for(i = 0; i < size; i++)

    {

        printf("%d ", arr[i]);

    }
```

```
        printf("\n");
}


int main()
{
    int arr[] = {46, 52, 21, 22, 11};
    int n = sizeof(arr)/sizeof(arr[0]);
    selectionSort(arr, n);
    printf("Sorted array: \n");
    printArray(arr, n);
    return 0;
}
```

Selection sort is an unstable sort i.e it might change the occurrence of two similar elements in the list while sorting. But it can also work as a stable sort when it is implemented using linked list.

Complexity Analysis of Selection Sort

Selection Sort requires two nested for loops to complete itself, one for loop is in the function selectionSort, and inside the first loop we are making a call to another function indexOfMinimum, which has the second(inner) for loop.

Hence for a given input size of n, following will be the time and space complexity for selection sort algorithm:

Worst Case Time Complexity [Big-O]: $O(n^2)$

Best Case Time Complexity [Big-omega]: $O(n^2)$

Average Time Complexity [Big-theta]: $O(n^2)$

Space Complexity: $O(1)$

External Sorting

The problem of sorting collections of records too large to fit in main memory. Because the records must reside in peripheral or external memory, such sorting methods are called *external sorts*. This is in contrast to *internal sorts*, which assume that the records to be sorted are stored in main memory. Sorting large collections of records is central to many applications, such as processing payrolls and other large business databases. As a consequence, many external sorting algorithms have been devised. Years ago, sorting algorithm designers sought to optimize the use of specific hardware configurations, such as multiple tape or *disk drives*. Most computing today is done on personal computers and low-end workstations with relatively powerful CPUs, but only one or at most two disk drives. The techniques presented here are geared toward optimized processing on a single disk drive. This approach allows us to cover the most important issues in external sorting while skipping many less important machine-dependent details.

When a collection of records is too large to fit in *main memory*, the only practical way to sort it is to read some records from disk, do some rearranging, then write them back to disk. This process is repeated until the file is sorted, with each record read perhaps many times. Given the high cost of *disk I/O*, it should come as no surprise that the primary goal of an external sorting algorithm is to minimize the number of times information must be read from or written to disk. A certain amount of additional CPU processing can profitably be traded for reduced disk access.

Before discussing external sorting techniques, consider again the basic model for accessing information from disk. The file to be sorted is viewed by the programmer as a sequential series of fixed-size *blocks*. Assume (for simplicity) that each block contains the same number of fixed-size data records. Depending on the application, a record might be only a few bytes—composed of little or nothing more than the key—or might be hundreds of bytes with a relatively small key field. Records are assumed not to cross block boundaries. These assumptions can be relaxed for special-purpose sorting applications, but ignoring such complications makes the principles clearer.

A sector is the basic unit of I/O. In other words, all disk reads and writes are for one or more complete sectors. Sector sizes are typically a power of two, in the range 512 to 16K bytes, depending on the operating system and the size and speed of the disk drive. The block size used for external sorting algorithms should be equal to or a multiple of the sector size.

Under this model, a sorting algorithm reads a block of data into a buffer in main memory, performs some processing on it, and at some future time writes it back to disk. *Recall that* reading or writing a block from disk takes on the order of one million times longer than a memory access. Based on this fact, we can reasonably expect that the records contained in a single block can be sorted by an internal sorting algorithm such as *Quicksort* in less time than is required to read or write the block.

Under good conditions, reading from a file in sequential order is more efficient than reading blocks in random order. Given the significant impact of seek time on disk access, it might seem obvious that sequential processing is faster. However, it is important to understand precisely under what circumstances sequential file processing is actually faster than random access, because it affects our approach to designing an external sorting algorithm.

Efficient sequential access relies on seek time being kept to a minimum. The first requirement is that the blocks making up a file are in fact stored on disk in sequential order and close together, preferably filling a small number of contiguous tracks. At the very least, the number of extents making up the file should be small. Users typically do not have much control over the layout of their file on disk, but writing a file all at once in sequential order to a disk drive with a high percentage of free space increases the likelihood of such an arrangement.

The second requirement is that the disk drive's I/O head remain positioned over the file throughout sequential processing. This will not happen if there is competition of any kind for the I/O head. For example, on a multi-user time-shared computer the sorting process might compete for the I/O head with the processes of other users. Even when the sorting process has sole control of the I/O head, it is still likely that sequential processing will not be efficient. Imagine the situation where all processing is done on a single disk drive, with the typical arrangement of a single bank of read/write heads that move together over a stack of platters. If the sorting process involves reading from an input file, alternated with writing to an output file, then the I/O head will continuously seek between the input file and the output file. Similarly, if two input files are being processed simultaneously (such as during a merge process), then the I/O head will continuously seek between these two files.

The moral is that, with a single disk drive, there often is no such thing as efficient sequential processing of a data file. Thus, a sorting algorithm might be more efficient if it performs a smaller number of non-sequential disk operations rather than a larger number of logically sequential disk operations that require a large number of seeks in practice.

As mentioned previously, the record size might be quite large compared to the size of the key. For example, payroll entries for a large business might each store hundreds of bytes of information including the name, ID, address, and job title for each employee. The sort key might be the ID number, requiring only a few bytes. The simplest sorting algorithm might be to process such records as a whole, reading the entire record whenever it is processed. However, this will greatly increase the amount of I/O required, because only a relatively few records will fit into a single disk block. Another alternative is to do a *key sort*. Under this method, the keys are all read and stored together in an *index file*, where each key is stored along with a pointer indicating the position of the corresponding record in the original data file. The key and pointer combination should be substantially smaller than the size of the original record; thus, the index file will be much smaller than the complete data file. The index file will then be sorted, requiring much less I/O because the index records are smaller than the complete records.

Once the index file is sorted, it is possible to reorder the records in the original database file. This is typically not done for two reasons. First, reading the records in sorted order from the record file requires a random access for each record. This can take a substantial amount of time and is only of value if the complete collection of records needs to be viewed or processed in sorted order (as opposed to a search for selected records). Second, database systems typically allow searches to be done on multiple keys. For example, today's processing might be done in order of ID numbers. Tomorrow, the boss might want information sorted by salary. Thus, there might be no single "sorted" order for the full record. Instead, multiple index files are often maintained, one for each sort key.

Simple Approaches to External Sorting

If your operating system supports virtual memory, the simplest "external" sort is to read the entire file into virtual memory and run an internal sorting method such as Quicksort. This approach allows the virtual memory manager to use its normal buffer pool mechanism to control disk accesses. Unfortunately, this might not always be a viable option. One potential drawback is that the size of virtual memory is usually limited to something much smaller than the disk space available.

Thus, your input file might not fit into virtual memory. Limited virtual memory can be overcome by adapting an internal sorting method to make use of your own buffer pool.

A more general problem with adapting an internal sorting algorithm to external sorting is that it is not likely to be as efficient as designing a new algorithm with the specific goal of minimizing disk I/O. Consider the simple adaptation of Quicksort to use a buffer pool. Quicksort begins by processing the entire array of records, with the first partition step moving indices inward from the two ends. This can be implemented efficiently using a buffer pool. However, the next step is to process each of the subarrays, followed by processing of sub-subarrays, and so on. As the subarrays get smaller, processing quickly approaches random access to the disk drive. Even with maximum use of the buffer pool, Quicksort still must read and write each record logn times on average. We can do much better. Finally, even if the virtual memory manager can give good performance using a standard Quicksort, this will come at the cost of using a lot of the system's working memory, which will mean that the system cannot use this space for other work. Better methods can save time while also using less memory.

Our approach to external sorting is derived from the Mergesort algorithm. The simplest form of external Mergesort performs a series of sequential passes over the records, merging larger and larger sublists on each pass. The first pass merges sublists of size 1 into sublists of size 2; the second pass merges the sublists of size 2 into sublists of size 4; and so on. A sorted sublist is called a *run*. Thus, each pass is merging pairs of runs to form longer runs. Each pass copies the contents of the file to another file. Here is a sketch of the algorithm.

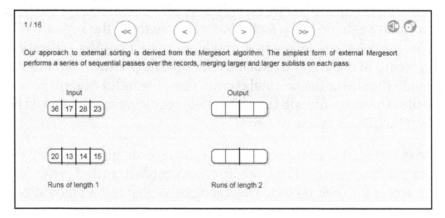

1. Split the original file into two equal-sized *run files*.

2. Read one block from each run file into input buffers.

3. Take the first record from each input buffer, and write a run of length two to an output buffer in sorted order.

4. Take the next record from each input buffer, and write a run of length two to a second output buffer in sorted order.

5. Repeat until finished, alternating output between the two output run buffers. Whenever the end of an input block is reached, read the next block from the appropriate input file. When an output buffer is full, write it to the appropriate output file.

6. Repeat steps 2 through 5, using the original output files as input files. On the second pass, the first two records of each input run file are already in sorted order. Thus, these two runs may be merged and output as a single run of four elements.

7. Each pass through the run files provides larger and larger runs until only one run remains.

This algorithm can easily take advantage of double buffering. Note that the various passes read the input run files sequentially and write the output run files sequentially. For sequential processing and double buffering to be effective, however, it is necessary that there be a separate I/O head available for each file. This typically means that each of the input and output files must be on separate disk drives, requiring a total of four disk drives for maximum efficiency.

Improving Performance

The external Mergesort algorithm just described requires that log n passes be made to sort a file of n records. Thus, each record must be read from disk and written to disk logn times. The number of passes can be significantly reduced by observing that it is not necessary to use Mergesort on small runs. A simple modification is to read in a block of data, sort it in memory (perhaps using Quicksort), and then output it as a single sorted run.

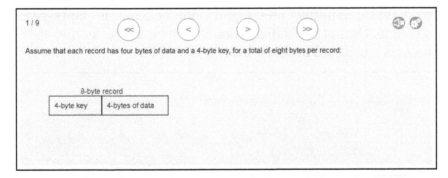

We can extend this concept to improve performance even further. Available main memory is usually much more than one block in size. If we process larger initial runs, then the number of passes required by Mergesort is further reduced. For example, most modern computers can provide tens or even hundreds of megabytes of RAM to the sorting program. If all of this memory (excepting a small amount for buffers and local variables) is devoted to building initial runs as large as possible, then quite large files can be processed in few passes.

Another way to reduce the number of passes required is to increase the number of runs that are merged together during each pass. While the standard Mergesort algorithm merges two runs at a time, there is no reason why merging needs to be limited in this way.

Over the years, many variants on external sorting have been presented, but all are based on the following two steps:

1. Break the file into large initial runs.

2. Merge the runs together to form a single sorted file.

Replacement Selection

Here we treat the problem of creating initial runs as large as possible from a disk file, assuming a fixed amount of RAM is available for processing. As mentioned previously, a simple approach is to allocate as much RAM as possible to a large array, fill this array from disk, and sort the array using Quicksort. Thus, if the size of memory available for the array is M records, then the input file can be broken into initial runs of length M. A better approach is to use an algorithm called replacement selection that, on average, creates runs of 2M records in length. Replacement selection is actually a slight variation on the Heapsort algorithm. The fact that Heapsort is slower than Quicksort is irrelevant in this context because I/O time will dominate the total running time of any reasonable external sorting algorithm. Building longer initial runs will reduce the total I/O time required.

Replacement selection views RAM as consisting of an array of size M in addition to an input buffer and an output buffer. (Additional I/O buffers might be desirable if the operating system supports double buffering, because replacement selection does sequential processing on both its input and its output.) Imagine that the input and output files are streams of records. Replacement selection takes the next record in sequential order from the input stream when needed, and outputs runs one record at a time to the output stream. Buffering is used so that disk I/O is performed one block at a time. A block of records is initially read and held in the input buffer. Replacement selection removes records from the input buffer one at a time until the buffer is empty. At this point the next block of records is read in. Output to a buffer is similar: Once the buffer fills up it is written to disk as a unit. This process is illustrated by figure below.

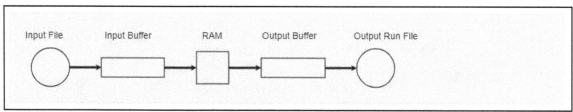

Overview of replacement selection.

Input records are processed sequentially. Initially RAM is filled with M records. As records are processed, they are written to an output buffer. When this buffer becomes full, it is written to disk. Meanwhile, as replacement selection needs records, it reads them from the input buffer. Whenever this buffer becomes empty, the next block of records is read from disk.

Replacement selection works as follows. Assume that the main processing is done in an array of size M records.

1. Fill the array from disk. Set LAST = M-1.

2. Build a min-heap. (Recall that a min-heap is defined such that the record at each node has a key value less than the key values of its children.)

3. Repeat until the array is empty:

a) Send the record with the minimum key value (the root) to the output buffer.

b) Let R be the next record in the input buffer. If R's key value is greater than the key value just output:

   i.   Then place R at the root.

   ii. Else replace the root with the record in array position LAST, and place R at position LAST. Set LAST = LAST - 1.

c) Sift down the root to reorder the heap.

When the test at step 3(b) is successful, a new record is added to the heap, eventually to be output as part of the run. As long as records coming from the input file have key values greater than the last key value output to the run, they can be safely added to the heap. Records with smaller key values cannot be output as part of the current run because they would not be in sorted order. Such values must be stored somewhere for future processing as part of another run. However, because the heap will shrink by one element in this case, there is now a free space where the last element of the heap used to be. Thus, replacement selection will slowly shrink the heap and at the same time use the discarded heap space to store records for the next run. Once the first run is complete (i.e., the heap becomes empty), the array will be filled with records ready to be processed for the second run. Here is a visualization to show a run being created by replacement selection.

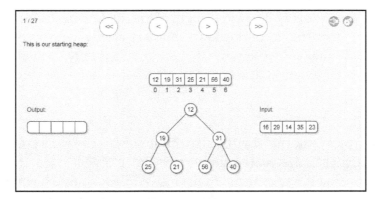

It should be clear that the minimum length of a run will be M records if the size of the heap is M, because at least those records originally in the heap will be part of the run. Under good conditions (e.g., if the input is sorted), then an arbitrarily long run is possible. In fact, the entire file could be processed as one run. If conditions are bad (e.g., if the input is reverse sorted), then runs of only size M result.

What is the expected length of a run generated by replacement selection? It can be deduced from an analogy called the snowplow argument. Imagine that a snowplow is going around a circular track during a heavy, but steady, snowstorm. After the plow has been around at least once, snow on the track must be as follows. Immediately behind the plow, the track is empty because it was just plowed. The greatest level of snow on the track is immediately in front of the plow, because this is the place least recently plowed. At any instant, there is a certain amount of snow S on the track. Snow is constantly falling throughout the track at a steady rate, with some snow falling "in front" of the plow and some "behind" the plow. During the next revolution of the plow, all snow S on the track is removed, plus half of what falls. Because everything is assumed to be in steady state, after one revolution S snow is still on the track, so 2S snow must fall during a revolution, and 2S snow is removed during a revolution (leaving S snow behind).

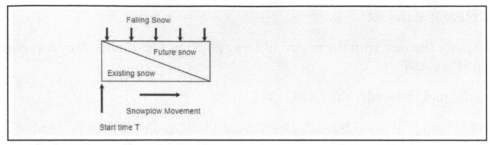

The snowplow analogy showing the action during one revolution of the snowplow.

A circular track is laid out straight for purposes of illustration, and is shown in cross section. At any time T, the most snow is directly in front of the snowplow. As the plow moves around the track, the same amount of snow is always in front of the plow. As the plow moves forward, less of this is snow that was in the track at time T; more is snow that has fallen since.

At the beginning of replacement selection, nearly all values coming from the input file are greater (i.e., "in front of the plow") than the latest key value output for this run, because the run's initial key values should be small. As the run progresses, the latest key value output becomes greater and so new key values coming from the input file are more likely to be too small (i.e., "after the plow"); such records go to the bottom of the array. The total length of the run is expected to be twice the size of the array. Of course, this assumes that incoming key values are evenly distributed within the key range (in terms of the snowplow analogy, we assume that snow falls evenly throughout the track). Sorted and reverse sorted inputs do not meet this expectation and so change the length of the run.

Multiway Merging

The second stage of a typical external sorting algorithm merges the runs created by the first stage. Assume that we have R runs to merge. If a simple two-way merge is used, then R runs (regardless of their sizes) will require log R passes through the file. While R should be much less than the total number of records (because the initial runs should each contain many records), we would like to reduce still further the number of passes required to merge the runs together. Note that two-way merging does not make good use of available memory. Because merging is a sequential process on the two runs, only one block of records per run need be in memory at a time. Keeping more than one block of a run in memory at any time will not reduce the disk I/O required by the merge process (though if several blocks are read from a file at once time, at least they take advantage of sequential access). Thus, most of the space just used by the heap for replacement selection (typically many blocks in length) is not being used by the merge process.

We can make better use of this space and at the same time greatly reduce the number of passes needed to merge the runs if we merge several runs at a time. Multiway merging is similar to two-way merging. If we have B runs to merge, with a block from each run available in memory, then the B-way merge algorithm simply looks at B values (the front-most value for each input run) and selects the smallest one to output. This value is removed from its run, and the process is repeated. When the current block for any run is exhausted, the next block from that run is read from disk.

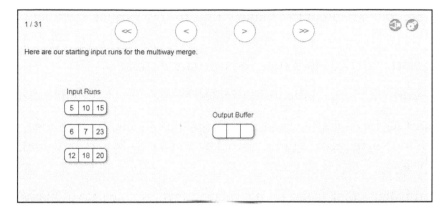

Conceptually, multiway merge assumes that each run is stored in a separate file. However, this is not necessary in practice. We only need to know the position of each run within a single file, and use seek to move to the appropriate block whenever we need new data from a particular run. Naturally, this approach destroys the ability to do sequential processing on the input file. However, if all runs were stored on a single disk drive, then processing would not be truly sequential anyway because the I/O head would be alternating between the runs. Thus, multiway merging replaces several (potentially) sequential passes with a single random access pass. If the processing would not be sequential anyway (such as when all processing is on a single disk drive), no time is lost by doing so.

Multiway merging can greatly reduce the number of passes required. If there is room in memory to store one block for each run, then all runs can be merged in a single pass. Thus, replacement selection can build initial runs in one pass, and multiway merging can merge all runs in one pass, yielding a total cost of two passes. However, for truly large files, there might be too many runs for each to get a block in memory. If there is room to allocate B blocks for a B-way merge, and the number of runs R is greater than B, then it will be necessary to do multiple merge passes. In other words, the first B runs are merged, then the next B, and so on. These super-runs are then merged by subsequent passes, B super-runs at a time.

How big a file can be merged in one pass? Assuming B blocks were allocated to the heap for replacement selection (resulting in runs of average length 2B blocks), followed by a B-way merge, we can process on average a file of size (2B^2) blocks in a single multiway merge. $2Bk^{+1}$ blocks on average can be processed in k B-way merges. To gain some appreciation for how quickly this grows, assume that we have available 0.5MB of working memory, and that a block is 4KB, yielding 128 blocks in working memory. The average run size is 1MB (twice the working memory size). In one pass, 128 runs can be merged. Thus, a file of size 128MB can, on average, be processed in two passes (one to build the runs, one to do the merge) with only 0.5MB of working memory. As another example, assume blocks are 1KB long and working memory is 1MB = 1024 blocks. Then 1024 runs of average length 2MB (which is about 2GB) can be combined in a single merge pass. A larger block size would reduce the size of the file that can be processed in one merge pass for a fixed-size working memory; a smaller block size or larger working memory would increase the file size that can be processed in one merge pass. Two merge passes allow much bigger files to be processed. With 0.5MB of working memory and 4KB blocks, a file of size 16~gigabytes could be processed in two merge passes, which is big enough for most applications. Thus, this is a very effective algorithm for single disk drive external sorting.

Table below shows a comparison of the running time to sort various-sized files for the following implementations:

(1) standard Mergesort with two input runs and two output runs.

(2) two-way Mergesort with large initial runs (limited by the size of available memory).

(3) R-way Mergesort performed after generating large initial runs. In each case, the file was composed of a series of four-byte records (a two-byte key and a two-byte data value), or 256K records per megabyte of file size.

We can see from this table that using even a modest memory size (two blocks) to create initial runs results in a tremendous savings in time. Doing 4-way merges of the runs provides another considerable speedup, however large-scale multi-way merges for R beyond about 4 or 8 runs does not help much because a lot of time is spent determining which is the next smallest element among the R runs.

A comparison of three external sorts on a collection of small records for files of various sizes. Each entry in the table shows time in seconds and total number of blocks read and written by the program. File sizes are in Megabytes. For the third sorting algorithm, on a file size of 4MB, the time and blocks shown in the last column are for a 32-way merge (marked with an asterisk). 32 is used instead of 16 because 32 is a root of the number of blocks in the file (while 16 is not), thus allowing the same number of runs to be merged at every pass.

File Size (Mb)	Sort 1	Sort 2 Memory size (in blocks)				Sort 3 Memory size (in blocks)		
		2	4	16	256	2	4	16
1	0.61 4,864	0.27 2,048	0.24 1,792	0.19 1,280	0.10 256	0.21 2,048	0.15 1,024	0.13 512
4	2.56 21,504	1.30 10,240	1.19 9,216	0.96 7,168	0.61 3,072	1.15 10,240	0.68 5,120	0.66* 2,048
16	11.28 94,208	6.12 49,152	5.63 45,056	4.78 36,864	3.36 20,480	5.42 49,152	3.19 24,516	3.10 12,288
256	220.39 1,769k	132.47 1,048K	123.68 983K	110.01 852K	86.66 589K	115.73 1,049K	69.31 524K	68.71 262K

We see from this experiment that building large initial runs reduces the running time to slightly more than one third that of standard Mergesort, depending on file and memory sizes. Using a multi-way merge further cuts the time nearly in half.

Distribution Sorts

Any sort algorithm where items are distributed from the input to multiple intermediate structures, which are then gathered and placed on the output.

Bucket Sort

Bucket sort is a comparison sort algorithm that operates on elements by dividing them into different buckets and then sorting these buckets individually. Each bucket is sorted individually using a separate sorting algorithm or by applying the bucket sort algorithm recursively. Bucket sort is mainly useful when the input is uniformly distributed over a range.

Assume one has the following problem in front of them:

One has been given a large array of floating point integers lying uniformly between the lower and upper bound. This array now needs to be sorted. A simple way to solve this problem would be to use another sorting algorithm such as Merge sort, Heap Sort or Quick Sort. However, these algorithms guarantee a best case time complexity of O(NlogN). However, using bucket sort, the above task can be completed in O(N) time. Let's have a closer look at it.

Consider one needs to create an array of lists, i.e of buckets. Elements now need to be inserted into these buckets on the basis of their properties. Each of these buckets can then be sorted individually using Insertion Sort. Consider the pseudo code to do so:

```
void bucketSort(float[] a,int n)
{
    for(each floating integer 'x' in n)
    {
        insert x into bucket[n*x];
    }
    for(each bucket)
    {
        sort(bucket);
    }
}
```

Time Complexity

If one assumes that insertion in a bucket takes O(1) time, then steps 1 and 2 of the above algorithm clearly take O(n) time.

Steps on How it Works

1. Create an empty array.

2. Loop through the original array and put each object in a "bucket".

3. Sort each of the non-empty buckets.

4. Check the buckets in order and then put all objects back into the original array.

Below is an image of an array, which needs to be sorted. We will use the Bucket Sort Algorithm, to sort this array:

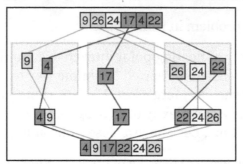

Bucket sort moves elements to buckets, then sorts the buckets.

And here is another image:

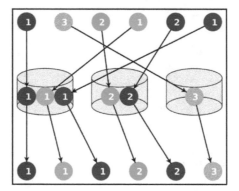

Bucket Sort: An Example

Here is an example of writing the Bucket Sort Algorithm based on the steps we provided earlier. Below, there is a function, which accepts the following parameter: an array and a key. The function returns the sorted array.

```js
bucketSort.js
function bucketSort(array, key) {
    key = key || function(x) { return x };
    var buckets = [],
        i, j, b, d = 0;
    for (; d < 32; d += 4) {
        for (i = 16; i--;)
            buckets[i] = [];
        for (i = array.length; i--;)
            buckets[(key(array[i]) >> d) & 15].push(array[i]);
        for (b = 0; b < 16; b++)
            for (j = buckets[b].length; j--;)
                array[++i] = buckets[b][j];
    }
    return a;
}
```

Characteristics of Bucket Sort

- Bucket sort assumes that the input is drawn from a uniform distribution.

- The computational complexity estimates involve the number of buckets.

- Bucket sort can be exceptionally fast because of the way elements are assigned to buckets, typically using an array where the index is the value.

- This means that more auxiliary memory is required for the buckets at the cost of running time than more comparison sorts.

- The average time complexity for Bucket Sort is $O(n + k)$. The worst time complexity is $O(n^2)$.

- The space complexity for Bucket Sort is $O(n+k)$.

Variants

Generic Bucket Sort

The most common variant of bucket sort operates on a list of n numeric inputs between zero and some maximum value M and divides the value range into n buckets each of size M/n. If each bucket is sorted using insertion sort, the sort can be shown to run in expected linear time (where the average is taken over all possible inputs). However, the performance of this sort degrades with clustering; if many values occur close together, they will all fall into a single bucket and be sorted slowly. This performance degradation is avoided in the original bucket sort algorithm by assuming that the input is generated by a random process that distributes elements uniformly over the interval $[0,1)$. Since there are n uniformly distributed elements sorted in to n buckets the probable number of inputs in each bucket follows a binomial distribution with $E(n_i) = 1$ and hence the entire bucket sort will be $O(n)$ despite the repeated use of $O(n^2)$ insertion sort.

ProxmapSort

Similar to generic bucket sort as described above, ProxmapSort works by dividing an array of keys into subarrays via the use of a "map key" function that preserves a partial ordering on the keys; as each key is added to its subarray, insertion sort is used to keep that subarray sorted, resulting in the entire array being in sorted order when ProxmapSort completes. ProxmapSort differs from bucket sorts in its use of the map key to place the data approximately where it belongs in sorted order, producing a "proxmap" a proximity mapping of the keys.

Histogram Sort

Another variant of bucket sort known as histogram sort or counting sort adds an initial pass that counts the number of elements that will fall into each bucket using a count array. Using this information, the array values can be arranged into a sequence of buckets in-place by a sequence of exchanges, leaving no space overhead for bucket storage.

Postman's Sort

The Postman's sort is a variant of bucket sort that takes advantage of a hierarchical structure of elements, typically described by a set of attributes. This is the algorithm used by letter-sorting machines in post offices: mail is sorted first between domestic and international; then by state, province or territory; then by destination post office; then by routes, etc. Since keys are not compared against each other, sorting time is $O(cn)$, where c depends on the size of the key and number of buckets. This is similar to a radix sort that works "top down," or "most significant digit first."

Shuffle Sort

The shuffle sort is a variant of bucket sort that begins by removing the first 1/8 of the n items to be sorted, sorts them recursively, and puts them in an array. This creates $n/8$ "buckets" to which the remaining 7/8 of the items are distributed. Each "bucket" is then sorted, and the "buckets" are concatenated into a sorted array.

Comparison with other Sorting Algorithms

Bucket sort can be seen as a generalization of counting sort; in fact, if each bucket has size 1 then bucket sort degenerates to counting sort. The variable bucket size of bucket sort allows it to use $O(n)$ memory instead of $O(M)$ memory, where M is the number of distinct values; in exchange, it gives up counting sort's $O(n + M)$ worst-case behavior.

Bucket sort with two buckets is effectively a version of quicksort where the pivot value is always selected to be the middle value of the value range. While this choice is effective for uniformly distributed inputs, other means of choosing the pivot in quicksort such as randomly selected pivots make it more resistant to clustering in the input distribution.

The n-way mergesort algorithm also begins by distributing the list into n sublists and sorting each one; however, the sublists created by mergesort have overlapping value ranges and so cannot be recombined by simple concatenation as in bucket sort. Instead, they must be interleaved by a merge algorithm. However, this added expense is counterbalanced by the simpler scatter phase and the ability to ensure that each sublist is the same size, providing a good worst-case time bound.

Top-down radix sort can be seen as a special case of bucket sort where both the range of values and the number of buckets is constrained to be a power of two. Consequently, each bucket's size is also a power of two, and the procedure can be applied recursively. This approach can accelerate the scatter phase, since we only need to examine a prefix of the bit representation of each element to determine its bucket.

Counting Sort

Counting sort is an algorithm for sorting a collection of objects according to keys that are small integers; that is, it is an integer sorting algorithm. It operates by counting the number of objects that have each distinct key value, and using arithmetic on those counts to determine the positions of each key value in the output sequence. Its running time is linear in the number of items and the difference between the maximum and minimum key values, so it is only suitable for direct use in situations where the variation in keys is not significantly greater than the number of items. However, it is often used as a subroutine in another sorting algorithm, radix sort, that can handle larger keys more efficiently.

Because counting sort uses key values as indexes into an array, it is not a comparison sort, and the $\Omega(n \log n)$ lower bound for comparison sorting does not apply to it. Bucket sort may be used for many of the same tasks as counting sort, with a similar time analysis; however, compared to counting sort, bucket sort requires linked lists, dynamic arrays or a large amount of preallocated memory to hold the sets of items within each bucket, whereas counting sort instead stores a single number (the count of items) per bucket.

The Algorithm

In summary, the algorithm loops over the items, computing a histogram of the number of times each key occurs within the input collection. It then performs a prefix sum computation (a second loop, over the range of possible keys) to determine, for each key, the starting position in the output array of the items having that key. Finally, it loops over the items again, moving each item into its sorted position in the output array.

In pseudocode, this may be expressed as follows:

```
# variables:

#    input -- the array of items to be sorted;

#    key(x) -- function that returns the key for item x

#    k -- a number such that all keys are in the range 0..k-1

#    count -- an array of numbers, with indexes 0..k-1, initially all zero

#    output -- an array of items, with indexes 0..n-1

#    x -- an individual input item, used within the algorithm

#    total, oldCount, i -- numbers used within the algorithm


# calculate the histogram of key frequencies:

for x in input:

    count[key(x)] += 1


# calculate the starting index for each key:

total = 0

for i in range(k):    # i = 0, 1, ... k-1

    oldCount = count[i]

    count[i] = total

    total += oldCount


# copy to output array, preserving order of inputs with equal keys:
```

```
for x in input:

    output[count[key(x)]] = x

    count[key(x)] += 1


return output
```

After the first for loop, count[i] stores the number of items with key equal to i. After the second for loop, it instead stores the number of items with key less than i, which is the same as the first index at which an item with key i should be stored in the output array. Throughout the third loop, count[i] always stores the next position in the output array into which an item with key i should be stored, so each item is moved into its correct position in the output array. The relative order of items with equal keys is preserved here; i.e., this is a stable sort.

Complexity Analysis

Because the algorithm uses only simple for loops, without recursion or subroutine calls, it is straightforward to analyze. The initialization of the count array, and the second for loop which performs a prefix sum on the count array, each iterate at most $k + 1$ times and therefore take $O(k)$ time. The other two for loops, and the initialization of the output array, each take $O(n)$ time. Therefore, the time for the whole algorithm is the sum of the times for these steps, $O(n + k)$.

Because it uses arrays of length $k + 1$ and n, the total space usage of the algorithm is also $O(n + k)$. For problem instances in which the maximum key value is significantly smaller than the number of items, counting sort can be highly space-efficient, as the only storage it uses other than its input and output arrays is the Count array which uses space $O(k)$.

Variant Algorithms

If each item to be sorted is itself an integer, and used as key as well, then the second and third loops of counting sort can be combined; in the second loop, instead of computing the position where items with key i should be placed in the output, simply append Count[i] copies of the number i to the output.

This algorithm may also be used to eliminate duplicate keys, by replacing the Count array with a bit vector that stores a one for a key that is present in the input and a zero for a key that is not present. If additionally the items are the integer keys themselves, both second and third loops can be omitted entirely and the bit vector will itself serve as output, representing the values as offsets of the non-zero entries, added to the range's lowest value. Thus the keys are sorted and the duplicates are eliminated in this variant just by being placed into the bit array.

For data in which the maximum key size is significantly smaller than the number of data items, counting sort may be parallelized by splitting the input into subarrays of approximately equal size, processing each subarray in parallel to generate a separate count array for each subarray, and then merging the count arrays. When used as part of a parallel radix sort algorithm, the key size (base of the radix representation) should be chosen to match the size of the split subarrays. The simplicity of the counting sort algorithm and its use of the easily parallelizable prefix sum primitive also make it usable in more fine-grained parallel algorithms.

Counting sort is not an in-place algorithm; even disregarding the count array, it needs separate input and output arrays. It is possible to modify the algorithm so that it places the items into sorted order within the same array that was given to it as the input, using only the count array as auxiliary storage; however, the modified in-place version of counting sort is not stable.

Radix Sort

Radix Sort is an algorithm that sorts a list of numbers and comes under the category of distribution sort. This sorting algorithm doesn't compare the numbers but distributes them, it works as follows:

1. Sorting takes place by distributing the list of number into a bucket by passing through the individual digits of a given number one-by-one beginning with the least significant part. Here, the number of buckets are a total of ten, which bare key values starting from 0 to 9.

2. After each pass, the numbers are collected from the buckets, keeping the numbers in order.

3. Now, recursively redistribute the numbers as in the above step '1' but with a following re-consideration: take into account next most significant part of the number, which is then followed by above step '2'.

Radix Sort arranges the elements in order by comparing the digits of the numbers.

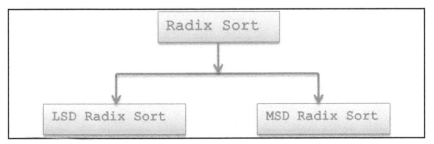

LSD Radix Sort

Least-significant-digit-first radix sort.

LSD radix sorts process the integer representations starting from the least significant digit and move the processing towards the most significant digit.

MSD Radix Sort

Most-significant-digit-first radix sort.

MSD radix sort starts processing the keys from the most significant digit, leftmost digit, to the least significant digit, rightmost digit. This sequence is opposite that of least significant digit (LSD) radix sorts.

Algorithm of Radix Sort

1. RADIX-SORT (A ,d)

2.

3. 1) for i ? 1 to d;

4.

5. 2) do use a stable sort to sort Array A on digit i // counting sort will do the job//

6.

c Fuction for radix sort

```
1. radix_sort(int arr[], int n)

2.

3. {

4.

5.    int bucket[10][5],buck[10],b[10];

6.

7.    int i,j,k,l,num,div,large,passes;

8.

9.

10.

11.   div=1;

12.

13.   num=0;

14.

15.   large=arr[0];

16.

17.

18.

19.   for(i=0 ; i< n ; i++)

20.

21.   {

22.
```

```
23.          if(arr[i] > large)

24.

25.              {

26.

27.                  large = arr[i];

28.

29.              }

30.

31.          while(large > 0)

32.

33.              {

34.

35.                  num++;

36.

37.                  large = large/10;

38.

39.              }

40.

41.          for(passes=0 ; passes < num ; passes++)

42.

43.              {

44.

45.                  for(k=0 ; k< 10 ; k++)

46.

47.                      {

48.

49.                          buck[k] = 0;

50.

51.                      }

52.
```

```
53.                for(i=0 ; i< n  ;i++)

54.

55.                {

56.

57.                        l = ((arr[i]/div)%10);

58.

59.                        bucket[l][buck[l]++] = arr[i];

60.

61.                }

62.

63.

64.

65.           i=0;

66.

67.           for(k=0 ; k < 10 ; k++)

68.

69.           {

70.

71.                        for(j=0 ; j < buck[k] ; j++)

72.

73.                    {

74.

75.                            arr[i++] = bucket[k][j];

76.

77.                    }

78.

79.           }

80.

81.           div*=10;

82.
```

```
83.              }

84.

85.   }

86.

87. }

88.
```

Implementation of Radix Sort

```
1.      #include<stdio.h>

2.

3.      #include<conio.h>

4.

5.

6.

7.      radix_sort(int array[], int n);

8.

9.      void main()

10.

11.     {

12.

13.             int array[100],n,i;

14.

15.             clrscr();

16.

17.             printf("Enter the number of elements to be sorted: ");

18.

19.             scanf("%d",&n);

20.

21.             printf("\nEnter the elements to be sorted: \n");

22.

23.             for(i = 0 ; i < n ; i++ )
```

```
24.
25.            {
26.
27.                    scanf("%d",&array[i]);
28.
29.            }
30.
31.
32.
33.            printf("\nBefore Radix Sort:");
34.
35.            for(i = 0; i < n; i++)
36.
37.            {
38.
39.                    printf("%d\t", array[i]);
40.
41.            }
42.
43.            printf("\n");
44.
45.            radix_sort(array,n);
46.
47.            printf("\nArray After Radix Sort: ");   //Array After Radix Sort
48.
49.            for(i = 0; i < n; i++)
50.
51.            {
52.
53.                    printf("%d\t", array[i]);
```

```
54.

55.            }

56.

57.            printf("\n");

58.

59.            getch();

60.

61.     }

62.

63.

64.

65.    radix_sort(int arr[], int n)

66.

67.     {

68.

69.            int bucket[10][5],buck[10],b[10];

70.

71.            int i,j,k,l,num,div,large,passes;

72.

73.

74.

75.            div=1;

76.

77.            num=0;

78.

79.            large=arr[0];

80.

81.

82.

83.            for(i=0 ; i < n ; i++)
```

```
84.

85.              {

86.

87.                   if(arr[i] > large)

88.

89.                   {

90.

91.                        large = arr[i];

92.

93.                   }

94.

95.                   while(large > 0)

96.

97.                   {

98.

99.                        num++;

100.

101.                       large = large/10;

102.

103.                  }

104.

105.                  for(passes=0 ; passes < num ; passes++)

106.

107.                  {

108.

109.                       for(k=0 ; k < 10 ; k++)

110.

111.                       {

112.

113.                            buck[k] = 0;
```

```
114.
115.                          }
116.
117.                          for(i=0 ; i < n   ;i++)
118.
119.                              {
120.
121.                                  l = ((arr[i]/div)%10);
122.
123.                                  bucket[l][buck[l]++] = arr[i];
124.
125.                              }
126.
127.
128.
129.                          i=0;
130.
131.                          for(k=0 ; k< 10 ; k++)
132.
133.                              {
134.
135.                                  for(j=0 ; j < buck[k] ; j++)
136.
137.                                      {
138.
139.                                          arr[i++] = bucket[k][j];
140.
141.                                      }
142.
143.                              }
```

```
144.

145.                              div*=10;

146.

147.                   }

148.

149.             }

150.

151.    }
```

OUTPUT

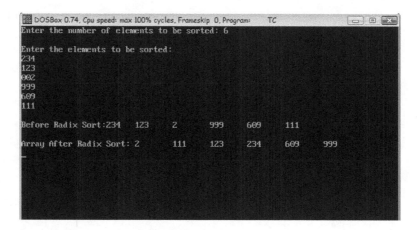

Consider a group of numbers. It is given by the list:

123, 002, 999, 609, 111

STEP1:

Sort the list of numbers according to the ascending order of least significant bit. The sorted list is given by:

111, 002, 123, 999, 609

STEP2:

Then sort the list of numbers according to the ascending order of 1st significant bit. The sorted list is given by:

609, 002, 111, 123, 999

STEP3:

Then sort the list of numbers according to the ascending order of most significant bit. The sorted list is given by:

002, 111, 123, 609, 999

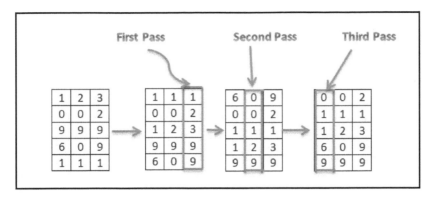

Analysis Of Radix sort	
Class	Sorting algoritdm
Data structure	Array
Worst case performance	O(K N)
Worst case space complexity	O(K N)

References

- MacIver, David R. (11 January 2010). "Understanding timsort, Part 1: Adaptive Mergesort". Retrieved 2015-12-05

- Know-your-sorting-algorithm-set-2-introsort-cs-sorting-weapon: geeksforgeeks.org, Retrieved 22 June 2020

- Bubble-sort-algorithm, data-structures-algorithms: tutorialspoint.com, Retrieved 31 July 2020

- Block-Merge-Sort-51222: algoritmy.net, Retrieved 19 March 2020

- Sorting-algorithm: whatis.techtarget.com, Retrieved 20 May 2020

- Selection-sorting, data-structures: studytonight.com, Retrieved 28 June 2020

- Edmonds, Jeff (2008), "5.2 Counting Sort (a Stable Sort)", How to Think about Algorithms, Cambridge University Press, pp. 72–75, ISBN 978-0-521-84931-9

Search Algorithms

Search algorithms are algorithms used to solve a search problem in order to retrieve the information stored in a data structure having discrete or continuous values. The appropriate search algorithm often depends on the data structure being searched. The concepts discussed in this chapter will help in gaining a better perspective about search algorithms and hash function.

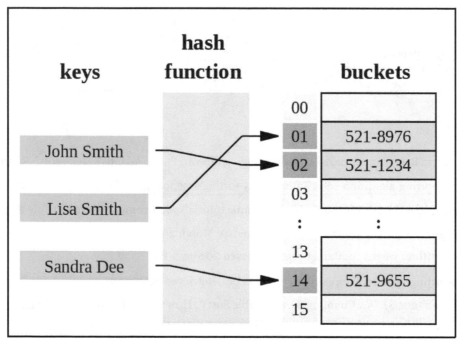

Visual representation of a hash table, a data structure that allows for fast retrieval of information.

In computer science, a search algorithm is an algorithm that retrieves information stored within some data structure. Data structures can include linked lists, arrays, search trees, hash tables, or various other storage methods. The appropriate search algorithm often depends on the data structure being searched. Searching also encompasses algorithms that query the data structure, such as the SQL SELECT command.

Search algorithms can be classified based on their mechanism of searching. Linear search algorithms check every record for the one associated with a target key in a linear fashion. Binary, or half interval searches, repeatedly target the center of the search structure and divide the search space in half. Comparison search algorithms improve on linear searching by successively eliminating records based on comparisons of the keys until the target record is found, and can be applied on data structures with a defined order. Digital search algorithms work based on the properties of digits in data structures that use numerical keys. Finally, hashing directly maps keys to records based on a hash function. Searches outside of a linear search require that the data be sorted in some way.

Search functions are also evaluated on the basis of their complexity, or maximum theoretical run time. Binary search functions, for example, have a maximum complexity of O(log(n)), or logarithmic time. This means that the maximum number of operations needed to find the search target is a logarithmic function of the size of the search space.

Classes

For Virtual Search Spaces

Algorithms for searching virtual spaces are used in constraint satisfaction problem, where the goal is to find a set of value assignments to certain variables that will satisfy specific mathematical equations and inequations / inequalities. They are also used when the goal is to find a variable assignment that will maximize or minimize a certain function of those variables. Algorithms for these problems include the basic brute-force search (also called "naïve" or "uninformed" search), and a variety of heuristics that try to exploit partial knowledge about structure of the space, such as linear relaxation, constraint generation, and constraint propagation.

An important subclass are the local search methods, that view the elements of the search space as the vertices of a graph, with edges defined by a set of heuristics applicable to the case; and scan the space by moving from item to item along the edges, for example according to the steepest descent or best-first criterion, or in a stochastic search. This category includes a great variety of general metaheuristic methods, such as simulated annealing, tabu search, A-teams, and genetic programming, that combine arbitrary heuristics in specific ways.

This class also includes various tree search algorithms, that view the elements as vertices of a tree, and traverse that tree in some special order. Examples of the latter include the exhaustive methods such as depth-first search and breadth-first search, as well as various heuristic-based search tree pruning methods such as backtracking and branch and bound. Unlike general metaheuristics, which at best work only in a probabilistic sense, many of these tree-search methods are guaranteed to find the exact or optimal solution, if given enough time. This is called "completeness".

Another important sub-class consists of algorithms for exploring the game tree of multiple-player games, such as chess or backgammon, whose nodes consist of all possible game situations that could result from the current situation. The goal in these problems is to find the move that provides the best chance of a win, taking into account all possible moves of the opponent(s). Similar problems occur when humans or machines have to make successive decisions whose outcomes are not entirely under one's control, such as in robot guidance or in marketing, financial, or military strategy planning. This kind of problem — combinatorial search — has been extensively studied in the context of artificial intelligence. Examples of algorithms for this class are the minimax algorithm, alpha–beta pruning, * Informational search and the A* algorithm.

For Sub-structures of a Given Structure

The name "combinatorial search" is generally used for algorithms that look for a specific sub-structure of a given discrete structure, such as a graph, a string, a finite group, and so on. The term combinatorial optimization is typically used when the goal is to find a sub-structure with a maximum (or minimum) value of some parameter. (Since the sub-structure is usually represented in the computer by a set of integer variables with constraints, these problems can be viewed as special cases of constraint satisfaction or discrete optimization; but they are usually formulated and solved in a more abstract setting where the internal representation is not explicitly mentioned.)

An important and extensively studied subclass are the graph algorithms, in particular graph traversal algorithms, for finding specific sub-structures in a given graph — such as subgraphs, paths, circuits, and so on. Examples include Dijkstra's algorithm, Kruskal's algorithm, the nearest neighbour algorithm, and Prim's algorithm.

Another important subclass of this category are the string searching algorithms, that search for patterns within strings. Two famous examples are the Boyer–Moore and Knuth–Morris–Pratt algorithms, and several algorithms based on the suffix tree data structure.

Search for the Maximum of a Function

In 1953, American statistician Jack Kiefer devised Fibonacci search which can be used to find the maximum of a unimodal function and has many other applications in computer science.

For Quantum Computers

There are also search methods designed for quantum computers, like Corley's algorithm, that are theoretically faster than linear or brute-force search even without the help of data structures or heuristics.

Linear Search

In computer science, linear search or sequential search is a method for finding a target value within a list. It sequentially checks each element of the list for the target value until a match is found or until all the elements have been searched.

Linear search runs in at worst linear time and makes at most n comparisons, where n is the length of the list. If each element is equally likely to be searched, then linear search has an average case of $n/2$ comparisons, but the average case can be affected if the search probabilities for each element vary. Linear search is rarely practical because other search algorithms and schemes, such as the binary search algorithm and hash tables, allow significantly faster searching for all but short lists.

Algorithm

Linear search sequentially checks each element of the list until it finds an element that matches the target value. If the algorithm reaches the end of the list, the search terminates unsuccessfully.

Basic Algorithm

Given a list L of n elements with values or records $L_0 \dots L_{n-1}$, and target value T, the following subroutine uses linear search to find the index of the target T in L.

1. Set i to 0.

2. If $L_i = T$, the search terminates successfully; return i.

3. Increase i by 1.

4. If $i < n$, go to step 2. Otherwise, the search terminates unsuccessfully.

With a Sentinel

The basic algorithm above makes two comparisons per iteration: one to check if L_i equals t, and the other to check if i still points to a valid index of the list. By adding an extra record L_n to the list (a sentinel value) that equals the target, the second comparison can be eliminated until the end of the search, making the algorithm faster. The search will reach the sentinel if the target is not contained within the list.

1. Set i to 0.

2. If $L_i = T$, go to step 4.

3. Increase i by 1 and go to step 2.

4. If $i < n$, the search terminates successfully; return i. Else, the search terminates unsuccessfully.

In an Ordered Table

If the list is ordered such that $L_0 \le L_1 \ldots \le L_{n-1}$, the search can establish the absence of the target more quickly by concluding the search once L_i exceeds the target. This variation requires a sentinel that is greater than the target.

1. Set i to 0.

2. If $L_i \ge T$, go to step 4.

3. Increase i by 1 and go to step 2.

4. If $L_i = T$, the search terminates successfully; return i. Else, the search terminates unsuccessfully.

Analysis

For a list with n items, the best case is when the value is equal to the first element of the list, in which case only one comparison is needed. The worst case is when the value is not in the list (or occurs only once at the end of the list), in which case n comparisons are needed.

If the value being sought occurs k times in the list, and all orderings of the list are equally likely, the expected number of comparisons is:

$$\begin{cases} n & \text{if } k = 0 \\ \dfrac{n+1}{k+1} & \text{if } 1 \le k \le n. \end{cases}$$

For example, if the value being sought occurs once in the list, and all orderings of the list are equally likely, the expected number of comparisons is $\dfrac{n+1}{2}$. However, if it is *known* that it occurs once, then at most $n-1$ comparisons are needed, and the expected number of comparisons is:

$$\frac{(n+2)(n-1)}{2n}$$

(for example, for $n = 2$ this is 1, corresponding to a single if-then-else construct).

Either way, asymptotically the worst-case cost and the expected cost of linear search are both $O(n)$.

Non-uniform Probabilities

The performance of linear search improves if the desired value is more likely to be near the beginning of the list than to its end. Therefore, if some values are much more likely to be searched than others, it is desirable to place them at the beginning of the list.

In particular, when the list items are arranged in order of decreasing probability, and these probabilities are geometrically distributed, the cost of linear search is only $O(1)$. If the table size n is large enough, linear search will be faster than binary search, whose cost is $O(\log n)$.

Application

Linear search is usually very simple to implement, and is practical when the list has only a few elements, or when performing a single search in an unordered list.

When many values have to be searched in the same list, it often pays to pre-process the list in order to use a faster method. For example, one may sort the list and use binary search, or build any efficient search data structure from it. Should the content of the list change frequently, repeated re-organization may be more trouble than it is worth.

As a result, even though in theory other search algorithms may be faster than linear search (for instance binary search), in practice even on medium-sized arrays (around 100 items or less) it might be infeasible to use anything else. On larger arrays, it only makes sense to use other, faster search methods if the data is large enough, because the initial time to prepare (sort) the data is comparable to many linear searches.

Linear search is the most simple of all searching techniques. It is also called sequential search. To find an element with key value='key',every element of the list is checked for key value='k' sequentially one by one.If such an element with key=k is found out, then the search is stopped. But if we eventually reach the end of the list & still the required element is not found then also we terminate the search as an unsuccessful one.

The linear search can be applied for both unsorted & sorted list

- Linear search for Unsorted list.
- Linear search for sorted list.

In case of unsorted list, we have to search the entire list every time i.e.we have to keep on searching the list till we find the required element or we reach the end of the list.this is because as elements are not in any order,so any element can be found just anywhere.

Algorithm

```
linear search(int x[],int n,int key)

{

 int i,flag = 0;

 for(i=0;i < n ; i++)

  {

  if(x[i]==key)

  {

  flag=1;

  break;

  }

  }

  if(flag==0)

  return(-1);

  else

 return(1);

}
```

Complexity

The number of comparisons in this case is n-1.So it is of o(n). The implementation af algo is simple but the efficiency is not good. Everytime we have to search the whole array (if the element with required value is not found out).

The efficiency of linear search can be increased if we take a previously sorted array say in ascending order. Now in this case, the basic algorithm remains the same as we have done in case of an unsorted array but the only difference is we do not have to search the entire array everytime. Whenever we encounter an element say y greater than the key to be searched, we conclude that there is no such element which is equal to the key, in the list. This is because all the elements in the list are in ascending order and all elements to the right of y will be greater or equal to y, ie greater than the key. So there is no point in continuing the search even if the end of the list has not been reached and the required element has not been found.

```
Linear search( int x[], int n, int key)

{
```

```
int i, flag=0;

for(i=0; i < n && x[i] <= key; i++)

{

if(x[i]==key)

{

flag=1;

break;

}

}

if(flag==1) /* Unsuccessful Search*/

return(-1);

else return(1); /*Successful search*/

}
```

Illustrative Explanation

The array to be sorted is as follows:

21 35 41 65 72

It is sorted in ascending order. Now let key = 40. At first 21 is checked as [x]=21.

It is smaller than 40. So next element is checked which is 35 that is also smaller than 40. So now 41 is checked.But 41 > 40 & all elements to the right of 41 are also greater than 40.So we terminate the search as an unsuccessful one and we may not have to search the entire list.

Complexity

Searching is NOT more efficient when key is in present in the list in case when the search key value lies between the minimum and the maximum element in the list. The Complexity of linear search both in case of sorted and unsorted list is the same. The average complexity for linear search for sorted list is better than that in unsorted list since the search need not continue beyond an element with higher value than the search value.

Binary Search

The most efficient method of searching a sequential file is binary search. This method is applicable to elements of a sorted list only. In this method, to search an element we compare it with the center element of the list. If it matches, then the search is successful and it is terminated. But if it does not match, the list is divided into two halves. The first half consists of 0th element to the center element whereas the second list consists of the element next to the center element to the last element. Now It is obvious that all elements in first half will be < or = to the center element and all element elements in the second half will be > than the center element. If the element to be searched is greater than the center element then searching will be done in the second half, otherwise in the first half.

Same process of comparing the element to be searched with the center element & if not found then dividing the elements into two halves is repeated for the first or second half. This process is repeated till the required element is found or the division of half parts gives a single element.

Algorithm for Binary Search

Illustrative Explanation

Let the array to be sorted is as follows:

```
11 23 31 33 65 68 71 89 100
```

Now let the element to be searched ie `key = 31` At first `hi=8 low=0` so `mid=4` and `x[mid]= 65` is the center element but `65 > 31`. So now `hi = 4-1=3`. Now `mid= (0 + 3)/2 = 1`, so `x[mid]= 23 < 31`. So again `low= 1 + 1 = 2`. Now `mid = (3 + 2)/2 = 2 & x[mid]= 31 = key`. So the search is successful. Similarly had the key been 32 it would have been an unsuccessful search.

Complexity

This is highly efficient than linear search. Each comparision in the binary search reduces the no. of possible candidates by a factor of 2. So the maximum no. of key comparisions is equal to log(2,n) approx. So the complexity of binary search is O(log n).

Limitations

Binary search algorithm can only be used if the list to be searched is in array form and not linked list. This is because the algorithm uses the fact that the indices of the array elements are consecutive integers. This makes this algorithm useless for lists with many insertions and deletions which can be implemented only when the list is in the form of a linked list.

But this can be overcome using *padded list.*

Hash Function

A hash function is any function that can be used to map data of arbitrary size to data of fixed size. The values returned by a hash function are called hash values, hash codes, digests, or simply hashes. One use is a data structure called a hash table, widely used in computer software for rapid data lookup. Hash functions accelerate table or database lookup by detecting duplicated records in a large file. An example is finding similar stretches in DNA sequences. They are also useful in cryptography. A cryptographic hash function allows one to easily verify that some input data maps to a given hash value, but if the input data is unknown, it is deliberately difficult to reconstruct it (or equivalent alternatives) by knowing the stored hash value. This is used for assuring integrity of transmitted data, and is the building block for HMACs, which provide message authentication.

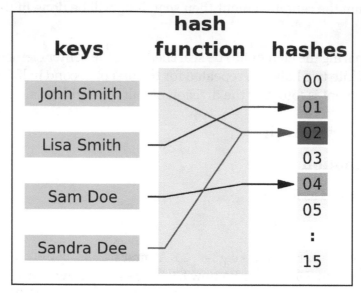

A hash function that maps names to integers from 0 to 15. There is a collision between keys "John Smith" and "Sandra Dee".

Hash functions are related to (and often confused with) checksums, check digits, fingerprints, lossy compression, randomization functions, error-correcting codes, and ciphers. Although these concepts overlap to some extent, each has its own uses and requirements and is designed and optimized differently. The Hash Keeper database maintained by the American National Drug Intelligence Center, for instance, is more aptly described as a catalogue of file fingerprints than of hash values.

Uses

Hash Tables

Hash functions are used in hash tables, to quickly locate a data record (e.g., a dictionary definition) given its search key (the headword). Specifically, the hash function is used to map the search key to an index; the index gives the place in the hash table where the corresponding record should be stored. Hash tables, in turn, are used to implement associative arrays and dynamic sets.

Typically, the domain of a hash function (the set of possible keys) is larger than its range (the number of different table indices), and so it will map several different keys to the same index. Therefore, each slot of a hash table is associated with (implicitly or explicitly) a set of records, rather than a single record. For this reason, each slot of a hash table is often called a *bucket*, and hash values are also called *bucket indices*.

Thus, the hash function only hints at the record's location — it tells where one should start looking for it. Still, in a half-full table, a good hash function will typically narrow the search down to only one or two entries.

Caches

Hash functions are also used to build caches for large data sets stored in slow media. A cache is generally simpler than a hashed search table, since any collision can be resolved by discarding or writing back the older of the two colliding items. This is also used in file comparison.

Bloom Filters

Hash functions are an essential ingredient of the Bloom filter, a space-efficient probabilistic data structure that is used to test whether an element is a member of a set.

Finding Duplicate Records

When storing records in a large unsorted file, one may use a hash function to map each record to an index into a table T, and to collect in each bucket $T[i]$ a list of the numbers of all records with the same hash value i. Once the table is complete, any two duplicate records will end up in the same bucket. The duplicates can then be found by scanning every bucket $T[i]$ which contains two or more members, fetching those records, and comparing them. With a table of appropriate size, this method is likely to be much faster than any alternative approach (such as sorting the file and comparing all consecutive pairs).

Protecting Data

A hash value can be used to uniquely identify secret information. This requires that the hash function is collision-resistant, which means that it is very hard to find data that will generate the same hash value. These functions are categorized into cryptographic hash functions and provably secure hash functions. Functions in the second category are the most secure but also too slow for most practical purposes. Collision resistance is accomplished in part by generating very large hash values. For example, SHA-1, one of the most widely used cryptographic hash functions, generates 160 bit values.

Finding Similar Records

Hash functions can also be used to locate table records whose key is similar, but not identical, to a given key; or pairs of records in a large file which have similar keys. For that purpose, one needs a hash function that maps similar keys to hash values that differ by at most m, where m is a small integer (say, 1 or 2). If one builds a table T of all record numbers, using such a hash function, then similar records will end up in the same bucket, or in nearby buckets. Then one need only check the records in each bucket $T[i]$ against those in buckets $T[i+k]$ where k ranges between $-m$ and m.

This class includes the so-called acoustic fingerprint algorithms, that are used to locate similar-sounding entries in large collection of audio files. For this application, the hash function must be as insensitive as possible to data capture or transmission errors, and to trivial changes such as timing and volume changes, compression, etc.

Finding Similar Substrings

The same techniques can be used to find equal or similar stretches in a large collection of strings, such as a document repository or a genomic database. In this case, the input strings are broken into many small pieces, and a hash function is used to detect potentially equal pieces, as above.

The Rabin–Karp algorithm is a relatively fast string searching algorithm that works in $O(n)$ time on average. It is based on the use of hashing to compare strings.

Geometric Hashing

This principle is widely used in computer graphics, computational geometry and many other disciplines, to solve many proximity problems in the plane or in three-dimensional space, such as finding closest pairs in a set of points, similar shapes in a list of shapes, similar images in an image database, and so on. In these applications, the set of all inputs is some sort of metric space, and the hashing function can be interpreted as a partition of that space into a grid of *cells*. The table is often an array with two or more indices (called a *grid file*, *grid index*, *bucket grid*, and similar names), and the hash function returns an index tuple. This special case of hashing is known as geometric hashing or *the grid method*. Geometric hashing is also used in telecommunications (usually under the name vector quantization) to encode and compress multi-dimensional signals.

Standard uses of Hashing in Cryptography

Some standard applications that employ hash functions include authentication, message integrity (using an HMAC (Hashed MAC)), message fingerprinting, data corruption detection, and digital signature efficiency.

Properties

Good hash functions, in the original sense of the term, are usually required to satisfy certain properties listed below. The exact requirements are dependent on the application, for example a hash function well suited to indexing data will probably be a poor choice for a cryptographic hash function.

Determinism

A hash procedure must be deterministic—meaning that for a given input value it must always generate the same hash value. In other words, it must be a function of the data to be hashed, in the mathematical sense of the term. This requirement excludes hash functions that depend on external variable parameters, such as pseudo-random number generators or the time of day. It also excludes functions that depend on the memory address of the object being hashed in cases that the address may change during execution (as may happen on systems that use certain methods of garbage collection), although sometimes rehashing of the item is possible.

The determinism is in the context of the reuse of the function. For example, Python adds the feature that hash functions make use of a randomized seed that is generated once when the Python process starts in addition to the input to be hashed. The Python hash is still a valid hash function when used in within a single run. But if the values are persisted (for example, written to disk) they can no longer be treated as valid hash values, since in the next run the random value might differ.

Uniformity

A good hash function should map the expected inputs as evenly as possible over its output range. That is, every hash value in the output range should be generated with roughly the same probability. The reason for this last requirement is that the cost of hashing-based methods goes up sharply as the number of *collisions*—pairs of inputs that are mapped to the same hash value—increases. If some hash values are more likely to occur than others, a larger fraction of the lookup operations will have to search through a larger set of colliding table entries.

Note that this criterion only requires the value to be *uniformly distributed*, not *random* in any sense. A good randomizing function is (barring computational efficiency concerns) generally a good choice as a hash function, but the converse need not be true.

Hash tables often contain only a small subset of the valid inputs. For instance, a club membership list may contain only a hundred or so member names, out of the very large set of all possible names. In these cases, the uniformity criterion should hold for almost all typical subsets of entries that may be found in the table, not just for the global set of all possible entries.

In other words, if a typical set of m records is hashed to n table slots, the probability of a bucket receiving many more than m/n records should be vanishingly small. In particular, if m is less than n, very few buckets should have more than one or two records. (In an ideal "perfect hash function", no bucket should have more than one record; but a small number of collisions is virtually inevitable, even if n is much larger than m).

When testing a hash function, the uniformity of the distribution of hash values can be evaluated by the chi-squared test.

Defined Range

It is often desirable that the output of a hash function have fixed size. If, for example, the output is constrained to 32-bit integer values, the hash values can be used to index into an array. Such hashing is commonly used to accelerate data searches. On the other hand, cryptographic hash functions produce much larger hash values, in order to ensure the computational complexity of brute-force inversion. For example, SHA-1, one of the most widely used cryptographic hash functions, produces a 160-bit value.

Producing fixed-length output from variable length input can be accomplished by breaking the input data into chunks of specific size. Hash functions used for data searches use some arithmetic expression which iteratively processes chunks of the input (such as the characters in a string) to produce the hash value. In cryptographic hash functions, these chunks are processed by a one-way compression function, with the last chunk being padded if necessary. In this case, their size, which is called *block size*, is much bigger than the size of the hash value. For example, in SHA-1, the hash value is 160 bits and the block size 512 bits.

Variable Range

In many applications, the range of hash values may be different for each run of the program, or may change along the same run (for instance, when a hash table needs to be expanded). In those situations, one needs a hash function which takes two parameters—the input data z, and the number n of allowed hash values.

A common solution is to compute a fixed hash function with a very large range (say, 0 to $2^{32} - 1$), divide the result by n, and use the division's remainder. If n is itself a power of 2, this can be done by bit masking and bit shifting. When this approach is used, the hash function must be chosen so that the result has fairly uniform distribution between 0 and $n - 1$, for any value of n that may occur in the application. Depending on the function, the remainder may be uniform only for certain values of n, e.g. odd or prime numbers.

We can allow the table size n to not be a power of 2 and still not have to perform any remainder or division operation, as these computations are sometimes costly. For example, let n be significantly less than 2^b. Consider a pseudorandom number generator (PRNG) function $P(\text{key})$ that is uniform on the interval $[0, 2^b - 1]$. A hash function uniform on the interval $[0, \text{n-1}]$ is $n\,P(\text{key})/2^b$. We can replace the division by a (possibly faster) right bit shift: $nP(\text{key}) >> b$.

Variable Range with Minimal Movement (Dynamic Hash Function)

When the hash function is used to store values in a hash table that outlives the run of the program, and the hash table needs to be expanded or shrunk, the hash table is referred to as a dynamic hash table.

A hash function that will relocate the minimum number of records when the table is – where z is the key being hashed and n is the number of allowed hash values – such that $H(z,n + 1) = H(z,n)$ with probability close to $n/(n + 1)$.

Linear hashing and spiral storage are examples of dynamic hash functions that execute in constant time but relax the property of uniformity to achieve the minimal movement property.

Extendible hashing uses a dynamic hash function that requires space proportional to n to compute the hash function, and it becomes a function of the previous keys that have been inserted.

Several algorithms that preserve the uniformity property but require time proportional to n to compute the value of $H(z,n)$ have been invented.

Data Normalization

In some applications, the input data may contain features that are irrelevant for comparison purposes. For example, when looking up a personal name, it may be desirable to ignore the distinction between upper and lower case letters. For such data, one must use a hash function that is compatible with the data equivalence criterion being used: that is, any two inputs that are considered equivalent must yield the same hash value. This can be accomplished by normalizing the input before hashing it, as by upper-casing all letters.

Continuity

"A hash function that is used to search for similar (as opposed to equivalent) data must be as continuous as possible; two inputs that differ by a little should be mapped to equal or nearly equal hash values."

Note that continuity is usually considered a fatal flaw for checksums, cryptographic hash functions, and other related concepts. Continuity is desirable for hash functions only in some applications, such as hash tables used in Nearest neighbor search.

Non-invertible

In cryptographic applications, hash functions are typically expected to be practically non-invertible, meaning that it is not realistic to reconstruct the input datum x from its hash value $h(x)$ alone without spending great amounts of computing time.

Hash Function Algorithms

For most types of hashing functions, the choice of the function depends strongly on the nature of the input data, and their probability distribution in the intended application.

Trivial Hash Function

If the data to be hashed is small enough, one can use the data itself (reinterpreted as an integer) as the hashed value. The cost of computing this "trivial" (identity) hash function is effectively zero. This hash function is perfect, as it maps each input to a distinct hash value.

The meaning of "small enough" depends on the size of the type that is used as the hashed value. For example, in Java, the hash code is a 32-bit integer. Thus the 32-bit integer `Integer` and 32-bit floating-point Float objects can simply use the value directly; whereas the 64-bit integer `Long` and 64-bit floating-point Double cannot use this method.

Other types of data can also use this perfect hashing scheme. For example, when mapping character strings between upper and lower case, one can use the binary encoding of each character, interpreted as an integer, to index a table that gives the alternative form of that character ("A" for "a", "8" for "8", etc.). If each character is stored in 8 bits (as in extended ASCII or ISO Latin 1), the table has only $2^8 = 256$ entries; in the case of Unicode characters, the table would have $17 \times 2^{16} = 1114112$ entries.

The same technique can be used to map two-letter country codes like "us" or "za" to country names ($26^2 = 676$ table entries), 5-digit zip codes like 13083 to city names (100000 entries), etc. Invalid data values (such as the country code "xx" or the zip code 00000) may be left undefined in the table or mapped to some appropriate "null" value.

Perfect Hashing

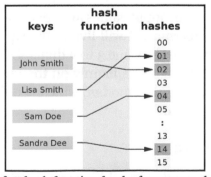

A perfect hash function for the four names shown.

A hash function that is injective—that is, maps each valid input to a different hash value—is said to be perfect. With such a function one can directly locate the desired entry in a hash table, without any additional searching.

Minimal Perfect Hashing

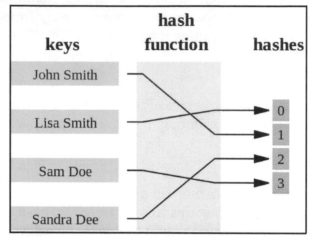

A minimal perfect hash function for the four names shown.

A perfect hash function for n keys is said to be minimal if its range consists of n *consecutive* integers, usually from 0 to $n-1$. Besides providing single-step lookup, a minimal perfect hash function also yields a compact hash table, without any vacant slots. Minimal perfect hash functions are much harder to find than perfect ones with a wider range.

Hashing Uniformly Distributed Data

If the inputs are bounded-length strings and each input may independently occur with uniform probability (such as telephone numbers, car license plates, invoice numbers, etc.), then a hash function needs to map roughly the same number of inputs to each hash value. For instance, suppose that each input is an integer z in the range 0 to $N-1$, and the output must be an integer h in the range 0 to $n-1$, where N is much larger than n. Then the hash function could be $h = z \bmod n$ (the remainder of z divided by n), or $h = (z \times n) \div N$ (the value z scaled down by n/N and truncated to an integer), or many other formulas.

Hashing Data with Other Distributions

These simple formulas will not do if the input values are not equally likely, or are not independent. For instance, most patrons of a supermarket will live in the same geographic area, so their telephone numbers are likely to begin with the same 3 to 4 digits. In that case, if m is 10000 or so, the division formula $(z \times m) \div M$, which depends mainly on the leading digits, will generate a lot of collisions; whereas the remainder formula $z \bmod m$, which is quite sensitive to the trailing digits, may still yield a fairly even distribution.

Hashing Variable-length Data

When the data values are long (or variable-length) character strings—such as personal names, web page addresses, or mail messages—their distribution is usually very uneven, with complicated dependencies. For example, text in any natural language has highly non-uniform distributions of characters, and character pairs, very characteristic of the language. For such data, it is prudent to use a hash function that depends on all characters of the string—and depends on each character in a different way.

In cryptographic hash functions, a Merkle–Damgård construction is usually used. In general, the scheme for hashing such data is to break the input into a sequence of small units (bits, bytes, words, etc.) and combine all the units $b[1], b[2], ..., b[m]$ sequentially, as follows:

```
S ← S0;                   // Initialize the state.

for k in 1, 2, ..., m do  // Scan the input data units:

  S ← F(S, b[k]);         // Combine data unit k into the state.

return G(S, n)            // Extract the hash value from the state.
```

This schema is also used in many text checksum and fingerprint algorithms. The state variable S may be a 32- or 64-bit unsigned integer; in that case, So can be 0, and $G(S,n)$ can be just $S \bmod n$. The best choice of F is a complex issue and depends on the nature of the data. If the units $b[k]$ are single bits, then $F(S,b)$ could be, for instance:

```
if highbit(S) = 0 then

   return 2 * S + b

 else

   return (2 * S + b) ^ P
```

Here $highbit(S)$ denotes the most significant bit of S; the '*' operator denotes unsigned integer multiplication with lost overflow; '^' is the bitwise exclusive or operation applied to words; and P is a suitable fixed word.

Special-purpose Hash Functions

In many cases, one can design a special-purpose (heuristic) hash function that yields many fewer collisions than a good general-purpose hash function. For example, suppose that the input data are file names such as FILE0000.CHK, FILE0001.CHK, FILE0002.CHK, etc., with mostly sequential numbers. For such data, a function that extracts the numeric part k of the file name and returns $k \bmod n$ would be nearly optimal. Needless to say, a function that is exceptionally good for a specific kind of data may have dismal performance on data with different distribution.

Rolling Hash

In some applications, such as substring search, one must compute a hash function h for every k-character substring of a given n-character string t; where k is a fixed integer, and n is k. The straightforward solution, which is to extract every such substring s of t and compute $h(s)$ separately, requires a number of operations proportional to $k \cdot n$. However, with the proper choice of h, one can use the technique of rolling hash to compute all those hashes with an effort proportional to $k + n$.

Universal Hashing

A universal hashing scheme is a randomized algorithm that selects a hashing function h among a family of such functions, in such a way that the probability of a collision of any two distinct keys is $1/n$, where n is the number of distinct hash values desired—independently of the two keys. Universal hashing ensures (in a probabilistic sense) that the hash function application will behave as well as if it were using a random function, for any distribution of the input data. It will, however, have more collisions than perfect hashing and may require more operations than a special-purpose hash function.

Hashing with Checksum Functions

One can adapt certain checksum or fingerprinting algorithms for use as hash functions. Some of those algorithms will map arbitrary long string data z, with any typical real-world distribution—no matter how non-uniform and dependent—to a 32-bit or 64-bit string, from which one can extract a hash value in 0 through $n - 1$.

This method may produce a sufficiently uniform distribution of hash values, as long as the hash range size n is small compared to the range of the checksum or fingerprint function. However, some checksums fare poorly in the avalanche test, which may be a concern in some applications. In particular, the popular CRC32 checksum provides only 16 bits (the higher half of the result) that are usable for hashing. Moreover, each bit of the input has a deterministic effect on each bit of the CRC32, that is one can tell without looking at the rest of the input, which bits of the output will flip if the input bit is flipped; so care must be taken to use all 32 bits when computing the hash from the checksum.

Multiplicative Hashing

Multiplicative hashing is a simple type of hash function often used by teachers introducing students to hash tables. Multiplicative hash functions are simple and fast, but have higher collision rates in hash tables than more sophisticated hash functions.

In many applications, such as hash tables, collisions make the system a little slower but are otherwise harmless. In such systems, it is often better to use hash functions based on multiplication—such as MurmurHash and the SBoxHash—or even simpler hash functions such as CRC32—and tolerate more collisions; rather than use a more complex hash function that avoids many of those collisions but takes longer to compute. Multiplicative hashing is susceptible to a "common mistake" that leads to poor diffusion—higher-value input bits do not affect lower-value output bits.

Hashing with Cryptographic Hash Functions

Some cryptographic hash functions, such as SHA-1, have even stronger uniformity guarantees than checksums or fingerprints, and thus can provide very good general-purpose hashing functions.

In ordinary applications, this advantage may be too small to offset their much higher cost. However, this method can provide uniformly distributed hashes even when the keys are chosen by a malicious agent. This feature may help to protect services against denial of service attacks.

Hashing by Nonlinear Table Lookup

Tables of random numbers (such as 256 random 32-bit integers) can provide high-quality nonlinear functions to be used as hash functions or for other purposes such as cryptography. The key to be hashed is split into 8-bit (one-byte) parts, and each part is used as an index for the nonlinear table. The table values are then added by arithmetic or XOR addition to the hash output value. Because the table is just 1024 bytes in size, it fits into the cache of modern microprocessors and allows very fast execution of the hashing algorithm. As the table value is on average much longer than 8 bits, one bit of input affects nearly all output bits.

This algorithm has proven to be very fast and of high quality for hashing purposes (especially hashing of integer-number keys).

Efficient Hashing of Strings

Modern microprocessors will allow for much faster processing, if 8-bit character strings are not hashed by processing one character at a time, but by interpreting the string as an array of 32 bit or 64 bit integers and hashing/accumulating these "wide word" integer values by means of arithmetic operations (e.g. multiplication by constant and bit-shifting). The remaining characters of the string which are smaller than the word length of the CPU must be handled differently (e.g. being processed one character at a time).

This approach has proven to speed up hash code generation by a factor of five or more on modern microprocessors of a word size of 64 bit.

Another approach is to convert strings to a 32 or 64 bit numeric value and then apply a hash function. One method that avoids the problem of strings having great similarity ("Aaaaaaaaaa" and "Aaaaaaaaab") is to use a Cyclic redundancy check (CRC) of the string to compute a 32- or 64-bit value. While it is possible that two different strings will have the same CRC, the likelihood is very small and only requires that one check the actual string found to determine whether one has an exact match. CRCs will be different for strings such as "Aaaaaaaaaa" and "Aaaaaaaaab". Although, CRC codes can be used as hash values they are not cryptographically secure since they are not collision-resistant.

Locality-Sensitive Hashing

Locality-sensitive hashing (LSH) is a method of performing probabilistic dimension reduction of high-dimensional data. The basic idea is to hash the input items so that similar items are mapped to the same buckets with high probability (the number of buckets being much smaller than the universe of possible input items). This is different from the conventional hash functions, such as those used in cryptography, as in this case the goal is to maximize the probability of "collision" of similar items rather than to avoid collisions.

One example of LSH is MinHash algorithm used for finding similar documents (such as web-pages):

Let h be a hash function that maps the members of A and B to distinct integers, and for any set S define $h_{min}(S)$ to be the member x of S with the minimum value of $h(x)$. Then $h_{min}(A) =$

$h_{min}(B)$ exactly when the minimum hash value of the union $A \cup B$ lies in the intersection $A \cap B$. Therefore,

$$Pr[h_{min}(A) = h_{min}(B)] = J(A,B). \text{ where J is Jaccard index.}$$

In other words, if r is a random variable that is one when $h_{min}(A) = h_{min}(B)$ and zero otherwise, then r is an unbiased estimator of $J(A,B)$, although it has too high a variance to be useful on its own. The idea of the MinHash scheme is to reduce the variance by averaging together several variables constructed in the same way.

Origins of the Term

The term "hash" offers a natural analogy with its non-technical meaning (to "chop" or "make a mess" out of something), given how hash functions scramble their input data to derive their output. In his research for the precise origin of the term, Donald Knuth notes that, while Hans Peter Luhn of IBM appears to have been the first to use the concept of a hash function in a memo dated January 1953, the term itself would only appear in published literature in the late 1960s, on Herbert Hellerman's *Digital Computer System Principles*, even though it was already widespread jargon by then.

List of Hash Functions

- Coalesced hashing
- Cuckoo hashing
- Hopscotch hashing
- NIST hash function competition
- MD5
- Bernstein hash
- Fowler-Noll-Vo hash function (32, 64, 128, 256, 512, or 1024 bits)
- Jenkins hash function (32 bits)
- Pearson hashing (64 bits)
- Zobrist hashing

Hashing Techniques

Introduction

Hashing is a method to store data in an array so that sorting, searching, inserting and deleting data is fast. For this every record needs unique key.

The basic idea is not to search for the correct position of a record with comparisons but to compute the position within the array. The function that returns the position is called the 'hash function' and the array is called a 'hash table'.

Why Hashing?

In the other type of searching, we have seen that the record is stored in a table and it is necessary to pass through some number of keys before finding the desired one. While we know that the efficient search technique is one which minimizesthese comparisons. Thus we need a search technique in which there is no unnecessary comparisons.

If we want to access a key in a single retrieval, then the location of the record within the table must depend only on the key, not on the location of other keys(as in other type of searching i.e. tree). The most efficient way to organize such a table is an array.It was possible only with hashing.

Hash Clash

Suppose two keys k1 and k2 are such that h(k1) equals h(k2).When a record with key two keys can't get the same position.such a situation is called hash collision or hash clash.

Methods of Dealing with Hash Clash

There are three basic methods of dealing with hash clash. They are:

1. Chaining

2. Rehashing

3. Separate Chaining

Chaining

It builds a link list of all items whose keys has the same value. During search,this sorted linked list is traversed sequentially fro the desired key.It involves adding an extra link field to each table position. There are three types of chaining:

1. Standard Coalsced Hashing

2. General Coalsced Hashing

3. Varied insertion coalsced Hashing

Standard Coalsced Hashing

It is the simplest of chaining methods. It reduces the average number of probes for an unsuccessful search. It efficiently does the deletion without affecting the efficiency.

General Coalsced Hashing

It is the generalization of standard coalesced chaining method. In this method, we add extra positions to the hash table that can be used to list the nodes in the time of collision.

Varied Insertion Coalsced Hashing

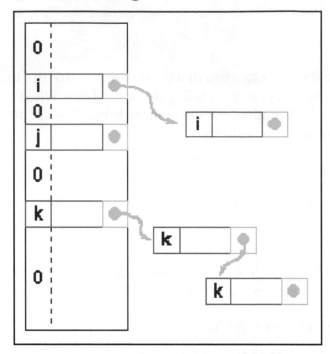

It is the combination of standard and general coalesced hashing. Under this method, the colliding item is inserted to the list immediately following the hash position unless the list forming from that position containing a cellar element.

Solving Hash Clashes by Linear Probing

The simplest method is that when a clash occurs, insert the record in the next available place in the table. For example in the table the next position 646 is empty. So we can insert the record with key 012345645 in this place which is still empty. Similarly if the record with key %1000 = 646 appears, it will be inserted in next empty space. This technique is called linear probing and is an example for resolving hash clashes called rehashing or open addressing.

Working of Linear Probing Algorithm

It works like this: If array location h(key) is already occupied by a record with a different key, rh is applied to the value of h(key) to find the other location where the record may be placed. If position rh(h(key))is also occupied,it too is rehashed to see if rh(rh(h(key))) is available. This process continues until an empty location is found. Thus we can write a search and insert algorithm using hashing as follows:

Algorithm

```
void insert( key, r )

typekey key; dataarray r;

  {
```

```
extern int n;

int i, last;

i = hashfunction( key ) ;

last = (i+m-1) % m;

 while ( i!=last && !empty(r[i]) && !deleted(r[i]) && r[i].k!=key )

 i = (i+1) % m;

  if (empty(r[i]) || deleted(r[i]))

   {

    /*** insert here ***/

   r[i].k = key;

   n++;

   }

 else Error /*** table full, or key already in table ***/;

}
```

Disadvantages of Linear Probing

It may happen, however, that the loop executes forever. There are two possible reasons for this. First, the table may be full so that it is impossible to insert any new record. This situation can be detected by keeping an account of the number of records in the table.

When the count equals the table size, no further insertion should be done. The other reason may be that the table is not full, too. In this type, suppose all the odd positions are emptyAnd the even positions are full and we want to insert in the even position by rh(i)=(i+2)%1000 used as a hash function. Of course, it is very unlikely that all the odd positions are empty and all the even positions are full.

However the rehash function rh(i)=(i+200)%1000 is used, each key can be placed in one of the five positions only. Here the loop can run infinitely, too.

Separate Chaining

As we have seen earlier, we can't insert items more than the table size. In some cases, we allocate space much more than required resulting in wastage of space. In order to tackle all these problems, we have a separate method of resolving clashes called separate chaining. It keeps a distinct link list for all records whose keys hash into a particular value. In this method, the items that end with a particular number (unit position) is placed in a particular link list as shown in the figure. The 10's, 100's not taken into account. The pointer to the node points to the next node and when there is no more nodes, the pointer points to NULL value.

Advantages of Seperate Chaining

1. No worries of filling up the table whatever be the number of items.

2. The list items need not be contiguous storage.

3. It allows traversal of items in hash key order.

Situation of Hash Clash

What would happen if we want to insert a new part number 012345645 in the table .Using he hash function key %1000 we get 645.Therefore for the part belongs in position 645.However record for the part is already being occupied by 011345645.Therefore the record with the key 012345645 must be inserted somewhere in the table resulting in hash clash.This is illustrated in the given table:

Position	Key	Record
0	258001201	
2	698321903	
3	986453204	
.		
.		
450	256894450	
451	158965451	
.		
.		
647	214563647	
648	782154648	
649	325649649	
.		
.		
997	011239997	
998	231452998	
999	011232999	

Double Hashing

A method of open addressing for a hash table in which a collision is resolved by searching the table for an empty place at intervals given by a different hash function, thus minimizing clustering. Double Hashing is another method of collision resolution, but unlike the linear collision resolution, double hashing uses a second hashing function that normally limits multiple collisions. The idea is that if two values hash to the same spot in the table, a constant can be calculated from the initial value using the second hashing function that can then be used to change the sequence of locations in the table, but still have access to the entire table.

Algorithm for double hashing

```
void insert( key, r )

typekey key; dataarray r;

{

extern int n;

int i, inc, last;

i = hashfunction( key ) ;

inc = increment( key );

last = (i+(m-1)*inc) % m;

while ( i!=last && !empty(r[i]) && !deleted(r[i]) && r[i].k!=key )

i = (i+inc) % m;

if ( empty(r[i]) || deleted(r[i]) )

{

/*** insert here ***/

r[i].k = key;

n++;

}

else Error /*** table full, or key already in table ***/;

}
```

Clustering

There are mainly two types of clustering:

Primary clustering

When the entire array is empty, it is equally likely that a record is inserted at any position in the array. However, once entries have been inserted and several hash clashes have been resolved, it doesn't remain true. For, example in the given above table, it is five times as likely for the record to be inserted at the position 994 as the position 401. This is because any record whose key hashes into 990, 991, 992, 993 or 994 will be placed in 994, whereas only a record whose key hashes into 401 will be placed there. This phenomenon where two keys that hash into different values compete with each other in successive rehashes is called primary clustering.

Cause of Primary Clustering

Any rehash function that depends solely on the index to be rehashed causes primary clustering.

Ways of Eleminating Primary Clustering

One way of eliminating primary clustering is to allow the rehash function to depend on the number of times that the function is applied to a particular hash value. Another way is to use random permutation of the number between 1 and e, where e is (table size -1, the largest index of the table). One more method is to allow rehash to depend on the hash value. All these methods allow key that hash into different locations to follow separate rehash paths.

Secondary Clustering

In this type, different keys that hash to the same value follow same rehash path.

Ways to Eliminate Secondary Clustering

All types of clustering can be eliminated by double hashing, which involves the use of two hash function h1(key) and h2(key).h1 is known as primary hash function and is allowed first to get the position where the key will be inserted. If that position is occupied already, the rehash function rh(i,key) = (i+h2(key))%table size is used successively until an empty position is found. As long as h2(key1) doesn't equal h2(key2),records with keys h1 and h2 don't compete for the same position. Therefore one should choose functions h1 and h2 that distributes the hashes and rehashes uniformly in the table and also minimizes clustering.

Deleting an Item from the Hash Table

It is very difficult to delete an item from the hash table that uses rehashes for search and insertion. Suppose that a record r is placed at some specific location. We want to insert some other record r1 on the same location. We will have to insert the record in the next empty location to the specified original location. Suppose that the record r which was there at the specified location is deleted.

Now, we want to search the record r1, as the location with record r is now empty, it will erroneously conclude that the record r1 is absent from the table. One possible solution to this problem is that the deleted record must be marked "deleted" rather than "empty" and the search must continue whenever a "deleted" position is encountered. But this is possible only when there are small numbers of deletions otherwise an unsuccessful search will have to search the entire table since most of the positions will be marked "deleted" rather than "empty".

Dynamic and Extendible Hashing

One of the serious drawbacks associated with hashing of external storage is its being insufficiently flexible. The contents of the external storage structure tend to grow and shrink unpredictably. The entire hash table structuring method that we have examined has a sharp space/time trade-off. Either the table uses a large amount of space for efficient access which results in wastage of large space an or it uses a small amount of space and accommodates growth very poorly and sharply increasing the access time fro overflow elements. So in order to tackle the above stated problems, we would like to develop a scheme that doesn't utilize too much extra space when a file is small but permits efficient access when it grows larger. Two such schemes are dynamic hashing and Extendible hashing.

Dynamic Hashing

Dynamic hashing is a hash table that grows to handle more items. The associated hash function must change as the table grows. Some schemes may shrink the table to save space when items are deleted.

Extendible Hashing

A hash table in which the hash function is the last few bits of the key and the table refer to buckets. Table entries with the same final bits may use the same bucket. If a bucket overflows, it splits, and if only one entry referred to it, the table doubles in size. If a bucket is emptied by deletion, entries using it are changed to refer to an adjoining bucket, and the table may be halved.

Hash Table Reordering

When a hash table is nearly full, many items given by their hash keys are not at their specified location. Thus, we have to make a lot of key comparisons before finding such items. If an item is not in the table, entire hash table has to be searched. Then, we come to the conclusion that the key is not in the table. In order to tackle this situation, many techniques came forward.

Amble and Knuth Method

In this method, all the records that hash into same locations are placed in descending order (assuming that the NULLKEY is the smallest one). Suppose we want to search a key, we need not rehash repeatedly until an empty slot is found. As soon as an item whose key is less than the search key is found in the table, we come to the conclusion that the search key is not in the table. At the time of insertion, if we want to insert a key k, if the rehash accesses a key smaller than k, the associated record with k replaces it and the insertion process continues with the replaced key.

The ordered hash table method can be used only in the technique in which a rehash depends only on the index and the key not in the technique in which a rehash function depends on the no of items the item is rehashed (unless that number is kept in the table).

Advantages of Amble and Knuth's Method

It reduces significantly the number of key comparisons necessary to determine that a key doesn't exist in the table.

Disadvantages of Amble and Knuth's Method

1. It doesn't change the average number of key comparisons required to find a key that is in the table.

2. The unsuccessful search needs same average number of probes as the successful search.

3. Average number of probes in insertion is not reduced in ordered table.

Brent's Method

This technique involves rehashing the search argument until an empty slot is found. Then each of the keys in rehash path is itself rehashed to determine if placing one of those keys in an empty slot would require fewer rehashes. If this is the case the search argument replaces the existing key in the table and the existing key is inserted in its empty rehash slot.

Binary Tree Hashing

Another method of reordering the hash table was developed by Gonnet and Munro and is called as binary tree hashing. It is seen as an improvement to Brent's algorithm. In this method, we assume to use double hashing. Whenever a key is inserted in the hash table, an almost complete binary tree is constructed. Figure below illustrates an example of such a tree in which the nodes are arranged according to the array representation of an almost complete binary tree.node(0) is the root and node(2*i+1)and node(2*i+2) are the left and right children of node(i) respectively. Each node of the tree contains an index into the hash table. In the explanation, node(i) will be referred to as index(i) and the key at that position is referred to as k(-1).

How to Construct a Tree

Firstly, we define the youngest right ancestor of node(i) or yra(i) as the node number of the father of the youngest son i.e. the right son. In the given figure, yra(12) is 1, since it is the left son of its father node(6) and its father is also a left child. So the youngest ancestor of node(12) is node(3) and is father is node(1). Similarly, yra(10) is 2 and yra(18) is 4 and yra(14) is 3. if node(i) is the right son, yra(i) is defined as the node number of its father (i-1)/2. Thus, yra(15) is 7 and yra(13) is 6. If node(i) has no ancestor i.e. is a right son, yra(i) is defined as (-1). Thus, yra(16) is -1. The binary tree is constructed according to the node number. The table construction continues until a NULLKEY and an empty position is found in the table.

How to Calculate Yra (i)

As we have seen above, the entire algorithm depends on the routine yra(i). Fortunately, yra(i) can be calculated very easily. It can be derived directly using this method. Find the binary representation of (i+1). Delete all the trailing zero bits along with one bit preceding them. Subtract 1 from the result and you will get the resulting binary number to get the value of yra(i).

Examples

1. yra(11):

11+1=12

Binary representation: 1100.

Removing 100, we get 1, which is binary representation of 1.

Therefore, yra(11)=0.

2. yra(17):

17+1=18

Binary representation: 10010.

Removing 10, we get 100, which is binary representation of 4.

Therefore, yra(11)=3.

3. yra(15):

15+1=16

Binary representation: 010000.

Removing 10000, we get 0, which is binary representation of 0.

Therefore, yra(11)=-1.

How to Insert a Key in the Table

Once the tree has been constructed, the keys along the path from the root to the last node are reordered in the hash table. Let, i be initialized to the last node of the tree. If yra(i) is non-zero, k(yra(i)) and its associated record are shifted from the table[index(yra(i))] to table[index(i)] and I is reset to yra(i). It is repeated until yra(i) is -1 at which point insertion is complete.

Example of Insertion

Suppose yra(21)=10 and index(10) is j, the key and record from j is shifted to u which is the right child. Then suppose yra(10) is 2, the record and key from position b is shifted to j which is the right child of index b.Finally since yra(2) is -1, key is inserted in position b.

Advantage of Binary Search Tree

Binary tree hashing yields results that are even closer to optimal than Brent's.

References

- Horvath, Adam. "Binary search and linear search performance on the .NET and Mono platform". Retrieved 19 April 2013

- Konheim, Alan (2010). "7. HASHING FOR STORAGE: DATA MANAGEMENT". Hashing in Computer Science: Fifty Years of Slicing and Dicing. Wiley-Interscience. ISBN 9780470344736

- Cam-Winget, Nancy; Housley, Russ; Wagner, David; Walker, Jesse (May 2003). "Security Flaws in 802.11 Data Link Protocols". Communications of the ACM. 46 (5): 35–39. doi:10.1145/769800.769823

- Knuth, Donald E. (2000). Sorting and searching (2. ed., 6. printing, newly updated and rev. ed.). Boston [u.a.]: Addison-Wesley. pp. 547–548. ISBN 0-201-89685-0

- Menezes, Alfred J.; van Oorschot, Paul C.; Vanstone, Scott A (1996). Handbook of Applied Cryptography. CRC Press. ISBN 0849385237

Permissions

Index